Brave the exam elements with CGP!

The current GCSE Geography climate is tougher than ever.
But don't worry, this CGP book creates a perfect revision environment...

It covers everything you'll need for the Edexcel A course, with
crystal-clear explanations, helpful diagrams and cracking case studies.

We've even included expert advice on fieldwork and essential geographical
skills — so you'll be fully prepared for the exams, come rain or shine.

CGP — still the best! ☺

Our sole aim here at CGP is to produce the highest quality books —
carefully written, immaculately presented and dangerously close to being funny.

Then we work our socks off to get them out to you
— at the cheapest possible prices.

Contents

Component 2:
The Human Environment

Topic 4 — Changing Cities

Topic 5 — Global Development

Topic 6 — Resource Management

Energy Resource Management

Water Resource Management

Component 3:
Geographical Investigations: Fieldwork and UK Challenges

Geographical Investigations — Fieldwork

Geographical Investigations — UK Challenges

Geographical Skills

Don't Forget

You __don't__ need to study __all__ of the content in Topics 1 and 6 — some of the sections are optional. See page 1 for more details.

Published by CGP

Editors:
Alex Billings, Claire Boulter, Ellen Burton, Kelsey Hammond, Katharine Howell, Claire Plowman.

Contributors:
Helena Mutton, Barbara Melbourne, Paddy Gannon.

Proofreading:
Nic Robinson

ISBN: 978 1 78908 301 9

With thanks to Emily Smith for the copyright research.

Printed by Elanders Ltd, Newcastle upon Tyne.
Clipart from Corel®

Based on the classic CGP style created by Richard Parsons.

Structure of the Course

'Know thy enemy', 'forewarned is forearmed'... There are many boring quotes that just mean <u>being prepared is a good thing</u>. <u>Don't</u> stumble <u>blindly</u> into a GCSE course — find out what you're facing.

See p.117-129 for more on geographical skills.

You'll have to do Three Exams

GCSE Edexcel Geography A is divided into <u>three components</u> — <u>The Physical Environment</u>, <u>The Human Environment</u> and <u>Geographical Investigations</u>. You'll have to do <u>three exams</u> — <u>one</u> on each of the three <u>components</u>. <u>Geographical skills</u> will be assessed in <u>all three</u> exams, but <u>fieldwork</u> (see p.113) will only be assessed in <u>Paper 3</u>. <u>All</u> your <u>exams</u> will take place at the <u>end of the course</u>.

Paper 1: The Physical Environment

Paper 1 is divided into <u>three sections</u> (A, B and C).
You <u>don't</u> have to answer questions on <u>all</u> of the topics in <u>Section A</u>.
<u>Section A: The Changing Landscapes of the UK</u>

*   The Changing Landscapes of the UK **plus**
*   **TWO FROM** Coastal Landscapes and Processes, River Landscapes and Processes **OR** Glaciated Upland Landscapes and Processes

<u>Section B: Weather Hazards and Climate Change</u>
<u>Section C: Ecosystems, Biodiversity and Management</u>

If you're not sure which of the optional topics to revise, check with your teacher.

Here's how <u>Paper 1</u> is structured:

	1 hour 30 minutes	94 marks in total	37.5% of your final mark

Paper 2: The Human Environment

Paper 2 is divided into <u>three sections</u> (A, B and C).
You <u>don't</u> have to answer questions on <u>all</u> of the topics in <u>Section C</u>.

<u>Section A: Changing Cities</u>
<u>Section B: Global Development</u>
<u>Section C: Resource Management</u>

*   Resource Management **plus**
*   **EITHER** Energy Resource Management **OR** Water Resource Management

Here's how <u>Paper 2</u> is structured:

	1 hour 30 minutes	94 marks in total	37.5% of your final mark

Paper 3: Geographical Investigations: Fieldwork and UK Challenges

Paper 3 is divided into <u>three sections</u> (A, B and C). For <u>Sections A</u> and <u>B</u> you need to answer questions about <u>fieldwork</u> in the environments you have chosen. Answer <u>all</u> the questions in <u>Section C</u>.

<u>Section A: Geographical Investigations — Physical Environments</u>
*   **EITHER** River Landscapes **OR** Coastal Landscapes

<u>Section B: Geographical Investigations — Human Environments</u>
*   **EITHER** Central/Inner Urban Areas **OR** Rural Settlements

There's more information about this paper on pages 113-116.

<u>Section C: UK Challenges</u>
*   These questions will be about <u>applying</u> what you have learnt for <u>Papers 1</u> and <u>2</u> to a <u>contemporary UK challenge</u>.

Here's how <u>Paper 3</u> is structured:

	1 hour 30 minutes	64 marks in total	25% of your final mark

In <u>each exam</u>, there will be one question which has <u>4 extra marks</u> available for <u>spelling</u>, <u>punctuation</u> and <u>grammar</u> as well as the use of <u>specialist terminology</u> (see p.117). These marks are <u>included</u> in the <u>total marks</u> given for each paper.

I'm all over those spelling marks.

May the course be with you...

It's worthwhile knowing all of this stuff so nothing comes as a shock to you. It also stops you from being the person who tried to answer every single question in the exam — there's a fine line between bravery and self-sabotage...

The UK Physical Landscape

Ah, the UK landscape. Majestic <u>mountains</u>, cracking <u>coasts</u> and raging <u>rivers</u> — I could go on all day...

The UK has large *Upland* and *Lowland Areas*, and *Important Rivers*

The UK's main <u>upland</u> areas (orange and red on the map below) tend to be in the <u>north</u> and <u>west</u> of the country, and <u>lowland</u> areas (green on the map) to the <u>south</u> and <u>east</u>.

Most <u>cities</u> are in <u>lowland</u> areas and often on the UK's main <u>rivers</u> — such as <u>London</u> (on the <u>Thames</u>), <u>Liverpool</u> (on the <u>Mersey</u>) and <u>Cardiff</u> (on the <u>Severn Estuary</u>).

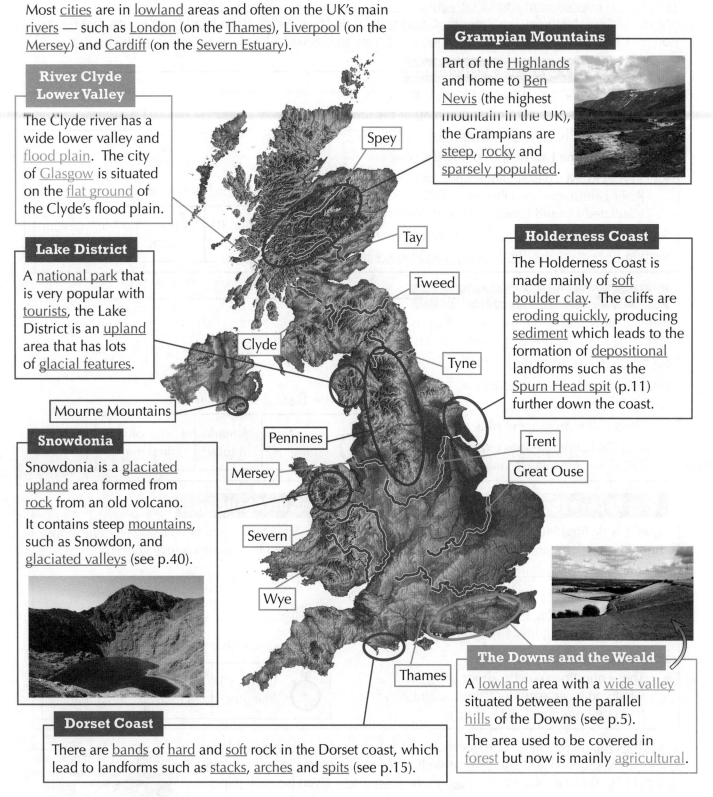

River Clyde Lower Valley

The Clyde river has a wide lower valley and <u>flood plain</u>. The city of <u>Glasgow</u> is situated on the <u>flat ground</u> of the Clyde's flood plain.

Lake District

A <u>national park</u> that is very popular with <u>tourists</u>, the Lake District is an <u>upland</u> area that has lots of <u>glacial features</u>.

Mourne Mountains

Snowdonia

Snowdonia is a <u>glaciated</u> <u>upland</u> area formed from <u>rock</u> from an old volcano.

It contains steep <u>mountains</u>, such as Snowdon, and <u>glaciated valleys</u> (see p.40).

Grampian Mountains

Part of the <u>Highlands</u> and home to <u>Ben Nevis</u> (the highest mountain in the UK), the Grampians are <u>steep</u>, <u>rocky</u> and <u>sparsely populated</u>.

Holderness Coast

The Holderness Coast is made mainly of <u>soft boulder clay</u>. The cliffs are <u>eroding quickly</u>, producing <u>sediment</u> which leads to the formation of <u>depositional</u> landforms such as the <u>Spurn Head spit</u> (p.11) further down the coast.

The Downs and the Weald

A <u>lowland</u> area with a <u>wide valley</u> situated between the parallel <u>hills</u> of the Downs (see p.5).

The area used to be covered in <u>forest</u> but now is mainly <u>agricultural</u>.

Dorset Coast

There are <u>bands</u> of <u>hard</u> and <u>soft</u> rock in the Dorset coast, which lead to landforms such as <u>stacks</u>, <u>arches</u> and <u>spits</u> (see p.15).

Map labels: Spey, Tay, Tweed, Clyde, Tyne, Trent, Great Ouse, Pennines, Mersey, Severn, Wye, Thames

I think you'll find the UK physical portrait is much easier to fit on a page...

This is a lovely little introduction to the rest of the UK changing landscapes section. You can actually revise it by looking through your holiday snaps or out the window on a long journey. Or by gazing at a lovely map...

Rocks and the UK Physical Landscape

There are three types of rock — hard, glam and punk... erm, I mean igneous, sedimentary and metamorphic...

There are Three Types of Rocks

Rock type depends on how the rock was formed:

1) Igneous — igneous rocks are formed when molten rock (magma) from the mantle cools down and hardens. The rock forms crystals as it cools. Igneous rocks are usually hard, e.g. granite and basalt.

2) Sedimentary — sedimentary rocks are formed when layers of sediment are compacted together until they become solid rock. Sedimentary rocks are usually softer and more easily eroded than igneous and metamorphic rocks, but some are still relatively hard.

- Sandstone is made of sand-sized particles which have been cemented together.
- Chalk is formed from tiny shells and the skeletons of dead sea creatures.

3) Metamorphic — metamorphic rocks are formed when other rocks (igneous, sedimentary or older metamorphic rocks) are changed by heat and pressure. The new rocks become harder and more compact, e.g. clay becomes slate and, with further pressure and heat, slate becomes schist.

Geological map of the UK *

Igneous
Sedimentary
Metamorphic

There Used to be More Tectonic Activity in the UK

The Earth's crust (outer layer) is divided into slabs called tectonic plates. These plates have moved over millions of years, shaping the landscape of the UK in three main ways:

1 Active Volcanoes

520 million years ago the land that now makes up the UK used to be much closer to the boundary of a tectonic plate than it is now. Volcanoes occur near some plate boundaries. Volcanic eruptions forced magma through the Earth's crust which cooled to form igneous rocks, e.g. granite and basalt.

2 Plate Collisions

1) Collisions between tectonic plates caused the rocks to be folded and uplifted, forming mountain ranges. Many of these areas remain as uplands, e.g. the Scottish Highlands, the Lake District and north Wales (Snowdonia) — the igneous granite is hard and more resistant to erosion.

2) The intense heat and pressure caused by plate collisions formed hard metamorphic rocks in northern Scotland and Northern Ireland.

3 Plate Movements — UK Position

1) Plate movements meant that 345-280 million years ago Britain was in the tropics and higher sea levels meant it was partly underwater — carboniferous limestone formed in the warm shallow seas. This can be seen in the uplands of the Peak District (northern England), south Wales and south west England.

2) The youngest rocks in the UK are the chalks and clays found in southern England. They formed in shallow seas and swamps. Chalks and clays are softer rocks that are more easily eroded — they form lowland landscapes.

The UK landscape rocks...

...and so will you if you can nail this page in the exam. Have a go at this question to check you've got it.
1) Give two characteristics of sedimentary rocks. [2]

Rocks and the UK Physical Landscape

Each rock type has different characteristics — and it's a good thing too, otherwise they'd be pretty boring to learn about. Oh, and I'd go grab a jumper if I were you — things get a little chilly at the bottom of the page...

The Characteristics of Different Rock Types Create Different Landscapes

Upland landscapes tend to be formed from harder rock types — igneous and metamorphic. Sedimentary rock is usually softer and gets eroded more easily, forming lowland landscapes.

Granite

1) Granite is igneous and forms upland landscapes.

2) It has lots of joints (cracks) which aren't evenly spread. The parts of the rock where there are more joints wear down faster. Areas that have fewer joints are weathered more slowly than the surrounding rock and stick out at the surface forming tors.

3) Granite is impermeable — it doesn't let water through. This creates moorlands — large areas of waterlogged land and acidic soil, with low-growing vegetation.

Slate and Schist

1) Slate and schist are metamorphic rocks.

2) Slate forms in layers creating weak planes in the rock. It is generally very hard and resistant to weathering but it is easily split into thin slabs.

3) Schist has bigger crystals than slate and also splits easily into small flakes.

4) Slate and schist often form rugged, upland landscapes. They are impermeable, which can lead to waterlogged and acidic soils.

Basalt

1) Basalt is an igneous rock made of volcanic lava. It is very hard and impermeable. It forms escarpments in UK uplands and cliffs at the coast.

2) As lava cools it can form columns. Cracks between the columns may be eroded by glaciation and the sea to form steps, e.g. the Giant's Causeway in Northern Ireland.

Chalk

1) Chalk is a sedimentary rock. It forms hills in UK lowlands and cliffs at the coast. One side of the hill is usually steep and the other side is more gentle.

2) Chalk is permeable — water flows through it and emerges as a spring where it meets impermeable rock.

Sandstone

1) Sandstone is a sedimentary rock made from sand. Sandstone can be hard or soft.

2) Softer sandstones form lowland landscapes. Harder sandstones can form upland landscapes, e.g. the Torridon hills in Scotland.

3) Sandstone is porous — it has small gaps in it, so it can store water in underground aquifers.

The Landscape Was Also Shaped By Ice

1) During the last glacial period (p.44), ice covered the UK roughly as far south as the line on this map, so glaciated landscapes are mostly found in upland areas in the north-west of the UK.

2) Ice is very powerful, so it was able to erode the landscape, carving out large U-shaped valleys in upland areas such as the Lake District.

3) Glaciation also affected lowland areas. Glaciers deposited lots of material as they melted. Landscapes formed by glacial meltwater and deposits extend south of where the ice sheets were. E.g. large parts of eastern England are covered in till (an unsorted mixture of clay, sand and rocks) deposited by melting glaciers.

Extent of ice during the last ice age

Chalk and granite — so different, they're like chalk and cheese...

Note: granite and cheese are not the same*. Anyhow, I know it's hard to believe that most of the UK was once buried under ice when we barely get enough snow to get a day off school, but it was, and it had a big impact on the landscape.

*This is the sort of critical revision advice you only get from CGP.

Landscape Processes — Physical

GEOGRAPHY SKILLS

It might look like nothing's changing, but <u>rocks</u> are constantly being <u>broken down</u>, <u>moved around</u> and <u>dumped</u>.

Physical Processes *Alter the Landscape*

1) <u>Physical processes</u> are constantly <u>changing</u> the <u>landscape</u> of the UK. They include:
   - <u>Weathering</u> — weathering is the <u>breakdown</u> of rock into smaller pieces.
     It can be <u>mechanical</u>, <u>chemical</u> or <u>biological</u> (see pages 7, 20 and 35).
   - <u>Erosion</u> — erosion <u>wears away</u> rock. During the last glacial period, <u>ice</u> eroded the landscape.
     <u>Rivers</u> and the <u>sea</u> now <u>constantly</u> erode the landscape.
   - <u>Post-glacial river processes</u> — <u>melting ice</u> at the <u>end</u> of <u>glacial periods</u> made rivers <u>much bigger</u>
     than normal with more <u>power</u> to <u>erode</u> the <u>landscape</u>. The ice also left <u>distinctive landforms</u> when
     it <u>melted</u>, e.g. hanging valleys (little valleys that are left at a higher level than the main valley).
   - <u>Slope processes</u> — including <u>mass movements</u>, e.g. rockfalls, slides, slumps and soil creep.
2) Physical processes are affected by <u>climate</u>. For example, a <u>cold</u> climate increases the likelihood of
   <u>freeze-thaw weathering</u> (see p.20 and p.35) and a <u>wet climate</u> increases the <u>number</u> of <u>streams</u> and <u>rivers</u>.

Physical Processes *Interact to Create Distinctive Upland Landscapes...*

<u>Snowdonia</u> is an <u>upland</u> landscape — the map shows <u>tightly packed contours</u> and there are lots of <u>rocky crags</u>.

<u>Llyn Idwal</u> is a <u>tarn</u> (lake). It sits in a corrie (basin) that was <u>hollowed out</u> by ice during glacial times.

<u>Freeze-thaw weathering</u> occurs on the <u>steep back wall</u> of the corrie. As the rocks are <u>broken up</u> there are <u>rock falls</u>, which form <u>scree slopes</u>.

This <u>large U-shaped valley</u> was eroded by ice — it has a <u>flat floor</u> and <u>steep sides</u>. The valley contains a <u>misfit river</u> that is <u>too small</u> to have created it.

There is lots of <u>rain</u> in <u>Snowdonia</u> and the rocks are mostly <u>impermeable</u>. This means there are lots of <u>streams</u> that are eroding the steep sides of the corrie and forming <u>gullies</u>.

... and Distinctive Lowland Landscapes

<u>The Downs and the Weald</u> are a <u>lowland</u> landscape — <u>chalk escarpments</u> (the Downs) lie either side of a <u>large flat area</u> of <u>clay</u> (the Weald). The valley is <u>flat</u> (the contour lines on the map are <u>widely spaced</u>).

<u>Dry valleys</u> are found in UK lowland landscapes. These are valleys with <u>no streams</u> visible (they flow <u>underground</u> in the <u>permeable chalk</u>). They formed during <u>glacial periods</u> when the <u>colder</u> climate led to more <u>freeze-thaw weathering</u> and <u>glacial snow melt</u> meant that <u>streams</u> had much <u>more water</u> in them than they do today.

Large rivers, e.g. the River Arun, <u>meander</u> on the <u>impermeable</u> clay, <u>widening</u> the valley floor (see p.18).

The UK has a <u>wet climate</u> — heavy rain can lead to <u>flooding</u>. The overflowing river <u>deposits silt</u> on the valley floor forming a <u>flood plain</u>.

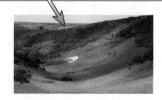

My Roman nose gives me a distinctive facial landscape...

Everything's interlinked — loads of different processes combine to create the different landscapes of the UK.
Make sure you can explain a few ways that physical processes interact to shape upland and lowland landscapes.

Landscape Processes — Human

GEOGRAPHY SKILLS

The UK is pretty <u>small</u> and there are quite <u>a lot</u> of <u>people</u> — wherever you go, the <u>actions</u> of people have <u>changed</u> the <u>landscape</u>. I know, those hedges don't naturally grow in straight lines at the edges of fields...

Humans *have* Changed the Landscape *Through Agriculture...*

1) People have <u>cleared</u> the land of <u>forest</u> to make space for <u>farming</u>.

2) Over time <u>hedgerows</u> and <u>walls</u> have been put in to mark out <u>fields</u>.

3) Different landscapes have been <u>adapted</u> for <u>different types</u> of farming:

- <u>Arable</u> — <u>flat land</u> with good <u>soil</u>, e.g. eastern England, is used for arable farming (growing <u>crops</u>).

- <u>Dairy</u> — warm and wet areas, e.g. south west England, are good for <u>dairy farming</u>. There are lots of <u>large, grassy fields</u>.

- <u>Sheep</u> — sheep farming takes place in the <u>harsher</u> conditions in the <u>uplands</u>. Sheep farming has led to a <u>lack of trees</u> on the hills (<u>young trees</u> are <u>eaten</u> or <u>trampled</u> before they get a chance to mature).

4) <u>OS®</u> <u>maps</u> show the influence of agriculture, including <u>field boundaries</u> and <u>drainage ditches</u> (dug to make the land dry enough for farming).

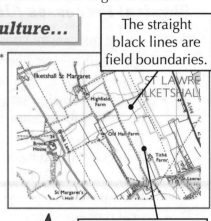

The straight black lines are field boundaries.

The straight blue lines are man-made drainage ditches.

...Forestry...

1) <u>Forestry</u> is the management of areas of <u>woodland</u> — they can be used for <u>timber</u>, <u>recreation</u> or <u>conservation</u>.

2) The UK used to be covered in <u>deciduous woodland</u>, but there is very <u>little</u> natural woodland <u>left</u>.

3) <u>Coniferous</u> (evergreen) forests have been planted for <u>timber</u>. The trees are often planted in <u>straight lines</u>. When areas are <u>felled</u>, the landscape is left <u>bare</u>. This affects <u>drainage</u> and can lead to increased <u>erosion</u>.

4) In some places, <u>deciduous</u> woodland is being <u>replanted</u> to try to <u>return</u> the area to a more <u>natural state</u>.

5) OS® maps show <u>forestry plantations</u> and areas that are being <u>managed</u>.

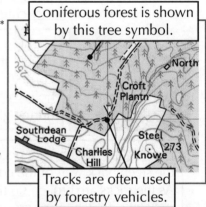

Coniferous forest is shown by this tree symbol.

Tracks are often used by forestry vehicles.

... and Settlement

1) Lots of factors influence <u>where settlements</u> have developed. For example, early settlers needed a <u>water supply</u>, flat land to <u>build</u> on or a place that could easily be <u>defended</u>.

2) These factors mean that the development of settlements has been concentrated in <u>lowland areas</u> and near <u>rivers</u> and <u>coasts</u>.

3) As settlements grew they further influenced the landscape. For example:

- land was <u>concreted</u> over for <u>roads</u> and <u>buildings</u>, which affected <u>drainage patterns</u>.

- some <u>rivers</u> were diverted through <u>underground channels</u>.

- some river channels were <u>straightened</u> or had <u>embankments</u> built to prevent flooding.

4) Most of the biggest cities are <u>ports</u> and <u>industrial areas</u>, e.g. London, Birmingham, Manchester and Portsmouth. These landscapes are <u>more urban</u> than natural.

5) Look for <u>buildings</u>, <u>railways</u>, <u>canals</u> and <u>embankments</u> to identify settlements on OS® maps.

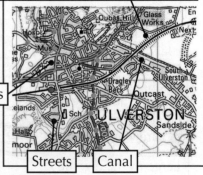

The land has been raised so the railway line is level — the dashed lines show embankments.

Built-up areas

Streets | Canal

EXAM QUESTION

I left my gutter at the altar — it was a drainage ditch...

Make sure you can recognise man-made features on OS® maps — they could well come up in the exam.

1) Explain two ways in which humans have influenced the landscape of the UK. [4]

Topic 1 — The Changing Landscapes of the UK

* © Crown copyright 2019 OS 100034841

Coastal Weathering and Erosion

For Topic 1, you need to study <u>two</u> landscapes out of three — <u>coasts</u>, <u>rivers</u> or <u>glaciers</u>. If you're <u>not</u> studying coasts, flip ahead to p.18. If you <u>are</u> doing coasts, crack on with these <u>physical processes</u>.

Rock is Broken Down by Mechanical, Chemical and Biological Weathering

1) <u>Mechanical weathering</u> is the <u>breakdown</u> of rock <u>without changing</u> its <u>chemical composition</u>. The main type of mechanical weathering that affects <u>coasts</u> in the <u>UK</u> is <u>salt weathering</u>:

> 1) The seawater <u>gets into cracks</u> in the rock.
> 2) When the water <u>evaporates</u>, <u>salt crystals</u> form. As the salt crystals form they <u>expand</u>, which puts <u>pressure</u> on the rock.
> 3) Repeated <u>evaporation</u> of saltwater and the <u>forming</u> of salt crystals <u>widens</u> the cracks and causes the rock to <u>break up</u>.

Freeze-thaw weathering is a similar process caused by the water in cracks expanding and contracting as it freezes and thaws — see p.20.

2) <u>Chemical weathering</u> is the breakdown of rock by <u>changing</u> its <u>chemical composition</u>. <u>Carbonation weathering</u> is a type of chemical weathering that happens in <u>warm</u> and <u>wet</u> conditions:

> 1) Rainwater has <u>carbon dioxide</u> dissolved in it, which makes it a <u>weak carbonic acid</u>.
> 2) Carbonic acid <u>reacts</u> with rock that contains <u>calcium carbonate</u>, e.g. chalk, so the <u>rocks</u> are <u>dissolved</u> by the rainwater.

3) <u>Biological weathering</u> is the breakdown of rocks by <u>living things</u>:
   - <u>Animals</u>, such as rabbits, <u>burrow</u> into soil on cliff tops.
   - <u>Plant roots</u> break down rocks by <u>growing into cracks</u> on their surfaces and <u>pushing them apart</u>.

Mass Movement is when Material Falls Down a Slope

1) Mass movement is the <u>shifting</u> of <u>rocks and loose material</u> down a slope, e.g. a cliff. It happens when the force of <u>gravity</u> acting on a slope is <u>greater than</u> the force <u>supporting</u> it.
2) Mass movements cause coasts to <u>retreat rapidly</u>.
3) They're <u>more likely</u> to happen when the material is <u>full of water</u> — it acts as a <u>lubricant</u>, and makes the material <u>heavier</u>.
4) <u>Undercutting</u> of a slope by <u>erosion</u> will <u>increase</u> the chance of mass movements. You need to know about <u>two</u> types of mass movement:

Slides: | Slumps:
Material shifts in a <u>straight line</u> | Material shifts with a <u>rotation</u>

There are Four Processes of Erosion

> 1) <u>Hydraulic action</u> — waves crash against rock and <u>compress</u> the <u>air</u> in the cracks, putting <u>pressure</u> on the rock. <u>Repeated compression</u> widens the cracks and makes bits of rock <u>break off</u>.
> 2) <u>Abrasion</u> — eroded particles in the water <u>scrape</u> and <u>rub</u> against rock, <u>removing small pieces</u>.
> 3) <u>Attrition</u> — eroded particles in the water <u>smash into each other</u> and break into <u>smaller fragments</u>. Their <u>edges</u> also get <u>rounded off</u> as they rub together.
> 4) <u>Solution</u> — dissolved <u>carbon dioxide</u> makes river and sea water slightly <u>acidic</u>. The acid <u>reacts</u> chemically with some rocks e.g. <u>chalk</u> and <u>limestone</u>, <u>dissolving</u> them.

The <u>waves</u> that carry out <u>erosional processes</u> are called <u>destructive waves</u>:
1) Destructive waves have a <u>high frequency</u> (10-14 waves per minute).
2) They're <u>high</u> and <u>steep</u>.
3) Their <u>backwash</u> (the movement of the water back <u>down</u> the beach) is <u>more powerful</u> than their <u>swash</u> (the movement of the water <u>up</u> the beach). This means material is <u>removed</u> from the coast.

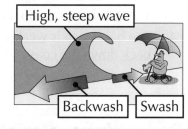

High, steep wave

Backwash | Swash

If you find yourself slumping — have a little break from revision...

This page is packed full of information, but you'll smash revision to bits by learning these processes one at a time.

Coastal Transport and Deposition

The material that's been eroded is moved around the coast and deposited by waves.

Transportation is the Movement of Material

Material is transported along coasts by a process called longshore drift:

1) Waves follow the direction of the prevailing (most common) wind.

2) They usually hit the coast at an oblique angle (any angle that isn't a right angle).

3) The swash carries material up the beach, in the same direction as the waves.

4) The backwash then carries material down the beach at right angles, back towards the sea.

5) Over time, material zigzags along the coast.

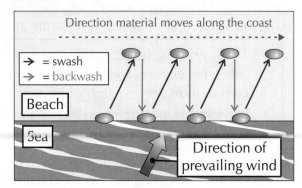

There are four other processes of transportation:

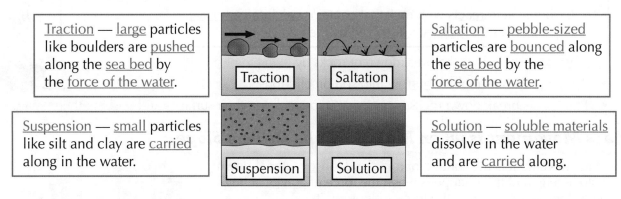

Traction — large particles like boulders are pushed along the sea bed by the force of the water.

Saltation — pebble-sized particles are bounced along the sea bed by the force of the water.

Suspension — small particles like silt and clay are carried along in the water.

Solution — soluble materials dissolve in the water and are carried along.

Deposition is the Dropping of Material

1) Deposition is when material being carried by the seawater is dropped on the coast. It occurs when water carrying sediment slows down so that it isn't moving fast enough to carry so much sediment.

2) Beaches are built up when the amount of deposition is greater than the amount of erosion.

3) The amount of material that's deposited on an area of coast is increased when:

- There's lots of erosion elsewhere on the coast, so there's lots of material available.
- There's lots of transportation of material into the area.

4) Low energy waves (i.e. slow waves) carry material to the coast but they're not strong enough to take a lot of material away — this means there's lots of deposition and very little erosion.

Waves that deposit more material than they erode are called constructive waves.

1) Constructive waves have a low frequency (6-8 waves per minute).

2) They're low and long.

3) The swash is powerful and it carries material up the coast.

4) The backwash is weaker and it doesn't take a lot of material back down the coast. This means material is deposited on the coast.

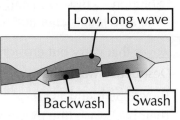

Depositing material on a beach? Sounds like littering to me.

Some more processes to learn here but none of them are tricky. You might find it useful to draw yourself a diagram of how longshore drift works — you'll get a feel for how the material is moved along the coast. Swashing stuff.

Coastal Landscapes

Erosion by waves forms many coastal landforms over long periods of time. But don't worry, you don't have to sit around for thousands of years to see what happens, it can all be explained with a few simple diagrams.

Coastlines can be Concordant or Discordant

1) The geological structure of a coastline influences the formation of erosional landforms.

2) Hard rocks like granite and chalk are more resistant, so it takes longer for them to be eroded and weathered by physical processes.

3) Softer rocks like clay and sandstone are less resistant, which means they are eroded more quickly.

4) Joints and faults are cracks and weaknesses in the rock. Rocks with lots of joints and faults erode faster.

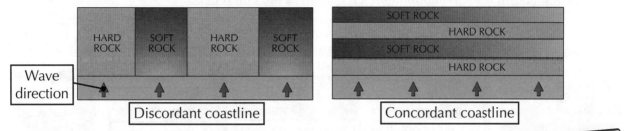

Wave direction

Discordant coastline

Concordant coastline

5) Some coastlines are made up of alternating bands of hard and soft rock that are at right angles to the coast — these are called discordant coastlines.

6) On a concordant coastline, the alternating bands of hard and soft rock are parallel to the coast.

7) Erosional landforms like bays and headlands are more common on discordant coastlines because the bands of rock are being eroded at different rates.

8) Concordant coastlines are eroded at the same rate along the coast. This means there are fewer erosional landforms.

The UK's Climate has an Impact on Coastal Erosion and Retreat

1) Weather in the UK varies with the seasons. Temperatures are coldest in winter, warm through spring, hottest in summer, then cool through autumn.

- Differences in temperature have an impact on processes along the coast, e.g. mild temperatures increase the rate of salt weathering (see page 7) because water evaporates more quickly.
- This can alter the landscape, e.g. weathering loosens material, which can lead to mass movement.

2) Storms are very frequent in many parts of the UK, especially in winter.

- The strong winds during storms create high energy, destructive waves, which increase erosion of the cliffs and cause coastal retreat.
- Intense rainfall can cause cliffs to become saturated, making mass movement (see page 7) more likely.
- Storms can dramatically change landforms — e.g. Porthcothan arch in Cornwall collapsed during a winter storm in 2014.

3) The prevailing (most common) winds in the UK are mostly warm south westerlies which bring storms from the Atlantic Ocean. The UK's south coast is exposed to these winds. Cold northerly winds are also common, especially on the east coast of the UK.

- Prevailing winds determine the direction of longshore drift, affecting where deposition happens.
- Prevailing winds also affect whether a coastline is exposed to storms or sheltered from them. More exposed coasts are more vulnerable to erosion and coastal retreat.

Even more discordant than my dad singing in the shower...

The physical processes shaping the coastal landscape are all affected by geology and climate. Make sure you know the difference between discordant and concordant coastlines — drawing a quick diagram of each one might help.

Coastal Landforms Caused by Erosion

Erosional processes wear away at cliffs and create lots of lovely landforms for you to learn about...

Waves Erode Cliffs to Form Wave-cut Platforms

1) Waves cause most erosion at the foot of a cliff (see diagrams below).

2) This forms a wave-cut notch, which is enlarged as erosion continues.

3) The rock above the notch becomes unstable and eventually collapses.

4) The collapsed material is washed away and a new wave-cut notch starts to form.

5) Repeated collapsing results in the cliff retreating.

6) A wave-cut platform is the platform that's left behind as the cliff retreats.

Hard rock cliffs tend to be more vertical, and soft rock cliffs tend to be more sloping.

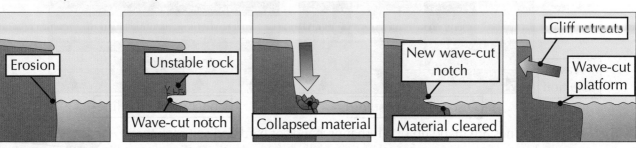

Headlands and Bays Form Along Discordant Coastlines

1) Soft rocks or rocks with lots of joints have low resistance to erosion. Hard rocks with a solid structure have a high resistance to erosion.

2) Headlands and bays form where there are alternating bands of resistant and less resistant rock along a coast.

3) The less resistant rock (e.g. clay) is eroded quickly and this forms a bay — bays have a gentle slope.

4) The resistant rock (e.g. chalk) is eroded more slowly and it's left jutting out, forming a headland — headlands have steep sides.

☐ = Less resistant rock
■ = Resistant rock
⇀ = Erosion

Headland   Bay

Headlands are Eroded to Form Caves, Arches and Stacks

1) Headlands are usually made of resistant rocks that have weaknesses like cracks.

2) Waves crash into the headlands and enlarge the cracks — mainly by hydraulic action and abrasion.

3) Repeated erosion and enlargement of the cracks causes a cave to form.

4) Continued erosion deepens the cave until it breaks through the headland — forming an arch, e.g. Durdle Door in Dorset.

5) Erosion continues to wear away the rock supporting the arch, until it eventually collapses.

6) This forms a stack — an isolated rock that's separate from the headland, e.g. Old Harry in Dorset.

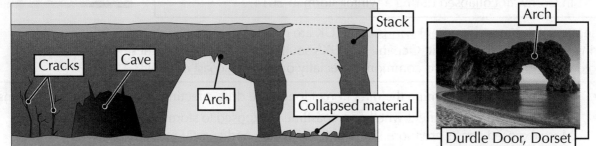

Durdle Door, Dorset

Erosion and gravity — they've always been arch enemies...

Just a few landforms to learn here, and as ever, learning the diagrams will help in the exam.

1) Explain how an arch, such as that shown above at Durdle Door, forms from a headland.   [2]

Coastal Landforms Caused by Deposition

Here are some more exciting <u>landforms</u> for you to learn about. This time it's all about <u>deposition</u>. Unfortunately you're going to be slightly disappointed — sandcastles won't be in the exam.

Beaches are Formed by Deposition

1) Beaches are found on coasts <u>between</u> the <u>high water mark</u> (the <u>highest point on the land</u> the <u>sea level</u> gets to) and the <u>low water mark</u> (the <u>lowest point</u> on the land the <u>sea level</u> gets to).

2) They're formed by <u>constructive waves</u> (see p.8) depositing material like <u>sand</u> and <u>shingle</u>.

3) <u>Sand</u> and <u>shingle beaches</u> have different <u>characteristics</u>:

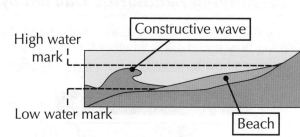

- <u>Sand</u> beaches are <u>flat</u> and <u>wide</u> — sand particles are small and the weak backwash <u>can</u> move them <u>back down</u> the beach, creating a <u>long, gentle slope</u>.
- <u>Shingle</u> beaches are <u>steep</u> and <u>narrow</u> — shingle particles are <u>large</u> and the weak backwash <u>can't</u> move them back down the beach. The shingle particles <u>build up</u> and create a <u>steep slope</u>.

Deposited Sediment Forms Spits and Bars

Spits

1) <u>Spits</u> are just <u>beaches</u> that <u>stick out</u> into the sea — they're <u>joined</u> to the coast at <u>one end</u>.

2) Spits form at <u>sharp bends</u> in the coastline, e.g. at a <u>river mouth</u>.

3) <u>Longshore drift</u> transports sand and shingle <u>past</u> the bend and <u>deposits</u> it in the sea.

4) Strong winds and waves can <u>curve</u> the end of the spit (forming a <u>recurved end</u>).

5) The <u>sheltered area</u> behind the spit is a <u>low energy environment</u> — it is <u>protected from waves</u>. Lots of material <u>accumulates</u> in this area, which means <u>plants</u> can grow there.

6) <u>Over time</u>, the sheltered area can become a <u>mud flat</u> or a <u>salt marsh</u>.

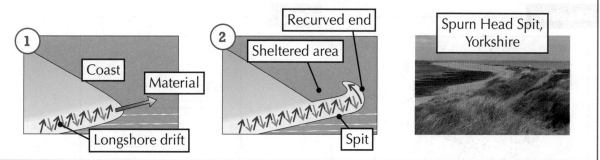

Bars

1) A bar is formed when a spit <u>joins two headlands together</u>.

2) The bar <u>cuts off</u> the bay between the headlands <u>from the sea</u>.

3) This means a <u>lagoon</u> is formed <u>behind</u> the bar.

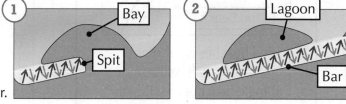

Depositional bars — they serve a delicious long beach iced tea...

Spits in geography have a very specific meaning. Don't get the wrong one and mess up your exam.

1) *Explain how spits are formed. You may include a diagram in your answer.* [4]

Identifying Coastal Landforms

I love <u>maps</u>, all geographers love maps. I can't get to sleep unless I've got one under my pillow. So I'm going to do you a favour and share my passion with you — check out these <u>coastal landforms</u>...

Identifying Landforms Caused by Erosion

You might be asked to <u>identify coastal landforms</u> on a <u>map</u> in the exam. The simplest thing they could ask is whether the map is showing <u>erosional</u> or <u>depositional landforms</u>, so here's how to <u>identify</u> a few <u>erosional landforms</u> to get you started:

Have a gander at pages 121-122 for more on reading maps.

Caves, Arches and Stacks

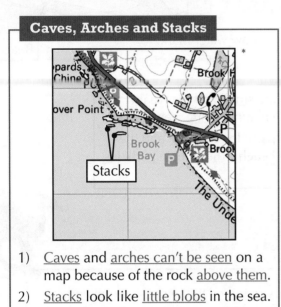

1) <u>Caves</u> and <u>arches can't be seen</u> on a map because of the rock <u>above them</u>.
2) <u>Stacks</u> look like <u>little blobs</u> in the sea.

Cliffs and Wave-cut Platforms

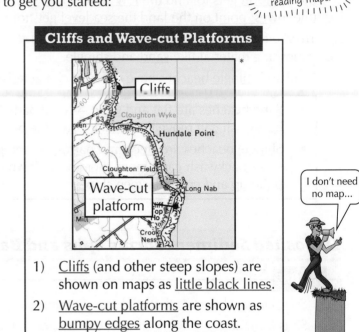

1) <u>Cliffs</u> (and other steep slopes) are shown on maps as <u>little black lines</u>.
2) <u>Wave-cut platforms</u> are shown as <u>bumpy edges</u> along the coast.

I don't need no map...

Identifying Landforms Caused by Deposition

<u>Identifying depositional landforms</u> is easy once you know that <u>beaches</u> are shown in <u>yellow</u> on maps. Here's how to <u>identify</u> a couple of <u>depositional landforms</u>:

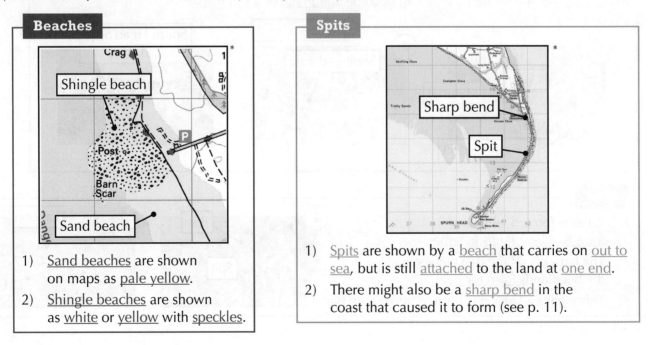

Beaches

1) <u>Sand beaches</u> are shown on maps as <u>pale yellow</u>.
2) <u>Shingle beaches</u> are shown as <u>white</u> or <u>yellow</u> with <u>speckles</u>.

Spits

1) <u>Spits</u> are shown by a <u>beach</u> that carries on <u>out to sea</u>, but is still <u>attached</u> to the land at <u>one end</u>.
2) There might also be a <u>sharp bend</u> in the coast that caused it to form (see p. 11).

Find the spit on the map — and then wipe it off...

There are some seriously easy marks up for grabs with map questions so make sure you learn this page. You could practise looking for landforms on any maps you can find, though you might struggle with the Tube map.

Topic 1 — The Changing Landscapes of the UK

Human Activity at the Coast

Ah, the <u>seaside</u>. Fish and chips, ice cream, being <u>mugged</u> by <u>seagulls</u>... you just can't beat it. The way <u>humans</u> <u>use</u> the coast can have an <u>effect</u> on the <u>landscape</u> and, you've guessed it, it's not always a <u>positive</u> thing...

Human Activities Affect Coastal Landscapes

Industry

1) Coastal <u>quarries</u> expose large areas of rock, making them more <u>vulnerable</u> to chemical <u>weathering</u> and <u>erosion</u>.

2) <u>Gravel</u> has been extracted from some <u>beaches</u> for use in the <u>construction industry</u>, e.g. for making concrete. This has <u>increased</u> the <u>risk</u> of <u>erosion</u> because there's <u>less</u> material to protect cliffs.

3) <u>Industrial growth</u> at <u>ports</u> has led to increased pressure to build on <u>salt marshes</u>. These areas provide <u>flat land</u> and <u>sheltered water</u>, which are ideal for <u>ports</u> and <u>industry</u>, but are also <u>natural flood barriers</u>. Building on them leaves the land <u>more vulnerable</u> to <u>erosion</u>.

Urbanisation

1) Coastal areas are popular places to <u>live</u> and <u>work</u>, so they often have lots of <u>development</u>, e.g. hotels and <u>infrastructure</u> (roads, rail, power lines etc.).

2) Coasts with lots of <u>settlement</u> may have more <u>coastal defences</u> than other areas because people want to <u>protect</u> their <u>homes</u> and <u>businesses</u>. This means the land is <u>better protected</u> against erosion.

3) However, building on coastal lowlands can <u>restrict</u> <u>sediment</u> supply to <u>beaches</u>, making them narrower. Narrow beaches <u>don't protect</u> the coast as well, which means the land is more <u>vulnerable</u> to erosion.

Agriculture

1) <u>Clearing</u> vegetation to make room for crops near the coast can <u>expose</u> the <u>soil</u> and underlying rock on clifftops, leaving them vulnerable to <u>weathering</u>.

2) <u>Marshland</u> is sometimes <u>reclaimed</u> and <u>drained</u> for agricultural use. This <u>reduces</u> the natural <u>flood barrier</u> that marshland provides.

3) Agricultural land has a <u>low economic value</u> which means it's often left <u>unprotected</u> and vulnerable to <u>erosion</u>.

Coastal Retreat and Flooding Affect People and the Environment

Effects on People

1) <u>Homes</u> and <u>businesses</u> in <u>low-lying coastal areas</u> are vulnerable to <u>flooding</u>. <u>Coastal recession</u> (retreat) means that the sea is <u>closer</u> to settlements, so they are <u>less protected</u> by beaches and cliffs during <u>storms</u> and <u>high tides</u>, increasing the <u>risk</u> of flooding.

2) Coastal <u>industries</u> may be shut down because of <u>flood damage</u> to <u>equipment</u> and <u>buildings</u>.

3) There's a risk of damage to <u>infrastructure</u> like <u>roads</u> and <u>rail networks</u> from flooding and coastal recession. For example, in 2014, winter storms caused <u>mass movement</u> on cliffs in <u>Dawlish, Devon</u> — this left some parts of the coastal railway lines <u>hanging</u> above the sea.

4) There's a <u>booming tourist industry</u> in coastal areas. Flooding and erosion can <u>put people off</u> visiting. <u>Businesses</u> that <u>rely on tourism</u> may <u>close</u>, leading to a loss of <u>livelihoods</u>.

5) In places with <u>rapid</u> coastal recession, e.g. <u>Happisburgh</u> in <u>Norfolk</u>, houses, businesses and farmland can be <u>lost</u> to the sea as cliffs <u>collapse</u>.

Sea level rise (p.46) also increases the risk of coastal flooding.

Effects on the Environment

1) The <u>force</u> of floodwater can <u>uproot</u> trees and plants, and <u>standing</u> floodwater drowns plants.

2) <u>Coastal flooding</u> brings <u>saltwater</u> into <u>freshwater ecosystems</u>. Increased salt levels in the soil and water can <u>damage</u> or <u>kill</u> organisms and reduce <u>soil fertility</u>.

3) Some <u>conservation areas</u> are threatened by coastal recession. For example, there are <u>lagoons</u> on the <u>Holderness coast</u> that are protected. The lagoons are separated from the sea by a <u>bar</u>. If this is <u>eroded</u> it will connect the lagoons to the <u>sea</u> and the ecosystems will be <u>destroyed</u>.

EXAM QUESTION

Building sandcastles — the most important coastal activity...

1) *Explain one way in which industry can affect coastal landscapes.* [2]

Coastal Defences

The aim of coastal management is to protect people and the environment from the impacts of erosion and flooding. Not all coastal areas can be managed though — the amount of money available is limited.

Coastal Defences Include Hard and Soft Engineering

Hard Engineering

Man-made structures built to control the flow of the sea and reduce flooding and erosion.

Soft Engineering

Schemes set up using knowledge of the sea and its processes to reduce the effects of flooding and erosion.

Different coastal defences lead to different changes in coastal landscapes — and have both costs and benefits:

Defence	What it is	Benefits	Costs
Sea Wall	• A wall made out of a hard material like concrete that reflects waves back to sea.	• It prevents erosion of the coast. • It also acts as a barrier to prevent flooding.	• It creates a strong backwash, which erodes under the wall. • Sea walls are very expensive to build and to maintain.
Rip-Rap	• Boulders that are piled up along the coast. (It's also sometimes called rock armour.) • The boulders act as a sea wall. The gaps between the rocks let water through, absorbing wave energy.	• By absorbing wave energy, rip-rap reduces erosion and flooding. • It's a fairly cheap defence.	• Boulders can be moved around by strong waves, so they need to be replaced. • Rip-rap prevents cliffs from being eroded, so there's no new material to replenish beaches. This can gradually lower the level of the beach.
Groynes	• Wooden or stone fences that are built at right angles to the coast. • They trap material transported by longshore drift, helping to build up the beach.	• They create wider beaches which slow the waves. This protects the land from flooding and erosion. • They're a fairly cheap defence.	• They starve beaches further down the coast of sand, making them narrower. Narrower beaches don't protect the coast as well, leading to greater erosion and floods.
Beach Nourishment	• Sand and shingle from elsewhere (e.g. from the seabed) or from lower down the beach are added to the upper part of beaches.	• It creates wider beaches which slow the waves. • This gives greater protection from flooding and erosion.	• Taking material from the seabed can kill organisms like sponges and corals. • It's a very expensive defence. • It has to be repeated.
Managed Retreat	• Removing an existing defence and allowing the land behind it to flood. • This land eventually becomes marshland, which protects the land behind it from flooding and erosion.	• It can be cheaper in the long run as it doesn't need maintaining. • The marshland can also provide new habitats for plants and animals.	• Choosing areas to flood can cause conflicts, e.g. flooding farmland affects farmers' livelihoods. • Saltwater can damage existing ecosystems.

Managed retreat — "Going forward, we're going backwards..."

Coastal defences change the landscape by preventing erosion or transport in some places and increasing it in others. Make sure you know at least a couple of the costs and benefits for each strategy so you'll be a winner in the exam.

Topic 1 — The Changing Landscapes of the UK

Coastal Landscape — Dorset Coast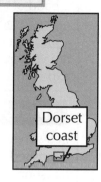

If <u>coastal landforms</u> are your thing (and let's face it, how could they not be), then the <u>Dorset coast</u> is paradise on Earth. It's got the lot — <u>headlands</u>, <u>bays</u>, <u>arches</u>, <u>stacks</u>, <u>coves</u>, <u>lagoons</u>...

The Dorset Coast is a Popular Tourist Destination in Southern England

1) The <u>Dorset coast</u> is located on the <u>south</u> coast of England.

2) It is called the <u>Jurassic Coast</u> because it has lots of <u>fossils</u> dating from the Jurassic period.

3) It also has a variety of <u>coastal landforms</u>, including <u>sandy beaches</u>, making it a popular tourist destination.

> Dorset coast

The Dorset Coast has Distinctive Geology...

1) The coastline is made from bands of <u>hard rock</u> and <u>soft rock</u>, forming a <u>concordant</u> coastline to the west, and a <u>discordant</u> coastline to the east. The rocks have been <u>eroded</u> at <u>different rates</u>, which has created the area's coastal landforms, e.g. <u>Lulworth Cove</u>.

2) <u>Soft rocks</u> like sandstone and clay are <u>easily eroded</u> by hydraulic action and abrasion, leading to faster rates of <u>coastal retreat</u> and the formation of <u>bays</u>, e.g. <u>Swanage Bay</u>.

3) The harder <u>chalk</u> and <u>limestone</u> cliffs are <u>weathered</u> and <u>eroded</u> more <u>slowly</u>, meaning that they stick out into the sea as exposed <u>headlands</u>. <u>Chalk</u> and <u>limestone</u> are vulnerable to erosion by <u>solution</u>, where the sea water <u>chemically reacts</u> with the rock, causing it to <u>dissolve</u>.

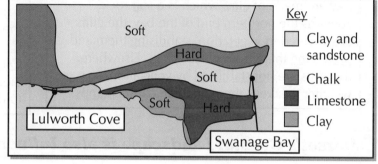

Key
- ☐ Clay and sandstone
- ▨ Chalk
- ■ Limestone
- ▥ Clay

...and a Distinctive Climate

1) The Dorset coast has <u>warm</u>, <u>dry</u> summers (around 21 °C in July) and <u>mild</u> and <u>wet</u> winters (average minimum temperature in January is about 3 °C).

2) <u>Salt weathering</u> is the dominant form of <u>mechanical</u> weathering, particularly in summer. The warm temperatures cause sea water to evaporate from rocks <u>quickly</u>, leaving a <u>build-up</u> of salt crystals in tiny <u>cracks</u> in the rock. The <u>mild</u> winters mean that it's usually <u>not cold enough</u> for <u>freeze-thaw weathering</u>.

3) The Dorset coast's <u>location</u> means that it's <u>exposed</u> to <u>prevailing winds</u> from the <u>south-west</u>. These can bring <u>storms</u> to the UK from the <u>Atlantic Ocean</u> with <u>high energy</u>, <u>destructive</u> waves which <u>increase erosion</u> of the cliffs.

4) Lots of <u>rain</u> makes Dorset's <u>chalk</u> and <u>limestone</u> cliffs vulnerable to <u>carbonation weathering</u> because the rainwater is <u>slightly acidic</u>.

5) Heavy rainfall can also cause soil and rocks to become <u>saturated</u> with water. This makes them <u>heavier</u>, <u>softer</u> and more <u>slippery</u>, making <u>mass movement</u> more likely. In the winter, when there is more <u>rainfall</u>, there are often <u>slides</u> and <u>slumps</u> on the clay cliffs.

> Mudslides and rock falls near Kimmeridge

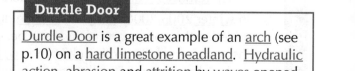

Dorset's Coastal Landforms Are Influenced by Physical Processes

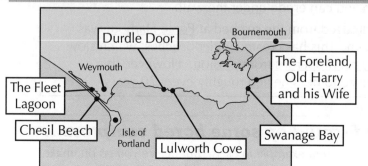

Durdle Door

<u>Durdle Door</u> is a great example of an <u>arch</u> (see p.10) on a <u>hard limestone headland</u>. <u>Hydraulic action</u>, <u>abrasion</u> and <u>attrition</u> by <u>waves</u> opened up a <u>crack</u> in the <u>headland</u>, which became a <u>cave</u> and then developed into an arch. The arch is being gradually broken down by <u>mechanical</u>, <u>chemical</u> and <u>biological weathering</u>.

Coastal Landscape — Dorset Coast

Lulworth Cove

Lulworth Cove is a small bay formed after a gap was eroded in a band of limestone. Behind the limestone is a band of clay. The clay is softer, so it has been eroded and transported away, forming the bay. The limestone cliffs forming the back wall of the bay are vulnerable to mass movement, and experience small slides and slumps.

Chesil Beach

Chesil Beach is a tombolo (a type of spit that extends out to an island). It joins the Isle of Portland to the mainland. It was formed by longshore drift transporting material that was deposited at the end of the last glacial period. Behind Chesil Beach is a shallow lagoon called The Fleet Lagoon.

Swanage Bay

In Swanage Bay, sand and shingle have been deposited, forming a beach. This material is transported by longshore drift from the south to the north of the bay. The beach has been losing material for decades. The cliffs backing Swanage Bay are made of clay, which is a soft rock. Towards the northern end of the bay, the cliffs are covered in vegetation, stabilising them and protecting them from weathering. Elsewhere, the cliffs are not stabilised by vegetation, so wet weather weakens them and can cause slumps.

The Foreland, Old Harry and his Wife

In between two areas of softer rock that have formed bays, there is a headland called The Foreland made from a band of harder rock (chalk). An arch at the end of the headland has collapsed to form a stack called Old Harry and a stump (a collapsed stack) called Old Harry's Wife. Salt and carbonation weathering, along with erosion, are gradually wearing down Old Harry and his Wife.

Dorset's Coastal Landscape is also Influenced by Human Activities

Tourism

1) The Dorset coast attracts large numbers of tourists. Coastal footpaths run along the cliff tops, and are gradually worn down as people repeatedly walk on them.

2) Vegetation along the cliff top may be trampled and worn away by repeated use of the footpaths. This can expose the underlying soil and rock to weathering and erosion by wind and rain.

Industry

1) A lot of quarrying has taken place along the coast, e.g. on the Isle of Portland, because limestone is a valuable building stone. This removed the more resistant limestone from the cliffs, leaving the rock underneath vulnerable to weathering and erosion.

2) Up until the 1960s, gravel was removed from Chesil Beach for use in the construction industry. Material was removed from the beach much more quickly than the sea could replenish it, so this began to damage the landform.

Coastal Management

1) New timber groynes were put in place along Swanage beach in 2005-6. They've helped to stop the loss of beach material. However, by stopping beach material from moving along the coast, they've starved areas further down the coast of sediment, making them narrower.

2) There are concrete sea walls in place along most of Swanage beach. These reflect waves back out to sea, preventing the erosion of the coast. But they can create a strong backwash, which removes sediment from the beach and can erode under the wall.

3) In winter 2005/2006, sand and shingle dredged from the sea bed at Poole Harbour was added to the upper parts of Swanage beach. This has created wider beaches, which slow the waves and help protect cliffs and coastal properties from erosion. However, this replenishment cost £5 million and will need to be repeated roughly every 20 years.

I heard Chesil Beach was actually formed by some bored sculptors...

You don't have to learn about Dorset if you've studied a different example in class. But before you go on, make sure you know the ins and outs of the landforms, physical processes and human impacts in your chosen area.

Revision Summary

Well this is most irregular. A revision summary partway through a topic? Absolute madness. I'm just glad the great old editor Cornelius Gerald Parsnipish never lived to see this — he'd be absolutely furious.

Anyway, you've coasted through the first part of the section — that means it's time to find out just how much of this information has been deposited in your noggin. Have a go at the questions below. If you're finding it tough, just look back at the pages in the section and then have another go. You'll be ready to move on to the next part when you can answer all of these questions without breaking a sweat.

Rocks and the UK Physical Landscape (p.2-4) ☐

1) a) How are igneous rocks formed?
   b) What are sedimentary rocks formed from?
   c) Describe how metamorphic rocks are formed.
2) Give two ways in which tectonic activity has shaped the UK landscape.
3) Outline the characteristics of slate and schist.
4) Explain how the UK landscape has been shaped by glacial periods.

Landscape Processes (p.5-6) ☑

5) Give three physical processes that alter the landscape.
6) a) Give an example of a lowland landscape.
   b) Outline how physical processes have created this landscape.
7) How does forestry change the landscape?
8) How does settlement alter the landscape?

Coastal Processes and Landforms (p.7-12) ☐

9) How does salt weathering break up rock?
10) What are the four types of erosion caused by waves? Explain how they work.
11) What are the characteristics of destructive waves?
12) How does longshore drift transport sediment along a coast?
13) What are the characteristics of constructive waves?
14) What is the difference between a discordant and a concordant coastline?
15) Give three ways that the UK's climate affects coastal erosion and retreat.
16) True or false: headlands and bays form along concordant coastlines.
17) Give two features of a shingle beach.
18) How do bars form?
19) What do stacks look like on a map?
20) On maps, what do speckles on top of yellow shading tell you?

Human Activity and Coastal Management (p.13-14) ☐

21) How does urbanisation affect the coast?
22) Explain how agriculture can affect the coast.
23) a) Give two effects of coastal flooding on people.
    b) Give two effects of coastal flooding on the environment.
24) What is the difference between hard and soft engineering? Give an example of each.
25) Name one disadvantage of using groynes for coastal management.
26) What is managed retreat?

UK Coastal Landscape — Example (p. 15-16) ☑

27) For a UK coastline you have studied:
    a) Name one erosional landform and one depositional landform.
    b) Describe the climate of the region.
    c) Give two examples of how human activities have affected the coastal landscape there.

River Landscapes

You're probably best off going to the loo <u>before</u> you start this. It's all about <u>flowing water</u>...

A River's Long Profile and Cross Profile Vary Over its Course

1) The <u>path</u> of a river as it <u>flows downhill</u> is called its <u>course</u>.

2) Rivers have an <u>upper course</u> (closest to the <u>source</u> of the river), a <u>middle course</u> and a <u>lower course</u> (closest to the <u>mouth</u> of the river).

3) Rivers form <u>channels</u> and <u>valleys</u> as they <u>flow downhill</u>.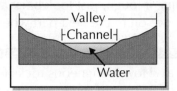

4) They <u>erode</u> the landscape — <u>wear it down</u>, then <u>transport</u> the material downstream where it's <u>deposited</u>.

5) The <u>shape</u> of the <u>valley</u> and <u>channel changes</u> along the river depending on whether <u>erosion</u> or <u>deposition</u> is having the most impact (is the dominant process).

6) The <u>long profile</u> of a river shows you how the <u>gradient</u> (steepness) <u>changes</u> over the different courses.

7) The <u>cross profile</u> shows you what a <u>cross section</u> of the river looks like.

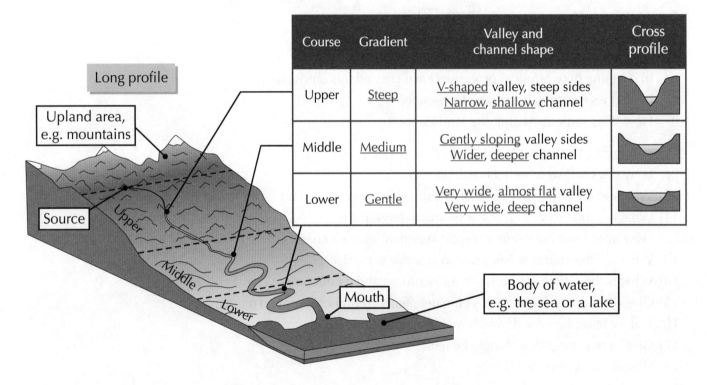

Course	Gradient	Valley and channel shape	Cross profile
Upper	<u>Steep</u>	<u>V-shaped</u> valley, steep sides Narrow, <u>shallow</u> channel	
Middle	<u>Medium</u>	<u>Gently sloping</u> valley sides <u>Wider</u>, <u>deeper</u> channel	
Lower	<u>Gentle</u>	Very wide, <u>almost flat</u> valley Very wide, <u>deep</u> channel	

Vertical and Lateral Erosion Change the Cross Profile of a River

Erosion can be <u>vertical</u> or <u>lateral</u> — both types happen at the <u>same time</u>, but one is usually <u>dominant</u> over the other at <u>different points</u> along the river:

There's more on vertical and lateral erosion on the next page.

Vertical erosion

This <u>deepens</u> the river valley (and channel), making it <u>V-shaped</u>. It's dominant in the <u>upper course</u> of the river. High <u>turbulence</u> causes the <u>rough, angular particles</u> to be scraped along the river bed, causing intense <u>downwards</u> erosion.

Lateral erosion

This <u>widens</u> the river valley (and channel) during the formation of <u>meanders</u> (see page 23). It's dominant in the <u>middle</u> and <u>lower courses</u>.

Don't show me that cross profile — just go with the flow...

Sit back, close your eyes and imagine gently babbling brooks. Then you'd best get on with learning this page. Make sure you can describe a river's long profile and its cross profile at different points along its course.

River Landscapes

EXAMPLE

Grab a paddle and hold on to your hat — it's time for a voyage along a northern river.

The River Eden's Landscape Changes Along its Course

1) The River Eden is in north-west England, between the mountains of the Lake District and the Pennines. It's 145 km long from source to mouth.

2) The River Eden's source is in the Pennine hills in south Cumbria. It flows north-west through Appleby-in-Westmorland and Carlisle. Its mouth is in the Solway Firth at the Scottish border.

Eden basin

A river basin is the area of land around a river where any rain that falls eventually makes its way into that river.

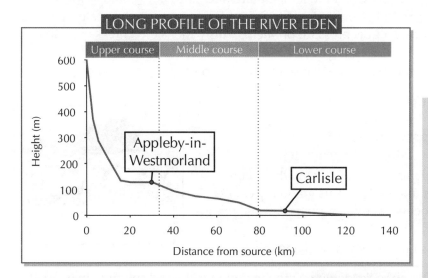

LONG PROFILE OF THE RIVER EDEN

Upper course | Middle course | Lower course

Appleby-in-Westmorland

Carlisle

Height (m) / Distance from source (km)

UPPER COURSE

- The source of the Eden is about 600 m above sea level in an area of hard, resistant rock.
- The valley is steep-sided due to vertical erosion and the channel has a steep gradient.
- The river channel is narrow and shallow — this means the discharge (see p.28) is low. The velocity (speed) is low due to friction from the rough channel sides and bed.
- The river carries large, angular stones.

River Eden at Appleby

MIDDLE COURSE

- The middle parts of the Eden basin are made from sandstone, a soft, less-resistant rock which is easily eroded by the river. This means that the river valley becomes wider because of lateral (sideways) erosion.

A meander at Salkeld

- The valley sides become gentle slopes and the gradient of the channel is less steep.
- The river channel also becomes wider and deeper. Discharge increases as more streams join the main river.
- The river flows faster than in the upper course as the channel sides are smoother, which leads to less friction.
- The river's sediment load is made up of smaller and more rounded rocks than it was in the upper course as erosion continues (see page 21).

LOWER COURSE

- In the lower course, the valley is very wide and flat.
- By the time the Eden reaches Carlisle, it's only a few metres above sea level.

- The river has a high velocity (it's flowing fast) because there's very little friction from the channel's smooth sides. It also has a very large discharge because two other rivers (the Caldew and the Petteril) join the Eden in Carlisle.
- The river channel is very wide and deep — in the centre of Carlisle, the Eden is more than 50 m wide. Material carried by the river is fine and well-rounded — most of it is carried by suspension or solution (see page 21).

River Eden at Carlisle

The Eden basin — a physical geographer's paradise...

You don't have to use this named river if you've studied another in class, just make sure you know how the river's landscape changes over its course. Splitting it up into the upper, middle and lower courses will make it easier to learn.

River Processes

There are a lot of <u>processes</u> that influence river landscapes — and they're not all just to do with the water flowing along the <u>channel</u>. <u>Weathering</u> and <u>mass movement</u> can occur throughout the entire <u>river valley</u>.

Weathering Helps Shape River Valleys

Weathering <u>breaks down rocks</u> on the valley and channel sides.
<u>Mechanical</u>, <u>chemical</u> and <u>biological</u> weathering can all take place in <u>river landscapes</u>.

1) <u>Mechanical weathering</u> is when rock is broken down <u>without</u> any changes to its <u>chemical composition</u>.

> For example, <u>freeze-thaw weathering</u> occurs when the temperature alternates <u>above</u> and <u>below</u> 0 °C (the <u>freezing point</u> of water). Water <u>expands</u> when it turns to ice, so when <u>rainwater</u> repeatedly <u>freezes</u> and <u>thaws</u> inside cracks in rocks, it puts pressure on them. This <u>widens the cracks</u> over time.

2) <u>Chemical weathering</u> is when rock is broken down because of <u>changes</u> to its <u>chemical composition</u>.

> - Some <u>minerals</u> that make up rocks are <u>soluble in water</u>, e.g. rock salt. The minerals <u>dissolve</u> in rainwater and are washed away, breaking the rock down. This is <u>dissolution weathering</u>.
> - <u>Rainwater</u> is slightly <u>acidic</u>, and this acid can <u>react</u> with certain minerals in rocks, causing them to <u>dissolve</u>. This gradually causes the rock to <u>break down</u>, in a process called <u>carbonation weathering</u>.

Dissolution weathering can also be known as solution weathering.

Carbonation weathering in Cumbria

3) <u>Biological weathering</u> is when rock is broken down by <u>living things</u>.

> In river landscapes, <u>plant roots</u> can break rocks down by growing into <u>cracks</u> and <u>splitting</u> them apart.

Mass Movements May Occur in River Landscapes

1) <u>Mass movement</u> is when <u>gravity</u> causes the movement of material <u>down a slope</u>.

> <u>Slides</u> and <u>slumps</u> are two types of <u>mass movement</u> that can take place in river landscapes. In slides, material shifts in a <u>straight line</u>, whereas in slumps, material shifts with a <u>rotation</u>.

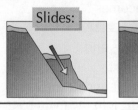
Slides: Slumps:

2) When a river <u>erodes</u> the base of a valley side (see next page), it can cause <u>undercutting</u> of the slope, which makes mass movements <u>more likely</u> to happen.

3) Mass movements are also more likely to occur when the valley sides are <u>saturated with water</u> after rain or flooding, as the water acts as a <u>lubricant</u> (it makes them <u>slippery</u>), and makes material <u>heavier</u>.

4) <u>Weathering</u> (see above) can also increase the likelihood of mass movements — when material has been <u>loosened</u> by <u>weathering</u>, it is held together more weakly.

5) Mass movement can add large amounts of material to the river's <u>load</u> (all of the solid material carried by a river).

Result of mass movement into the River Spey in the Scottish Highlands

---

EXAM QUESTION

How do you arrest a Viking? 'Freeze, Thor!'

If you're not feeling too weathered after all that information, have a go at this question:
1) Give one impact that biological weathering might have on a river landscape. [1]

Topic 1 — The Changing Landscapes of the UK

River Processes

Rivers <u>scrape</u> and <u>smash rocks up</u>, <u>push</u> them about, then <u>dump</u> them when they've had enough...

There are Four Processes of Erosion That Act in the River Channel

1) <u>Hydraulic action</u>

> The <u>force</u> of the water <u>breaks rock particles away</u> from the <u>river channel</u>.

I'm taking hydraulic action against this revision.

2) <u>Abrasion</u>

> Eroded <u>rocks</u> picked up by the river <u>scrape</u> and <u>rub</u> against the <u>channel</u>, wearing it away. <u>Most erosion</u> happens by <u>abrasion</u>.

3) <u>Attrition</u>

> Eroded <u>rocks</u> picked up by the river <u>smash into each other</u> and break into <u>smaller fragments</u>. Their <u>edges</u> also get <u>rounded off</u> as they rub together. The <u>further</u> material travels, the more <u>eroded</u> it gets — attrition causes <u>particle size</u> to <u>decrease</u> between a river's <u>source</u> and its <u>mouth</u>.

4) <u>Solution</u>

> River water <u>dissolves</u> some types of rock, e.g. <u>chalk</u> and <u>limestone</u>.

The faster a river's flowing, the more erosion happens.

Transportation is the Movement of Eroded Material by the River

The <u>material</u> a river has <u>eroded</u> is <u>transported downstream</u>.
There are <u>four processes</u> of transportation:

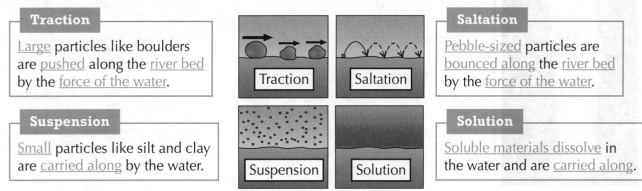

Traction

<u>Large</u> particles like boulders are <u>pushed</u> along the <u>river bed</u> by the <u>force of the water</u>.

Saltation

<u>Pebble-sized</u> particles are <u>bounced along</u> the <u>river bed</u> by the <u>force of the water</u>.

Suspension

<u>Small</u> particles like silt and clay are <u>carried along</u> by the water.

Solution

<u>Soluble materials dissolve</u> in the water and are <u>carried along</u>.

Deposition is When a River Drops Eroded Material

Deposition is when a river <u>drops</u> the <u>eroded material</u> it's <u>transporting</u>.

It happens when a river <u>slows down</u> (<u>loses velocity</u>).

There are a <u>few reasons</u> why rivers slow down and deposit material:

> 1) The <u>volume</u> of <u>water</u> in the river <u>falls</u>.
> 2) The <u>amount</u> of <u>eroded material</u> in the water <u>increases</u>.
> 3) The water is <u>shallower</u>, e.g. on the <u>inside of a bend</u>.
> 4) The river <u>reaches</u> its <u>mouth</u>.

Oi!

I can't bear the suspension — just go ahead and dump me...

There are lots of very similar names to remember here — try not to confuse saltation, solution and suspension. And yes, confusingly, solution is both a process of erosion and transportation. Now saltate on over to the next page...

River Landforms — Erosion

If you don't know anything about <u>waterfalls</u> then you haven't been watching enough <u>shampoo adverts</u>. Now's your chance to find out how <u>geology</u> and <u>erosion</u> influence their formation (as well as other landforms).

Geology Influences the Formation of River Landforms

1) Rivers flowing through areas of <u>hard rock</u> have a <u>slower</u> rate of erosion because hard rocks are <u>more resistant</u>, whereas areas with <u>softer rocks</u> will experience <u>more erosion</u>.

2) Landscapes with <u>more resistant rocks</u> tend to have <u>steeper valley sides</u>. Landscapes with <u>less resistant rocks</u> have <u>gentle sloping valley sides</u>.

3) The course of a river will always follow the path of least resistance, so in areas where <u>both</u> soft and hard rocks are present, rivers prefer to erode the <u>softer</u> rocks.

4) The types of <u>landforms</u> that develop in a landscape depend on the geology. Landforms are often found at the <u>boundary</u> between hard and soft rocks.

Waterfalls and Gorges are Found in the Upper Course of a River

1) <u>Waterfalls</u> form where a river flows over an area of <u>hard rock</u> followed by an area of <u>softer rock</u>.

2) The <u>softer rock</u> is <u>eroded</u> (by <u>hydraulic action</u> and <u>abrasion</u> — see previous page) <u>more</u> than the <u>hard rock</u>, creating a '<u>step</u>' in the river.

3) As water goes over the step it <u>erodes</u> <u>more and more</u> of the softer rock.

4) A <u>steep drop</u> is eventually created, which is called a <u>waterfall</u>.

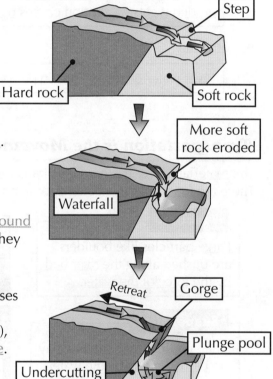

5) The <u>hard rock</u> is eventually <u>undercut</u> by erosion. It becomes <u>unsupported</u> and <u>collapses</u>.

6) The collapsed rocks are <u>swirled around</u> at the foot of the waterfall where they <u>erode</u> the softer rock by <u>abrasion</u>. This creates a deep <u>plunge pool</u>.

7) Over time, <u>more undercutting</u> causes <u>more collapses</u>. The waterfall will <u>retreat</u> (move back up the channel), leaving behind a steep-sided <u>gorge</u>.

Interlocking Spurs are Nothing to do with Cowboys

1) In the <u>upper course</u> of a river most of the <u>erosion</u> is <u>vertically downwards</u>. This creates <u>steep-sided</u>, <u>V-shaped valleys</u>.

2) The rivers <u>aren't powerful enough</u> to <u>erode</u> <u>laterally</u> (sideways) — they have to <u>wind around</u> the <u>high hillsides</u> (spurs) that stick out into their paths on either side.

3) These hillsides are often made of a <u>resistant</u> rock which the river <u>can't erode</u>, so the river erodes the <u>less resistant</u> rock <u>between</u> the spurs as it winds down the valley.

4) The <u>hillsides that interlock</u> with each other (like a zip if you were looking from above) as the river winds around them are called <u>interlocking spurs</u>.

Interlocking spurs along a river in Shropshire

Topic 1 — The Changing Landscapes of the UK

River Landforms — Erosion and Deposition

When a river's <u>eroding</u> and <u>depositing</u> material, <u>meanders</u> and <u>ox-bow lakes</u> can form.
Australians have a different name for <u>ox-bow lakes</u> — billabongs. Stay tuned for more incredible facts.

Meanders are Formed by Erosion and Deposition

Rivers develop <u>large bends</u> called <u>meanders</u> in their <u>middle</u> and <u>lower courses</u>, in areas where there are both <u>shallow</u> and <u>deep</u> sections in the channel:

1) The <u>current</u> (the flow of the water) is <u>faster</u> on the <u>outside</u> of the bend because the river channel is <u>deeper</u> (there's <u>less friction</u> to <u>slow</u> the water down).

2) So the outside of the bend is a <u>high-energy</u> environment, meaning more <u>erosion</u> (<u>abrasion</u> and <u>hydraulic action</u> — see p.21) takes place there, forming steep-sided <u>river cliffs</u>.

3) The inside of the bend is a <u>low-energy</u> environment. The <u>current</u> is <u>slower</u> there because the river channel is <u>shallower</u> (there's <u>more friction</u> to <u>slow</u> the water down).

4) So eroded material is <u>deposited</u> on the <u>inside</u> of the bend.

5) Over time, this material builds up to form a <u>point bar</u> — a crescent-shaped gentle <u>slope</u> made of <u>sand</u> or <u>stones</u>.

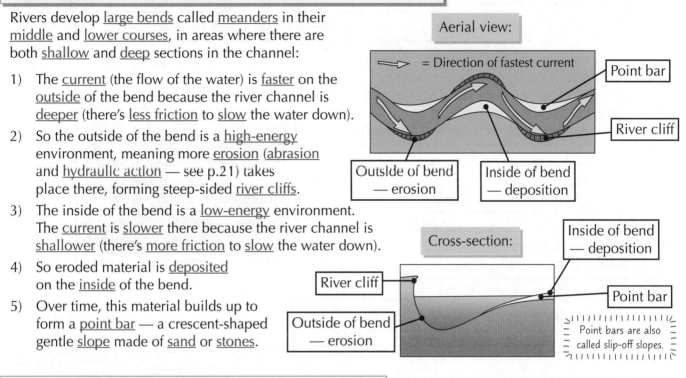

Aerial view:

⟹ = Direction of fastest current

Point bar

River cliff

Outside of bend — erosion

Inside of bend — deposition

Cross-section:

Inside of bend — deposition

River cliff

Point bar

Outside of bend — erosion

Point bars are also called slip-off slopes.

Ox-Bow Lakes are Formed from Meanders

Meanders get <u>larger</u> over time — they can eventually turn into an <u>ox-bow lake</u>:

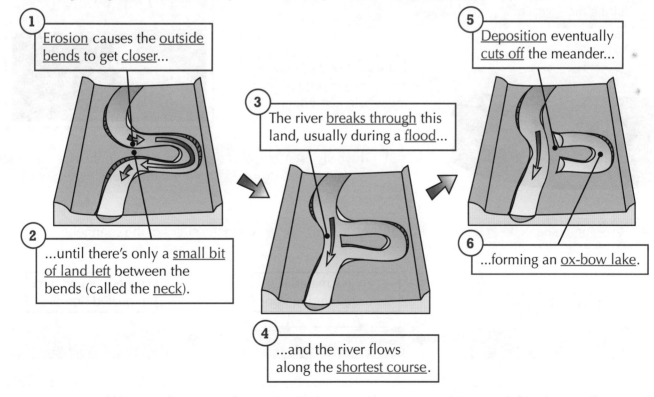

1 <u>Erosion</u> causes the <u>outside bends</u> to get <u>closer</u>...

2 ...until there's only a <u>small bit of land left</u> between the bends (called the <u>neck</u>).

3 The river <u>breaks through</u> this land, usually during a <u>flood</u>...

4 ...and the river flows along the <u>shortest course</u>.

5 <u>Deposition</u> eventually <u>cuts off</u> the meander...

6 ...forming an <u>ox-bow lake</u>.

Fun fact — 'meanders' is a rubbish anagram of 'dreamers'

In the exam, don't be afraid to draw diagrams of river landforms — examiners love a good diagram and they can help make your answer clear. Oh, and bonus CGP grammar tip: say "Her and me" or "She and I", not "Me and 'er"...

River Landforms — Deposition

When rivers dump material they don't do it by text message — they make attractive landforms instead.
You saw point bars on the previous page, but here are two more depositional landforms you need to know.

Flood Plains are Flat Areas of Land that Flood

1) The flood plain is the wide valley floor on either side of a river which occasionally gets flooded.

2) When a river floods onto the flood plain, the water slows down and deposits the eroded material that it's transporting. This builds up the flood plain (makes it higher).

Flood plain

3) Meanders migrate (move) across the flood plain, making it wider.

4) Meanders also migrate downstream, flattening out the valley floor.

5) The deposition that happens on the point bars of meanders (see previous page) also builds up the flood plain.

Levees are Natural Embankments

1) Levees are natural embankments (raised bits) along the edges of a river channel.

Flood plains and levees are both found in the lower course of a river.

Levees

2) During a flood, eroded material is deposited over the whole flood plain.

3) The heaviest material is deposited closest to the river channel, because it gets dropped first when the river slows down.

4) Over time, the deposited material builds up, creating levees along the edges of the channel.

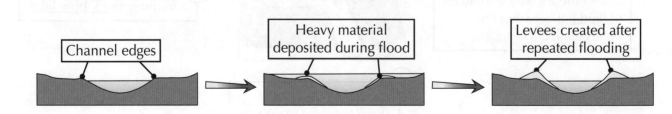

Channel edges | Heavy material deposited during flood | Levees created after repeated flooding

EXAM QUESTION

Oh, I just love a levee — it must be my cheery deposition...

These depositional landforms might not be as exciting as waterfalls, but you still need to know about them. Once you've read this page, try this question to see how much information has been deposited in your brain.

1) Explain how levees are formed. [3]

Identifying River Landforms

GEOGRAPHY SKILLS

You can know all the facts about <u>rivers</u>, but if you don't know what their <u>features</u> look like on <u>maps</u> then some of the exam questions will be a wee bit tricky. Here's something I prepared earlier...

Contour Lines *Tell you the Direction a River Flows*

<u>Contour lines</u> are the <u>orange lines</u> drawn all over maps. They tell you about the <u>height</u> of the land (in metres) by the numbers marked on them, and the <u>steepness</u> of the land by how <u>close together</u> they are (the <u>closer</u> they are, the <u>steeper</u> the slope).

It sounds obvious, but rivers <u>can't</u> flow uphill. Unless gravity's gone screwy, a river flows <u>from higher</u> contour lines <u>to lower</u> ones. Have a look at this map of Cawfell Beck:

Take a peek at pages 121-122 for more on reading maps.

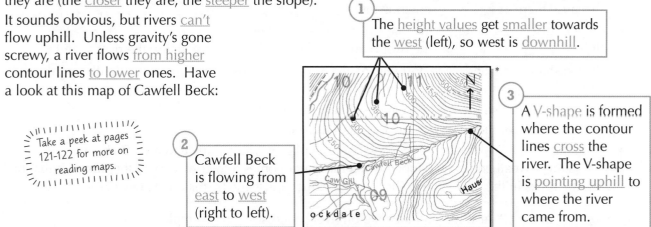

1 The <u>height values</u> get <u>smaller</u> towards the <u>west</u> (left), so west is <u>downhill</u>.

2 Cawfell Beck is flowing from <u>east</u> to <u>west</u> (right to left).

3 A <u>V-shape</u> is formed where the contour lines <u>cross</u> the river. The V-shape is <u>pointing uphill</u> to where the river came from.

Maps contain *Evidence for River Landforms*

Exam questions might ask you to look at a <u>map</u> and give the <u>evidence</u> for a <u>landform</u>. Remember, different landforms are found in the <u>upper</u> and <u>lower course</u> — you can use this evidence to help you <u>identify</u> them.

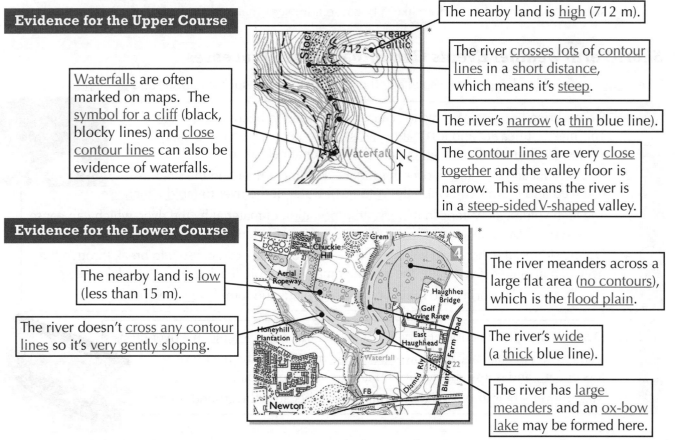

Evidence for the Upper Course

<u>Waterfalls</u> are often marked on maps. The <u>symbol for a cliff</u> (black, blocky lines) and <u>close contour lines</u> can also be evidence of waterfalls.

The nearby land is <u>high</u> (712 m).

The river <u>crosses lots</u> of <u>contour lines</u> in a <u>short distance</u>, which means it's <u>steep</u>.

The river's <u>narrow</u> (a <u>thin</u> blue line).

The <u>contour lines</u> are very <u>close together</u> and the valley floor is narrow. This means the river is in a <u>steep-sided V-shaped</u> valley.

Evidence for the Lower Course

The nearby land is <u>low</u> (less than 15 m).

The river doesn't <u>cross any contour lines</u> so it's <u>very gently sloping</u>.

The river meanders across a large flat area (<u>no contours</u>), which is the <u>flood plain</u>.

The river's <u>wide</u> (a <u>thick</u> blue line).

The river has <u>large meanders</u> and an <u>ox-bow lake</u> may be formed here.

My contours are largely a result of too much chocolate...

It's important to understand what maps are showing, so read this page like there's no tomorrow, then find a map and explain to anyone who'll listen the evidence it provides for the many beautiful and varied features of rivers.

Topic 1 — The Changing Landscapes of the UK

Climate, Weather and River Landscapes

The weather and climate in the UK play a big role in shaping river landscapes.

The Climate Has an Influence on River Landscapes in the UK

1) Rainfall has a big impact on river processes and landscapes. Some areas of the UK, e.g. north-west Scotland, have more rainfall than others, e.g. south-east England.

- Rivers in wetter climates have a higher discharge (see p.28) because there's more water entering the river channel.

  See p.21 for more on the processes of erosion.

- Higher discharge increases the rate of erosion — if a river has a higher volume of water, it has more power to erode the river banks and bed. This adds material to the river's load.

- It also shapes the landscape, forming V-shaped valleys in the river's upper course (through vertical erosion) and a wide, flat flood plain in the lower course (through lateral erosion).

- Transportation also increases when there's a higher discharge because the river has more energy to carry material.

- Chemical weathering (see p.20) occurs more in places with a rainy climate. Both carbonation and dissolution weathering can happen when rainwater comes into contact with the minerals that make up the rocks in the river valley. This can affect the landscape by making valley sides less stable.

2) Temperature in the UK also has an influence on river processes. For example:

- During winter, temperatures can often drop below freezing, especially at night. This leads to freeze-thaw weathering (see p.20).

- In the summer, the higher temperatures speed up the rate of chemical reactions, so the rate of chemical weathering tends to increase.

- This can affect the shape of a river landscape — weathering means mass movements such as rockfalls become more likely, because it loosens material on the valley sides.

Short-Term Weather Events Can Impact River Processes

River processes and landscapes are also affected by weather events, such as storms and droughts:

Storms

1) Storms bring heavy rainfall, which causes the ground to become saturated. This makes it heavier and less stable. Mass movement is then more likely — river banks may slide or slump into the river channel (see p.20).

2) Heavy rain can flow quickly over the surface and into a river and the streams that feed into it. This can cause the volume of water in the river to rapidly increase.

3) The high volume of water can increase transportation of material by the river, which can cause more erosion by abrasion and hydraulic action — particularly in the upper course of the river.

4) During storms, the increased volume and velocity of a river can cause it to break through the neck of a meander. Eventually, the meander may be cut off, leaving an ox-bow lake (see p.23).

5) Floods caused by storms also build up the flood plain and form levees (see p.24).

Droughts

1) During a drought (a period of very little rainfall), the water volume in a river drops.

2) Less erosion occurs, because lower discharge means that the river has less energy, and is less able to pick up and transport material.

3) Mass movement is also less likely to take place, because the ground is dry.

Success in the exam might depend on weather you've revised this page...

The fact that more rainfall makes rivers bigger and more powerful might seem like common sense, but it's the details that'll really impress in the exam — so, make sure you know how the UK's weather and climate affect the different river processes. I'm sure you've reached peak excitement about rivers by now, but keep it together for just a bit longer...

Topic 1 — The Changing Landscapes of the UK

Human Activity in River Landscapes

<u>Human</u> activities like building, farming and industry can have a <u>big impact</u> on the landscape, and <u>rivers</u> are <u>no exception</u> — it's time to look at how we've been <u>sticking our oar in</u>.

River Processes and Landscapes are Affected by Urbanisation...

1) There has been an increase in the amount of land in the UK taken up by <u>urban areas</u>. In many places, buildings have been constructed on <u>flood plains</u>.

2) Urban areas have a lot of <u>impermeable</u> surfaces, e.g. <u>tarmac</u> and <u>concrete</u>. Water <u>can't infiltrate</u> (soak) into these surfaces. So, when it rains, more water <u>flows quickly overland</u> (called <u>surface runoff</u>), and <u>gutters</u> and <u>drains</u> quickly take this runoff to rivers. This rapidly increases the <u>volume</u> of water in the river (the river discharge).

3) Because more rainwater gets into a river in a <u>shorter space of time</u> in urban areas, the river has more <u>energy</u>, which may <u>increase</u> the amount of <u>erosion</u> and <u>transportation</u> that takes place.

4) In urban areas, rivers are often <u>managed</u> to reduce the <u>risk</u> of flooding (next page). River defences can cause <u>major changes</u> to the river landscape — see page 30.

...Agriculture...

1) <u>Irrigation</u> (supplying crops with water) may involve <u>taking water</u> from a river. A reduction in the amount of water in a river <u>decreases</u> its ability to <u>erode</u> and <u>transport</u> material, and it may <u>deposit</u> material instead.

2) <u>Ploughing</u> of farmland <u>exposes soil</u>, allowing it to be washed away into rivers when it rains. This gives rivers a <u>larger sediment load</u>, which leads to <u>more deposition</u> occurring downstream.

3) Farmland may have <u>drainage systems</u> that remove water from the soil and move it into rivers. After heavy rainfall, these cause water to move more <u>quickly</u> into a river, increasing its <u>discharge</u> and temporarily causing higher rates of <u>erosion</u>.

> Urbanisation, agriculture and industry can all lead to the removal of vegetation (deforestation), which can have a big impact on river processes (see next page).

...and Industry

1) Just like urbanisation, <u>industry</u> leads to more <u>impermeable surfaces</u>, which increases <u>runoff</u> into rivers.

2) <u>Air pollution</u> from factories and vehicles can make <u>rainwater</u> more <u>acidic</u>, which results in more <u>chemical weathering</u> of the river landscape (see p.20).

3) Many major industrial areas developed on rivers, as they're accessible by <u>boat</u>. <u>Dredging</u> (the <u>removal of sediment</u> from the river bed) creates <u>deeper channels</u>, allowing large boats to fit. This means the river has a <u>faster flow</u> and more <u>energy</u> for <u>erosion</u>. It also reduces the likelihood of <u>flooding</u>, because the river can hold more water.

4) <u>Boats</u> themselves can also affect river processes — their motors <u>disturb</u> the water, which can lead to <u>increased erosion</u> of the river banks.

A dredger

EXAM QUESTION

Ploughing through this revision will increase your knowledge load

These are just some of the ways humans affect river landscapes. Make sure you're totally happy with everything on this page, then have a go at this lovely exam question to see what you've learnt:

1) Explain one way that industry affects river processes. [2]

River Flooding

River flooding is becoming more and more frequent in the UK. Luckily for you, I've got just the page to tell you all about the reasons why it happens. So find yourself a spot of high ground and get reading...

River Flooding is Influenced by Physical Factors

1) River discharge is the volume of water that flows in a river per second.
2) When the discharge increases, the level of the river increases, because there's more water in the channel.
3) Flooding occurs when the river level gets so high that it spills over its banks.
4) There are physical factors that can increase discharge, and therefore cause flooding:

Prolonged Rainfall

After a long period of rain, the soil becomes saturated. Any further rainfall can't infiltrate, which increases runoff into rivers. This increases discharge quickly, so flooding is more likely.

Heavy Rainfall

Heavy rainfall means the water arrives too rapidly for infiltration, so there's a lot of runoff. This increases discharge quickly, increasing the risk of a flood.

You might see the probability of a flood happening written as a ratio, e.g. 1:200. This means that there's a one in two hundred (0.5%) chance of a flood of that size happening in any given year.

Geology (rock type)

Clay soils and some rocks, e.g. granite and shale, are impermeable (i.e. they don't allow infiltration) so runoff is increased. When it rains, discharge increases quickly, which can cause a flood.

Relief

Relief is the change in the height of the land. If a river is in a steep-sided valley, water will reach the river channel much faster because water flows more quickly on steeper slopes. Discharge increases rapidly, increasing the flood risk.

There can also be Human Causes of River Flooding

Changing the land use, e.g. by building on it or removing trees, can increase the flood risk.

Building

1) Buildings are often made from impermeable materials, e.g. concrete, and they're surrounded by roads made from tarmac (also impermeable).
2) Impermeable surfaces increase runoff and drains quickly take runoff to rivers — discharge increases quickly, so there's a greater risk of flooding.

Deforestation

1) Vegetation intercepts rainwater — rainwater lands on plants and is stored there before evaporating.
2) Plants also take up water from the soil. This allows more rainwater to infiltrate the soil instead of running over the surface.
3) When vegetation is removed, there's less interception and infiltration, so more rainwater goes straight to streams and rivers by surface runoff.
4) This increases discharge and makes flooding more likely.

Runoff? Run away more like...

Make sure you've got your head around the physical and human factors that influence river flooding, then have a go at this exam question before the floodwaters wash away your pen and paper:

1) *Explain how changing land use can increase the risk of flooding.* [3]

River Flooding

Now you know the causes of river flooding, let's have a look at some of the <u>impacts</u>. Then it's time for some <u>rising</u> and <u>falling limbs</u>. Best do some warm-up stretches first — I don't want any injuries.

Flooding Affects People...

1) People can be <u>killed</u> or injured by <u>floodwater</u>.

2) Floodwater is often <u>contaminated</u> with <u>sewage</u>, which can lead to a lack of <u>clean drinking water</u>.

3) <u>Possessions</u> can be <u>damaged</u> or washed away.

4) People can be made <u>homeless</u> as their properties are <u>inundated</u> or <u>damaged</u>.

5) The flooding of <u>electrical sub-stations</u> can leave homes and businesses without <u>power</u> for <u>several days</u>.

6) <u>Businesses</u> may be forced to <u>shut down</u> because of <u>flood damage</u> and disrupted <u>power supplies</u>. This leads to a <u>loss of livelihoods</u>.

7) Important services such as <u>schools</u> and <u>hospitals</u> may have to close.

8) <u>Transport links</u> can be affected, e.g. floods can damage <u>roads</u> and <u>railways</u>, and sweep away <u>bridges</u>.

2015 floods in Carlisle

...and the Environment

1) Floodwater <u>contaminated</u> with <u>sewage</u> and <u>rubbish</u> can <u>pollute</u> rivers, damaging <u>wildlife habitats</u>.

2) <u>Farmland</u> can be <u>ruined</u> by <u>silt</u> and <u>sediment</u> deposited <u>after a flood</u>.

3) River banks are <u>eroded</u>, causing <u>huge changes</u> to the <u>river landscape</u>, e.g. <u>widening</u> of the <u>river channel</u> and increased <u>deposition</u> downstream.

4) The <u>force</u> of floodwater can <u>uproot</u> trees and plants, and <u>standing</u> floodwater may cause those that survive the initial wave of water to <u>die</u>.

Farmland ruined by flooding

Storm Hydrographs are Used to Analyse Discharge During a Flood

GEOGRAPHY SKILLS

1) River discharge is measured in <u>cumecs</u> — cubic metres per second (m³/s).

2) <u>Storm hydrographs</u> show the changes in river discharge around the time of a <u>storm</u>:

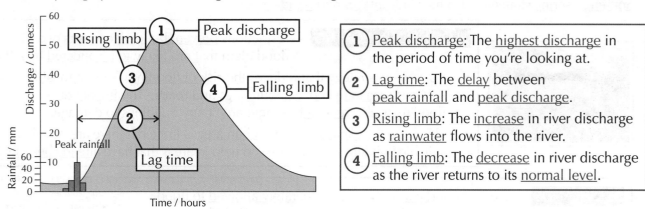

① <u>Peak discharge</u>: The <u>highest discharge</u> in the period of time you're looking at.

② <u>Lag time</u>: The <u>delay</u> between <u>peak rainfall</u> and <u>peak discharge</u>.

③ <u>Rising limb</u>: The <u>increase</u> in river discharge as <u>rainwater</u> flows into the river.

④ <u>Falling limb</u>: The <u>decrease</u> in river discharge as the river returns to its <u>normal level</u>.

3) Lag time happens because most rainwater <u>doesn't land directly</u> in the river channel — there's a <u>delay</u> as rainwater <u>gets to the channel</u>.

4) It gets there by <u>surface runoff</u>, <u>infiltration</u> (soaking into the ground) and flowing <u>slowly underground</u>.

Revision lag time — the time between starting and getting bored...

Hydrographs look scary, but they're not too bad — just keep going until the knowledge infiltrates your brain.
Make sure you understand the main impacts of river flooding too, and you'll be home and dry... until the next page.

River Defences

Floods can be <u>devastating</u>, but there are a number of different <u>strategies</u> to stop them or lessen the blow.

Engineering can Reduce the Risk of Flooding or its Effects

There are <u>two</u> types of strategy to <u>deal with flooding</u>:

1) <u>Hard engineering</u> — <u>man-made structures</u> built to <u>control the flow</u> of rivers and <u>reduce flooding</u>.

2) <u>Soft engineering</u> — schemes set up using <u>knowledge</u> of a <u>river</u> and its <u>processes</u> to <u>reduce the effects of flooding</u>.

Different <u>hard engineering</u> strategies have different <u>advantages</u> and <u>disadvantages</u>:

DAMS AND RESERVOIRS — <u>dams</u> (huge walls) are built <u>across</u> the rivers, usually in the <u>upper course</u>. A <u>reservoir</u> (artificial lake) is formed <u>behind</u> the dam.

- Reservoirs <u>store water</u>, especially during periods of prolonged or heavy rain, <u>reducing</u> the <u>risk of flooding</u>. The water in the reservoir can be used as <u>drinking water</u> and to <u>generate hydroelectric power</u> (HEP).

- However, dams are <u>very expensive</u> to build, and creating a reservoir can <u>flood existing settlements</u>. Eroded material is <u>deposited</u> in the <u>reservoir</u> and <u>not</u> along the river's <u>natural course</u>. This means <u>farmland</u> downstream can become <u>less fertile</u>, and the formation of some <u>depositional landforms</u>, e.g. levees, downstream may be <u>slowed down</u> or <u>prevented</u>.

CHANNELISATION — this can involve the river channel being <u>widened</u>, <u>deepened</u> or <u>straightened</u>. <u>Meanders</u> are <u>cut out</u> by building <u>artificial straight channels</u>. Sometimes the river <u>beds</u> and <u>banks</u> might be lined with <u>concrete</u>.

- Channelisation <u>reduces flood risk</u>, because:

  1) <u>deeper</u> or <u>wider</u> channels can <u>hold more water</u>.

  2) with a <u>straighter channel</u>, water moves out of the area <u>more quickly</u>. This is because it doesn't have to travel around a series of meanders.

  3) <u>concrete</u> beds and banks reduce the friction between the water and the channel. This increases river <u>velocity</u> so water moves out of the area <u>more quickly</u>.

- However, <u>flooding</u> may happen <u>downstream</u> instead, as water is <u>carried there faster</u>. The water's also <u>flowing faster</u> downstream, which may speed up the formation of <u>erosional</u> landforms (see p.22-23).

<u>Soft engineering</u> strategies also have <u>advantages</u> and <u>disadvantages</u>:

FLOOD PLAIN ZONING — restrictions <u>prevent building</u> on parts of a flood plain that are <u>likely to be affected</u> by a flood.

- It's a cheap strategy that reduces the <u>risk of flooding</u> — <u>impermeable surfaces aren't created</u>, e.g. buildings and roads. The <u>impact</u> of flooding is also <u>reduced</u> — there aren't any buildings to damage.

- However, the <u>expansion</u> of an <u>urban area</u> is <u>limited</u> if there are no other suitable building sites. It's also no help in areas that have <u>already been built on</u>.

WASHLANDS — areas of <u>flood plains</u> that are <u>deliberately allowed to flood</u> during <u>wet periods</u>, in order to reduce flooding elsewhere.

- Washlands <u>store water</u> when river discharge is high, which <u>reduces</u> the <u>flood risk</u> in areas where floods could cause a lot of <u>damage</u>. Washlands can also provide a <u>wetland habitat</u> for many rare species, and they're <u>inexpensive</u>.

- However, these areas can then not be used for anything else, e.g. <u>farming</u> or <u>building</u>.

> Soft engineering tends to allow natural river processes to continue, so the landscape is more likely to evolve as it would have done without human interference.

Flood your mind — with knowledge of flood defence schemes...

Make sure you have the advantages and disadvantages of each flood defence strategy stashed away in your brain.

River Landscape — River Eden

You need to know about <u>one named UK river landscape</u> — these pages are about the <u>River Eden</u> in Cumbria, but you might have studied a different river in class. You can stick to that one if you prefer.

The River Eden is in North-West England

1) The River Eden flows from the Pennine hills in south Cumbria to the <u>Solway Firth</u> at the <u>Scottish border</u>.

2) It passes through several urban areas, and provides <u>drinking water</u> to <u>Carlisle</u>, a city situated in the north of the Eden basin.

3) The river basin is a largely <u>rural</u> area, with many <u>scenic</u> landscapes that are popular with <u>tourists</u>.

4) It also contains important <u>landscapes</u> and <u>habitats</u> — the River Eden has been chosen as a <u>Special Area of Conservation</u> and a <u>Site of Special Scientific Interest</u> (SSSI).

Carlisle

River Eden and its tributaries

Area drained by the River Eden

North Pennines

Lake District

You've already seen a bit about the Eden basin on p.19.

The Local Geology has Influenced the Formation of the Landscape

1) The River Eden runs through the <u>Vale of Eden</u>, which is the name for the large valley between the <u>mountains</u> of the Lake District and the north Pennines.

2) The <u>geology</u> of the Eden basin has influenced how the landscape has developed:

- The <u>harder rocks</u> around the edge of the Eden basin have remained as <u>high ground</u> as they are more <u>resistant</u> to <u>erosion</u>. However, exposed <u>limestone</u> is vulnerable to slow <u>carbonation weathering</u> (p.20).

- <u>Igneous</u> rocks, such as those found in the west of the Eden basin, tend to be <u>impermeable</u> (i.e. water <u>won't soak</u> into the rock). Because water can't soak into the ground, high rainfall causes lots of <u>surface streams</u> to form, which have a lot of power to erode <u>vertically</u>, creating <u>steep-sided</u> V-shaped valleys. <u>Waterfalls</u> (see p.22) have formed where there is a <u>change</u> from <u>hard</u> rock to <u>softer</u> rock, e.g. <u>Hell Gill Force</u> near the <u>source</u> of the river Eden.

- Through the <u>middle</u> and <u>lower courses</u> of the Eden, the river <u>valley</u> is made up of sandstone (a <u>softer</u> rock). The river's increasing <u>volume</u> and <u>energy</u> in its lower course mean that there's lots of <u>lateral</u> (sideways) <u>erosion</u> of the sandstone. This <u>widens</u> the river channel and forms <u>meanders</u> and steep <u>river cliffs</u>.

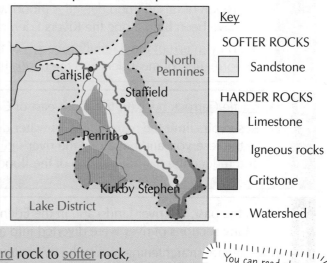

Key

SOFTER ROCKS

Sandstone

HARDER ROCKS

Limestone

Igneous rocks

Gritstone

Watershed

North Pennines

Carlisle

Staffield

Penrith

Kirkby Stephen

Lake District

You can read about how the river Eden's landscape changes over its course on p.19.

The Landscape is also Influenced by the Climate

Cumbria is on the <u>west coast</u> of the UK, facing the prevailing <u>south-westerly</u> winds. As a result, the <u>climate</u> is <u>mild</u> and <u>wet</u>, with <u>cool summers</u> and <u>mild winters</u>. The climate has helped shape the Eden's landscape:

1) Cumbria is one of the <u>wettest</u> parts of the UK*, often experiencing periods of <u>intense</u> rainfall that <u>rapidly increase</u> the volume of water in the River Eden. The <u>high volume</u> of water can increase <u>transportation</u> of material, which can cause more erosion by <u>abrasion</u> — particularly in the <u>upper course</u>, where it has carved out <u>V-shaped valleys</u>.

2) In winter, the <u>higher ground</u> in the Eden basin can <u>regularly freeze</u>. This allows <u>freeze-thaw weathering</u> to slowly <u>break up</u> the exposed rock of the valley sides in the upper course of the river. If the valley sides are weakened, sudden <u>mass movements</u> become more likely.

Head to p.20 for more on freeze-thaw weathering.

*Trust me, I live there.

Topic 1 — The Changing Landscapes of the UK

River Landscape — River Eden

Human Activities have Caused Changes to the Landscape

Deforestation and agriculture have both had an impact on the River Eden's landscape:

Deforestation

1) Natural woodland and heathland have been cleared from many upland areas in the Eden basin.

2) This increases surface runoff when it rains, and means that more water ends up in river channels more quickly.

3) This increase in volume gives rivers more energy for erosion, and can cause sliding and slumping of the river banks.

Farming

1) Some upland areas have been drained of moisture to make them more suitable for farming.

2) This reduces the stability of the soil, meaning that more soil is washed into the river channel by rain.

3) The increased load of the river increases deposition downstream, changing the flood plain landscape from its natural state.

The River Landscape has been Altered by Management Schemes

The River Eden has been managed to meet the needs of the people in the area. Management strategies have influenced the river landscape. For example:

Flood Defences

1) 10 km of raised flood defences (flood walls and embankments) have been built along the Rivers Eden and Caldew in Carlisle.

2) They interrupt the natural processes of the river and can prevent the natural formation of meanders and the deposition of sediment on the flood plain.

Reservoirs

1) Castle Carrock beck (to the south-east of Carlisle) has been dammed to create a reservoir.

2) Reservoirs limit the natural flow of water downstream. Material carried by the river is deposited in the reservoir and not along the river's natural course. This can increase erosion downstream, and reduce the natural buildup of the flood plain in the lower course of the river.

Channel Management

1) In the past, the river landscape in the Eden basin was changed by channel straightening. Many sections of river were diverted into artificial channels to try to reduce flooding.

2) Channel straightening makes the water flow more quickly than it naturally would, which can increase erosion and decrease deposition. In the artificial channel, conditions aren't right for meanders to form as they normally would — so the natural river landscape is changed.

3) More recently, some areas of the Eden basin have been restored to their original state by having artificial meanders put in, e.g. on the River Lyvennet to the south-west of Appleby.

4) The meanders slow the river's flow, increasing deposition. This encourages the river to begin to meander more naturally, and allows the natural build-up of the flood plain.

Planting Trees

1) Near Dalston (south of Carlisle), the landscape has been changed by the planting of 1000 trees to reduce flooding and also to reduce erosion by stabilising the soil.

2) Trees intercept rainfall and reduce surface runoff. This prevents rapid increases in the volume of water in the river because it takes longer for water to reach the river channel.

3) As a result, the river will have less energy, reducing lateral and vertical erosion, meaning that meanders may take longer to form.

Castle Carrock beck — the best dammed stream this side of Carlisle...

Whether you choose this river landscape or a different one you've studied, make sure you know how it's been formed and the main factors influencing its change. And now, would you look at that — it's the end of rivers.

Revision Summary

Wat-er load of fun that was. Now it's time to see how much information your brain has soaked up. I think you'll be surprised — I reckon about 16 litres of knowledge has been taken in. Have a go at the questions below and then go back over the section to check your answers.

If Rivers is <u>not</u> one of the options that you've chosen, do a little celebratory dance, then move directly onto some lovely revision of Glaciated Upland Landscapes.

River Landscapes and Processes (p.18-21) ☑

1) What does a river's long profile show?
2) Describe the cross profile of a river's lower course.
3) What is the difference between vertical and lateral erosion?
4) Compare the sediment size and shape in a river's upper and lower courses.
5) How does a river's discharge change along its course?
6) Describe the process of freeze-thaw weathering.
7) What is mass movement?
8) What's the difference between abrasion and attrition?
9) Name two processes of transportation.
10) When does deposition occur?

River Landforms (p.22-25) ☐

11) Where do waterfalls form?
12) What are interlocking spurs?
13) a) Where is the current fastest on a meander?
    b) What feature of a meander is formed where the flow is fastest?
14) How does a point bar form?
15) Name the landform created when a meander is cut off by deposition.
16) What is a flood plain?
17) What do contour lines on a map show?
18) Give two pieces of map evidence for a waterfall.
19) Give two pieces of map evidence for a river's lower course.

Climate, Weather and Human Activity in River Landscapes (p26-27) ☐

20) Describe one way that temperature affects the processes that happen in river valleys.
21) Why is mass movement more likely during a storm?
22) How does the presence of nearby impermeable surfaces affect river processes?
23) Describe one impact of industry on river landscapes.

River Flooding and Defences (p.28-30) ☐

24) What is river discharge?
25) Describe two physical factors that can cause floods.
26) Explain how cutting down trees can increase flooding.
27) Give two impacts that flooding has on the environment.
28) What is lag time?
29) Describe how channelisation reduces the risk of a flood.
30) What is flood plain zoning?

River Landscape — Example (p.31-32) ☐

31) For a named UK river landscape:
    a) Describe how the geology has shaped the landscape.
    b) Explain two ways in which human activity has changed the landscape.

Glacial Erosion

Glaciers are masses of ice that fill valleys and hollows and slowly move downhill. The UK might not have any glaciers any more, but it did in the past, and they can seriously carve up the landscape through erosion.

Much of the UK Used to be Covered in Ice

1) There have been lots of glacial (cold) periods during the last 2.6 million years.

2) During some glacial periods, parts of the UK were covered in a massive ice sheet.

3) The map shows the maximum extent of ice cover during the last glacial period, 20 000 years ago.

4) Ice covered most of Scotland, Ireland and Wales and came as far south as the Bristol Channel in England.

5) During this period, the climate had a major impact on physical processes. Temperatures were up to 10 °C colder.

6) When the climate warmed up again, glaciers began to stop moving and melt (stagnate).

7) This was due to changes in their glacial mass balance — the balance between inputs (e.g. snowfall) and outputs (e.g. meltwater). As the climate became warmer, glaciers were losing more ice than they were gaining, causing a negative mass balance. This meant the glaciers began to retreat.

8) As glaciers in the last glacial period grew, moved and melted, they shaped the landscape through the erosion, transportation and deposition of material.

There's more on glacial periods on page 44.

Maximum extent of ice during the last glacial period (approximate).

ice sheet

Scotland

Leeds

Wales

Ireland

Bristol Channel

London

Glaciers Erode the Landscape as They Move

1) The weight of the ice in a glacier makes it move downhill (advance), eroding the landscape as it goes.

2) The moving ice erodes the landscape in two ways:

- Plucking occurs when meltwater at the base, back or sides of a glacier freezes onto the rock. As the glacier moves forward it pulls pieces of rock out.

- Abrasion is where bits of rock stuck in the ice grind against the rock below the glacier, wearing it away (it's a bit like the glacier's got sandpaper on the bottom of it).

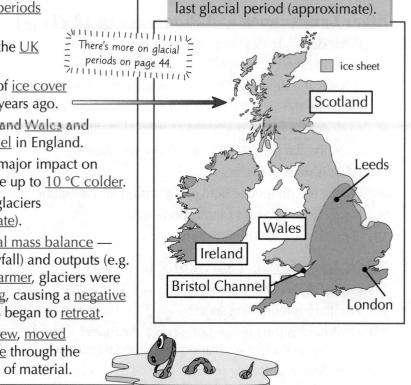

the ice moves in a circular motion

plucking breaks bits of rock off the mountain face and makes the wall steeper

abrasion grinds and gouges the valley floor

3) At the top end of the glacier the ice doesn't move in a straight line — it moves in a circular motion called rotational slip. This can erode hollows in the landscape and deepen them into bowl shapes.

Plucking and abrasion — beauty treatments glacier style...

Freezin' fiddlesticks — imagine half the UK covered in ice. Just thinking about it is making me feel chilly.
Make sure you know the difference between plucking and abrasion, then shiver on over to the next page...

Glacial Landforms and Processes

Glaciers can produce some really cracking <u>landforms</u>, so let's have a look at some...

Glacial Erosion Produces Distinctive Landforms

An <u>arête</u> is a <u>narrow</u>, <u>steep-sided ridge</u> formed when <u>two</u> glaciers flow in <u>parallel valleys</u>. The glaciers erode the <u>sides</u> of the valleys, which sharpens the <u>ridge between them</u> giving it a jagged profile. (E.g. Striding Edge, Lake District)

<u>Truncated spurs</u> are cliff-like edges on the valley side formed when <u>ridges</u> of land (spurs) that stick out into the main valley are <u>cut off</u> as the glacier moves past.

<u>Hanging valleys</u> are valleys formed by <u>smaller glaciers</u> (called <u>tributary glaciers</u>) that flow into the <u>main glacier</u>. The glacial trough is eroded much <u>more deeply</u> by the <u>larger glacier</u>, so when the glaciers melt the valleys are left at a <u>higher level</u>.

<u>Corries</u> begin as hollows containing a small glacier. As the ice moves by <u>rotational slip</u>, it <u>erodes</u> the hollow into a steep-sided, <u>armchair shape</u> with a lip at the bottom end. When the ice melts it can leave a small circular <u>glacial lake</u> called a <u>tarn</u>.

A <u>roche moutonnée</u> is a mass of rock on the valley floor. The <u>upstream</u> (stoss) side is <u>smooth</u>, because it was smoothed by <u>abrasion</u> as the glacier went over it. The <u>downstream</u> (lee) side is steep and <u>rough</u> where the glacier <u>plucked</u> at it.

ice flow →

smoothed by abrasion

← plucking

<u>Glacial troughs</u> are <u>steep-sided</u> valleys with <u>flat</u> <u>bottoms</u>. They start off as a <u>V-shaped</u> river valley but change to a <u>U-shape</u> as the glacier erodes the sides and bottom, making it <u>deeper</u> and <u>wider</u>. (E.g. Nant Ffrancon, Snowdonia)

Physical Processes Operate on These Landforms Today

1) <u>Relict</u> upland glacial landscapes were <u>once</u> shaped by <u>glacial processes</u>, but are no longer affected by glaciers <u>today</u>. However, <u>other</u> physical processes are <u>still</u> operating on them:

- <u>Mechanical weathering</u> is when rock is <u>broken down</u> where it is, <u>without</u> any changes to its chemical composition. <u>Freeze-thaw weathering</u> is a type of mechanical weathering that occurs in glacial landscapes when <u>water</u> gets into <u>cracks</u> in rocks. The water <u>freezes</u> and <u>expands</u>, putting <u>pressure</u> on the rock. The ice then <u>thaws</u>, <u>releasing</u> the pressure. If this process is <u>repeated</u>, it can make bits of the rock <u>fall off</u>.
- <u>Mass movement</u> is when material falls <u>down</u> a <u>slope</u>. Soil can move slowly by <u>soil creep</u> — when <u>water</u> adds <u>weight</u> to the soil and makes it <u>expand</u>, the particles move downslope. Other types of mass movement in glaciated uplands are <u>faster</u>. <u>Rock falls</u> are when material <u>breaks up</u> into <u>small</u> blocks that <u>fall</u> down a slope, and <u>rock slides</u> are when a <u>large number</u> of rocks shift as <u>one mass</u>.

2) The <u>weather</u> and <u>climate</u> in the UK today have an influence on these physical processes:

- In <u>winter</u>, there can be significant <u>diurnal</u> (daily) <u>variations</u> in temperature — fluctuating from <u>above</u> freezing in the <u>day</u> to <u>below</u> freezing at <u>night</u>. This results in <u>freeze-thaw weathering</u>.
- The climate is generally <u>rainy</u>. This makes <u>mass movements</u> common, because <u>rainwater</u> acts as a <u>lubricant</u> and makes material <u>heavier</u>. <u>Seasonal</u> variations make this more common in <u>winter</u>.

Truncated spurs — when Tottenham finish their match early...

Knowing those landforms will help you sound clever next time you're up a mountain. Oh, and it'll help in the exam too.

Glacial Transportation and Deposition

Glaciers aren't too choosy when it comes to picking things up along their paths. Sand, clay, rocks, your grocery shopping — they'll carry pretty much anything. They'll also drop it wherever they please...

Glaciers Transport and Deposit Material called Till

1) Glaciers can move material (such as sand, clay and rocks) over very large distances — this is called transportation. This unsorted mixture of material is called till.

2) The material is frozen in the glacier, carried on its surface, or pushed in front of it. It's called bulldozing when the ice pushes loose material in front of it.

3) When the ice carrying the material melts, the material is deposited (dropped) on the valley floor, forming landforms such as moraines and drumlins (see below).

4) Most glacial deposits aren't sorted by size and weight like river deposits — rocks of all shapes and sizes are mixed up together.

Different Types of Moraine are Created by Glacial Deposition

Depending on their position, there are different kinds of moraine:

1) Ground moraines are eroded material that is dragged along the base of the glacier and then deposited over a wide area on the valley floor as the ice melts.

2) Terminal moraines build up at the snout (end) of the glacier — marking the furthest point reached by the ice. Material that's abraded and plucked from the valley floor is transported at the front of the glacier, and then deposited as semicircular mounds as the ice retreats.

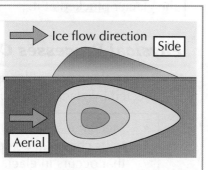

Ground moraine

Terminal moraine

Deposition and Erosion Interact to form Drumlins and Crags and Tails

Drumlins

1) Drumlins are elongated hills made up of till that was eroded from elsewhere by a glacier, and transported within it.

2) This material gathered at the base of the glacier. It was then deposited when the ice at the bottom of the glacier melted.

3) Over time, the material built up, forming hills beneath the glacier.

4) The continuing ice flow over these hills shaped them, making them round, blunt and steep at the upstream (stoss) end, and tapered, pointed and gently sloping at the downstream end (the lee side).

Ice flow direction
Side
Aerial

Crag and Tail

1) Crags and tails are outcrops of rock with smooth inclines behind them.

2) The crag is made from the more resistant rock, which is hit by the glacier first (stoss side). The glacier erodes the material around the crag, leaving it as a steep hill.

3) The tail is made from softer rock which was protected by the crag. As the glacier passed, the rock was eroded into a smooth slope.

4) Some tails are made via deposition when the glacier drops till after it passes over the crag. The till is then smoothed by the passing glacier.

Ice flow direction
Side
Crag Tail
Aerial

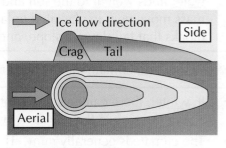

I could tell you a great story about crags...

...but that's a tail for another time. For now, have a crack at this practice exam question instead.

1) Describe the formation of ground moraines. [2]

Identifying Glacial Landforms

GEOGRAPHY SKILLS

In the exam you might be asked to spot glacial landforms on an OS® map. If the thought of map-reading has you in a cold sweat, don't panic. It's no problem when you know how — here are a few tips for you...

Use Contour Lines to Spot Corries and Arêtes on a Map

Contour lines are the orange lines drawn all over maps. They tell you about the height of the land by the numbers marked on them, and the steepness of the land by how close together the lines are (the closer they are, the steeper the slope). Here are a few tips on how to use them to spot arêtes and corries on a map:

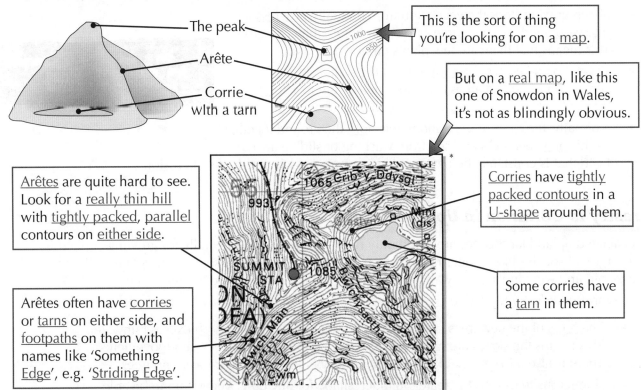

The peak

Arête

Corrie with a tarn

This is the sort of thing you're looking for on a map.

But on a real map, like this one of Snowdon in Wales, it's not as blindingly obvious.

Arêtes are quite hard to see. Look for a really thin hill with tightly packed, parallel contours on either side.

Arêtes often have corries or tarns on either side, and footpaths on them with names like 'Something Edge', e.g. 'Striding Edge'.

Corries have tightly packed contours in a U-shape around them.

Some corries have a tarn in them.

You can also use Maps to Spot Glacial Troughs

You might be asked to spot a glacial trough on a map extract.
This map of Nant Ffrancon (a glacial trough) in Wales shows the classic things to look out for:

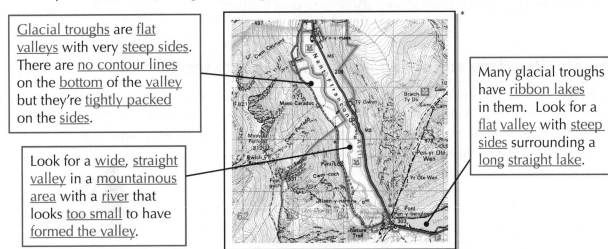

Glacial troughs are flat valleys with very steep sides. There are no contour lines on the bottom of the valley but they're tightly packed on the sides.

Look for a wide, straight valley in a mountainous area with a river that looks too small to have formed the valley.

Many glacial troughs have ribbon lakes in them. Look for a flat valley with steep sides surrounding a long straight lake.

Some corries have tarns, others have drama and hotpots...

There's lots of potential here for easy marks in the exam, just study the map carefully and say what you see. Make sure you refer to the map in your answer though — there's more about using maps on pages 121-122.

Topic 1 — The Changing Landscapes of the UK

Human Activity in Glaciated Landscapes

For <u>thousands</u> of years, <u>people</u> have been living in glaciated upland areas and using them for <u>forestry</u> and <u>farming</u>. These activities can seriously <u>meddle</u> in important <u>physical processes</u>...

Glaciated Upland Landscapes are Used for Keeping Livestock

1) <u>Sheep farming</u> is common in <u>upland</u> glaciated areas because the <u>steep slopes</u> and <u>poor soils</u> make it <u>unsuitable</u> for most other types of farming (like growing crops).

2) This has had major <u>impacts</u> on the glaciated landscape:

   - Sheep grazing stops the vegetation from <u>naturally progressing</u> into <u>woodland</u>, as young trees are eaten before they can grow. This means that there are few plants other than grass.

   - Vegetation takes in <u>excess water</u> from the soil. A <u>lack</u> of vegetation in upland areas can cause heavy rain to <u>saturate</u> the soil and begin to run <u>overland</u> — this can lead to <u>flooding</u>.

   - Normally, the <u>roots</u> of trees and plants <u>hold</u> the ground together — this <u>prevents</u> rocks and soil from washing or sliding away. Land that is constantly being grazed has few trees, so is at risk of <u>soil erosion</u>.

Forestry is Common in Upland Areas

1) Glaciated upland landscapes are commonly used for <u>forestry</u> — especially for growing <u>coniferous</u> (<u>evergreen</u>) species like spruces rather than <u>native</u> trees. Coniferous species can <u>cope</u> well with the <u>cold</u> and <u>wet</u> climate. They also grow <u>quickly</u>, which means more timber to sell.

2) The forestry industry has led to <u>changes</u> in glaciated upland landscapes, for example:

   - The <u>roots</u> of the new trees can help to <u>hold soil together</u> and <u>absorb</u> excess rainwater. This means the <u>slopes</u> are more <u>stable</u>, reducing the likelihood of <u>mass movements</u>. There is also a lower risk of <u>flooding</u> after heavy rain than if there were no trees.

   - <u>Coniferous</u> trees tend to create <u>too much shade</u> for any other vegetation to be able to grow underneath them. This <u>lack of ground vegetation</u> in coniferous plantations means that when trees are <u>felled</u> for <u>timber</u>, the ground is completely <u>exposed</u>. This increases the risk of <u>soil erosion</u>, <u>mass movements</u> and <u>flooding</u>.

   - <u>Machinery</u> used in forestry can also affect physical processes, e.g. heavy machines <u>compress</u> the soil. This makes it harder for water to be <u>absorbed</u> by the soil, increasing the risk of <u>flooding</u>.

Settlements Also Have an Impact on Physical Processes

1) There aren't many <u>large</u> settlements in glaciated upland landscapes, because they're <u>tricky</u> places to build in. However, there are many <u>villages</u> and <u>small towns</u> that have grown from <u>farming communities</u>.

2) The growing <u>tourism</u> industry (see p.39) has <u>increased</u> the need for <u>building</u> in upland areas.

3) Building and expanding settlements in upland areas leads to the <u>removal of vegetation</u> (see above) to make space for new buildings. Building settlements also increases the amount of ground covered with <u>impermeable surfaces</u> (ones that rain cannot get through). This <u>increases</u> the amount of water that <u>runs over</u> the land into rivers, instead of being <u>stored</u> in soil and plants, which puts the area at risk of <u>flooding</u>.

An ice cream sundae — my preferred glaciated landscape...

Human activities in upland glaciated landscapes might not be thrilling to read about, but it might come up in the exam, so get it learnt. Throwing in impressive words like 'impermeable surfaces' will add extra pizzazz to your answers.

Development in Glaciated Landscapes

More and more stuff is being <u>built</u> in upland landscapes, and I'm not talking about just the odd shed or patio...

Glaciated Landscapes can Provide Water Storage and Supply

Glaciated upland landscapes are often full of <u>rivers</u> and <u>lakes</u>, and get a lot of <u>rain</u>. This, combined with their <u>steep</u> valleys, makes them good sites for <u>water storage</u> using <u>dams</u> and <u>reservoirs</u>. These can be used to <u>supply</u> water to settlements. Water storage developments in glaciated uplands can have <u>pros</u> and <u>cons</u>:

Advantages
- The UK is prone to water <u>shortages</u> in <u>summer</u>. Having <u>additional</u> water storage can help <u>prevent</u> shortages.
- The water industry creates <u>jobs</u> in the area for local people.

Disadvantages
- <u>Dams</u> and reservoirs are extremely <u>expensive</u> to <u>build</u> and <u>maintain</u>.
- <u>Habitats</u> are <u>destroyed</u> when vegetation is <u>cleared</u> and areas are <u>flooded</u> to create reservoirs.

Tourism and Recreation can Cause Significant Problems

Glaciated areas have <u>dramatic</u> landscapes, making some of them very popular with tourists. Tourists can use upland areas for <u>recreational activities</u> like mountain biking, climbing and walking. This <u>changes</u> the landscape because it requires the <u>development</u> of <u>roads</u>, <u>paths</u> and <u>buildings</u> to cater for tourists' activities.

Advantages
- Tourism can create <u>employment</u> opportunities for local people.
- If the scenery and wildlife are <u>making money</u> for the area, they may be <u>more likely</u> to become <u>protected</u> and <u>better kept</u>.

Disadvantages
- Walkers cause <u>footpath erosion</u> which destroys <u>vegetation</u> and <u>soil</u>. Some also leave <u>waste</u> behind which doesn't <u>break down</u>, especially in the <u>cold</u> climate.
- Climbing supports can cause rocks to become loose and <u>unsafe</u>.

Renewable Energy Generation is a Growing Industry

Some upland areas provide opportunities for <u>renewable energy generation</u>. <u>Dams</u> can be used for <u>hydroelectric power</u>, and many upland landscapes are exposed to the <u>wind</u>, which is ideal for creating <u>wind farms</u>.

Advantages
- <u>Renewable</u> energy sources are better for the <u>environment</u> than fossil fuels (see p.101).
- Developing renewable energy sources, e.g. building dams, can create <u>jobs</u> for <u>local people</u>.

Disadvantages
- <u>Dams</u> and <u>wind farms</u> can negatively impact <u>animals</u>, e.g. wind turbines can kill birds.
- Some people feel that structures like dams <u>spoil</u> the <u>scenery</u>, which can discourage <u>tourists</u> from visiting the area.

Conservation can Protect Glaciated Landscapes

With all of these <u>developments</u> going on, <u>measures</u> have been put in place to <u>conserve</u> upland glaciated landscapes, e.g. <u>protecting species</u>, <u>replanting forests</u> and <u>preventing building</u> in some places.

Advantages
- Conservation ensures that <u>habitats</u> for plants and animals remain intact.
- By <u>preventing</u> development, conservation can prevent <u>imbalances</u> in natural cycles — e.g. building <u>houses</u> changes the <u>water cycle</u> by increasing <u>run-off</u>, which can lead to <u>flooding</u>.

Disadvantages
- Preventing development could <u>limit</u> the <u>growth</u> of the local <u>economy</u>.
- Conservation measures can be <u>unpopular</u> with <u>other users</u> of glaciated uplands, e.g. restricting <u>livestock grazing</u> can affect farmers' <u>livelihoods</u>.

What do you call a man who likes to hold back water..?

Adam — obviously. If only the answer to this exam question was as obvious:

1) Give two advantages and two disadvantages of tourism in upland glaciated landscapes. [4]

Glaciated Landscape — Snowdonia

EXAMPLE

Snowdonia is a great place to look for glacial landforms. It may not be covered in ice now, but it's sure seen a lot in the past. It's a lovely example of glaciated landscape, but you might've done a different one in class.

Snowdonia *is a* Glaciated Landscape *in North Wales*

1) Snowdonia is a National Park in a mountainous area in north Wales. Historically, it has been an important region for mining, and more recently it is a major tourist destination. The area contains several Sites of Special Scientific Interest and Special Areas of Conservation.

2) Like most upland glaciated landscapes, it is formed mainly from metamorphic (slate) and igneous (basalt) rock types (there's more on rock types on p.3).

3) It has been repeatedly covered by ice during glacial periods (see p.34).

4) The upland areas of Snowdonia (e.g. the Glyders — mountains to the north-east of Snowdon) show many of the landforms from p.35.

5) Here's how some of the glacial features found on the Glyders and the surrounding area were formed:

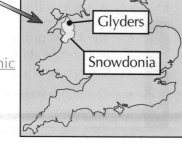

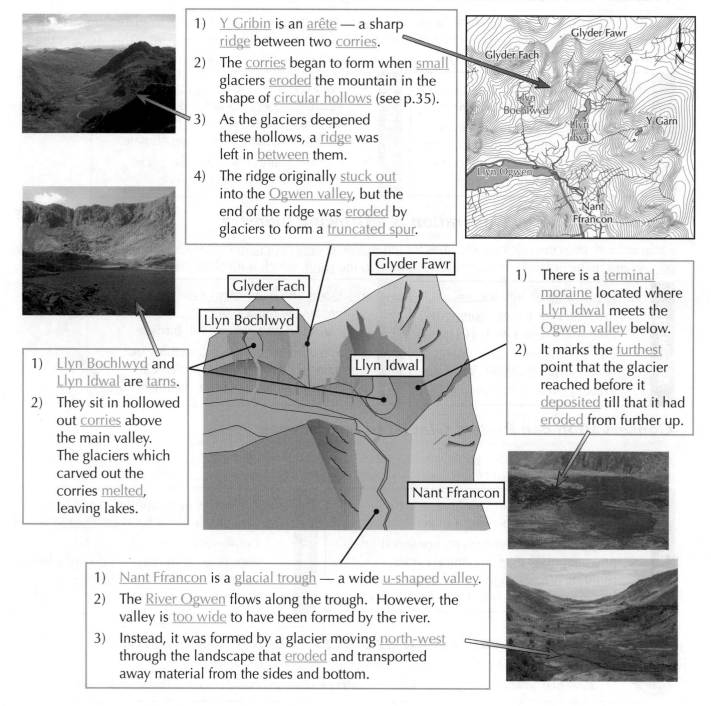

1) Y Gribin is an arête — a sharp ridge between two corries.

2) The corries began to form when small glaciers eroded the mountain in the shape of circular hollows (see p.35).

3) As the glaciers deepened these hollows, a ridge was left in between them.

4) The ridge originally stuck out into the Ogwen valley, but the end of the ridge was eroded by glaciers to form a truncated spur.

1) There is a terminal moraine located where Llyn Idwal meets the Ogwen valley below.

2) It marks the furthest point that the glacier reached before it deposited till that it had eroded from further up.

1) Llyn Bochlwyd and Llyn Idwal are tarns.

2) They sit in hollowed out corries above the main valley. The glaciers which carved out the corries melted, leaving lakes.

1) Nant Ffrancon is a glacial trough — a wide u-shaped valley.

2) The River Ogwen flows along the trough. However, the valley is too wide to have been formed by the river.

3) Instead, it was formed by a glacier moving north-west through the landscape that eroded and transported away material from the sides and bottom.

Glaciated Landscape — Snowdonia

Snowdonia *Attracts Millions of Tourists*

1) Snowdonia National Park receives about <u>4 million visitors</u> a year. The <u>attractions</u> for visitors include:
   - <u>Beautiful scenery</u> — large <u>lakes</u> (e.g. Bala Lake) and <u>mountains</u>
     (e.g. Snowdon, which is Wales's <u>highest</u> mountain).
   - <u>Cultural attractions</u> — e.g. Ffestiniog Steam Railway and Portmeirion (a tourist village).
   - <u>Activities</u> — e.g. rock-climbing, mountain biking, water sports, birdwatching and fishing.

2) <u>Tourism</u> is having big impacts on the area:
   - <u>Snowdon</u> is the most <u>popular mountain</u> for walkers, with around <u>500 000</u> people visiting the mountain each year, but this has led to severe <u>erosion</u> around the main <u>footpaths</u>.
   - Tourists damage <u>vegetation</u> by parking on grass verges and <u>trampling</u> rare plants.
   - Using <u>boats</u> on the <u>lakes</u> causes <u>noise</u> pollution, can increase <u>erosion</u> of banks and can <u>pollute</u> the water with <u>fuel</u>.
   - Over <u>90%</u> of visitors arrive by <u>car</u>, which bring <u>noise</u> and <u>air</u> pollution to the area.
   - The growing tourist industry needs more <u>infrastructure</u> to accommodate visitors. This may lead to <u>deforestation</u> which impacts on <u>physical processes</u> (see p.35).

Farming *has been* Changing the Landscape *for Many Years*

1) People have <u>farmed</u> in Snowdonia for over <u>9000 years</u>. During this time, large areas of <u>natural vegetation</u> have been <u>cleared</u> for fields.

2) Most land in Snowdonia is <u>unsuitable</u> for growing crops — the terrain is too <u>rocky</u> and <u>steep</u> to use machinery and the weather is too <u>cold</u> and <u>wet</u>. Instead, the main agricultural products are <u>livestock</u>. <u>Cattle</u> are farmed in <u>valleys</u>, where the best grazing ground is found. <u>Hardy</u> types of <u>sheep</u> such as <u>Welsh Mountain Sheep</u>, which have been <u>bred</u> to survive <u>harsh</u> conditions, are grazed in the <u>hills</u>.

3) <u>Grazing</u> prevents the growth of <u>woodland</u>. Trees are important for preventing <u>flooding</u> and <u>soil erosion</u> (see p.38).

Mining *has also Influenced the Area*

1) Snowdonia is known for its enormous stores of <u>slate</u>, <u>copper</u> and <u>gold</u>. These were <u>mined</u> in the region as early as <u>600 BC</u>.

2) Many <u>quarries</u> were dug to extract the rock and precious metals, causing <u>huge changes</u> to the landscape. <u>Vegetation</u>, <u>soil</u> and <u>rock</u> were removed in vast quantities.

A disused quarry

3) There are still a few quarries operating in Snowdonia (e.g. Penrhyn Slate Quarry), but the majority have now <u>closed</u>. However, they have <u>permanently changed</u> the landscape.

Renewable Energy *is now Generated in the Area*

1) Snowdonia is a great location for <u>renewable energy generation</u>. The <u>rivers</u> and <u>lakes</u> are good sites for <u>hydroelectric</u> energy installations, like Dinorwig Power Station in Gwynedd.

2) Hydroelectric energy installations can <u>change the landscape</u> by <u>flooding</u> surrounding areas for reservoirs and by <u>altering</u> the paths of <u>rivers</u>. E.g. in 1965 the <u>Tryweryn Valley</u>, including the village of Capel Celyn, was <u>flooded</u> to create the <u>Llyn Celyn reservoir</u>, which has a hydroelectric power station.

3) The <u>exposed</u> landscapes in Snowdonia are suitable for <u>wind farms</u>, e.g. Hafoty Ucha wind farm near Bala. However, <u>not many</u> wind farms have been constructed in the National Park, as wind <u>turbines</u> have a big <u>visual impact</u> on the landscape.

EXAM QUESTION

Don't you dare steal any of my quarry jokes — they're mine

Examiners love examples, so keep Snowdonia in mind. They might ask you something like...
   1) Describe one way that human activities have changed a named UK glaciated upland landscape. [4]

Revision Summary

Time to whip off your hat and scarf and warm up with some revision questions. The bad news is that if you don't know the answers you're going to have to dip back into the icy depths of this topic. Once you're confident of all the answers I recommend that you indulge in some kind of recreational activity. Don't disappear for too long though, there's plenty more revision where this topic came from.

You only have to study two from Coasts, Rivers and Glacial Landscapes, so if this is not one of you chosen themes, you are released from the grip of winter to go frolic in pastures new — turn over to Weather and Climate Change.

Glacial Erosion and Glacial Landforms (p.34-35) ☑

1) Describe the maximum extent of ice in the UK during the last ice age.
2) Describe two ways that ice erodes the landscape.
3) What is rotational slip?
4) What is a corrie?
5) What other feature is sometimes found in corries?
6) How does a roche moutonnée form?
7) Explain how a hanging valley forms.
8) What is a glacial trough?
9) Explain what freeze-thaw weathering is.
10) Name two kinds of mass movement.
11) Describe one way that the current UK climate can affect physical processes on glaciated landscapes.

Glacial Transportation and Deposition (p.36) ☑

12) What is bulldozing?
13) Describe the formation of terminal moraines.
14) Describe what a drumlin looks like.
15) How is a crag and tail formed?

Identifying Glacial Landforms (p.37) ☑

16) What do contour lines show?
17) How would you identify an arête on a map?
18) How would you identify a corrie on a map?
19) Describe what a glacial trough looks like on a map.

Human Activity in Glaciated Landscapes (p.38-39) ☑

20) Give one way that farming can affect physical processes in glaciated upland landscapes?
21) How can forestry impact on physical processes in glaciated upland landscapes?
22) Describe two ways in which tourism can change glaciated upland landscapes.
23) Give two disadvantages of renewable energy development in glaciated landscapes.
24) Describe one benefit of conservation activities in glaciated landscapes.

Glaciated Landscape — Example (p.40-41) ☑

25) a) Describe three features of a glaciated upland landscape that you have studied.
    b) Explain how these features were formed.
26) For a named upland area, list three ways that human activities have changed the landscape.

Global Atmospheric Circulation & Heat Transfer

Let's kick things off with a load of <u>hot air</u>. And further down the page we'll get into some <u>hot water</u>...

Winds Transfer Heat from the Equator to the Poles

1) The <u>Sun</u> heats the Earth's surface <u>unevenly</u> — <u>insolation</u> (the <u>solar radiation</u> that reaches the Earth's surface) is <u>greater</u> at the equator than the poles.

2) The differences in <u>temperature</u> cause differences in <u>air pressure</u> (see below).

3) <u>Winds</u> blow <u>FROM</u> the areas of <u>high</u> pressure <u>TO</u> the areas of <u>low pressure</u>. This helps to <u>transfer</u> heat energy <u>away</u> from the equator and <u>redistributes</u> it around the Earth.

4) Winds are part of <u>global atmospheric circulation</u> loops (called <u>cells</u>). These loops have <u>warm rising air</u> which creates a <u>low pressure belt</u>, and <u>cool falling air</u> which creates a <u>high pressure belt</u>.

5) There are <u>three cells</u> in each hemisphere — the <u>Hadley</u>, <u>Ferrel</u> and <u>Polar</u> cells.

---

1) At the <u>equator</u> the <u>Sun warms</u> the Earth, which transfers heat to the air above, causing it to <u>rise</u>. This creates a <u>low pressure belt</u>. As the air rises, it <u>cools</u> and <u>condenses</u> forming <u>clouds</u> and <u>rain</u>.

2) This cool, dry air <u>moves away</u> from the equator. At 30° north and south of the equator, this air <u>sinks</u>. This creates a <u>high pressure belt</u> with <u>cloudless skies</u> and <u>very low rainfall</u>.

---

3) The cool air reaches the ground surface and moves as surface winds either <u>back to the equator</u> or <u>towards the poles</u>.

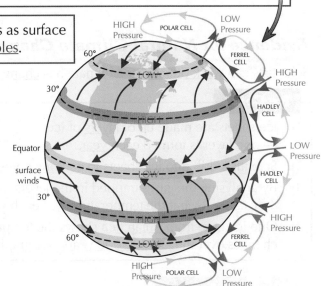

- Surface winds blowing towards the <u>equator</u> are called <u>trade winds</u>.
- Trade winds blow from the SE in the southern hemisphere and from the NE in the northern hemisphere. At the equator, these <u>trade winds meet</u> and heat from the sun causes them to rise and form <u>clouds</u>.
- Surface winds blowing towards the <u>poles</u> are called <u>westerlies</u>. They blow from the NW in the southern hemisphere and from the SW in the northern hemisphere.

---

4) At <u>60° north and south of the equator</u>, the warmer surface winds meet colder air from the poles. The warmer air is less dense than the cold air so it is forced to <u>rise</u>, creating <u>low pressure</u> and <u>rain</u>.

5) At the <u>poles</u> the <u>cool air sinks</u>, creating <u>high pressure</u>. Air in this area of high pressure is <u>drawn back</u> towards areas of lower pressure nearer the equator as <u>surface winds</u>.

Heat is also Transferred by Ocean Currents

1) Ocean currents are large scale movements of water that <u>transfer</u> heat energy from <u>warmer</u> to <u>cooler</u> regions.

2) <u>Surface currents</u> are caused by <u>winds</u> and help transfer heat <u>away</u> from the Equator, e.g. the <u>Gulf Stream</u> brings warm water from the <u>Caribbean</u> and keeps <u>Western Europe</u> warmer than it would otherwise be.

3) There are also <u>deep ocean currents</u> driven by differences in <u>water density</u>.

~ deep cold currents ~ shallow warm currents

4) When water <u>freezes</u> at the poles, the surrounding water gets <u>saltier</u>, increasing its <u>density</u>.

5) As it gets denser, it <u>sinks</u>, causing <u>warmer</u> water to flow in at the surface — creating a current.

6) This <u>warmer</u> water is <u>cooled</u> and <u>sinks</u>, continuing the <u>cycle</u>. This cycle of cooling and sinking moves water in a big <u>loop</u> round the Earth — this is known as the <u>thermohaline circulation</u>.

Natural Climate Change

We British like to talk about the weather, so global climate change should give us plenty to go on...

The Earth's Climate is Always Changing

Climate change is any significant change in the Earth's climate over a long period. The climate constantly changes — it always has, and it always will.

1) The Quaternary period is the most recent geological time period, spanning from about 2.6 million years ago to the present day.

2) In the period before the Quaternary, the Earth's climate was warmer and quite stable. Then things changed a lot.

The Quaternary period includes the whole of human history.

3) During the Quaternary, global temperature has shifted between cold glacial periods that last for around 100 000 years, and warmer interglacial periods that last for around 10 000 years.

4) The last glacial period ended around 15 000 years ago. Since then the climate has been warming.

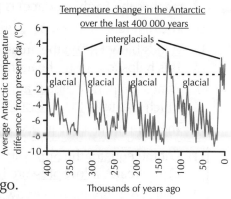

Temperature change in the Antarctic over the last 400 000 years

Evidence for Natural Climate Change Comes from Many Sources

Scientists can work out how the climate has changed over time using a range of methods. For example:

Ice Cores

1) Ice sheets are made up of layers of ice — one layer is formed each year.

2) Scientists drill into ice sheets to get long cores of ice.

3) By analysing the gases trapped in the layers of ice, they can tell what the temperature was each year.

4) One ice core from Antarctica shows the temperature changes over the last 400 000 years (see graph above).

Historical Sources

1) Since the 1850s global temperatures have been measured accurately using thermometers. This gives a reliable but short-term record of temperature change.

2) Historical sources (e.g. diaries and paintings) can extend the record of climate change a bit further back.

3) For example, historical diaries can show what the climate was like in the past, e.g. by giving the number of days of rain or snow and the dates of harvests (an early harvest suggests warm weather).

4) Paintings of fairs and markets on frozen rivers show that winters in Europe were regularly much colder 500 years ago than they are now.

Dear Diary, Today was bloomin' FREEZING!

Tree Rings

1) As a tree grows, it forms a new ring each year — the tree rings are thicker in warm, wet conditions.

2) Scientists take cores and count the rings to find the age of a tree. The thickness of each ring shows what the climate was like.

3) Tree rings are a reliable source of evidence of climate change for the past 10 000 years.

Pollen Records

1) Pollen from plants gets preserved in sediment, e.g. at the bottom of lakes or in peat bogs.

2) Scientists can identify and date the preserved pollen to show which species were living at that time.

3) Scientists know the conditions that plants live in now, so preserved pollen from similar plants shows that climate conditions were similar.

Ice sheets — what polar bears use to make their ice beds...

There were no thermometers 2.6 million years ago but scientists can reconstruct climates using these clever methods. Climate change is a hot topic (sorry), so make sure you learn this stuff inside out and sideways before your exam.

Natural Climate Change

This page is all about the natural causes of climate change, from the Earth's wobble to the Sun's complexion. Some of it looks a bit tricky, but have a good look at the diagrams and you shouldn't have any trouble.

There Are Natural Causes of Climate Change

1 Milankovitch Cycles

1) Milankovitch cycles are variations in the way the Earth moves as it orbits the Sun.
   - Stretch — the path of the Earth's orbit around the Sun changes from an almost perfect circle to an ellipse (an oval) and back again about every 96 000 years.
   - Tilt — the Earth is tilted at an angle as it orbits the Sun. This tilt (or axis) changes over a cycle of about 41 000 years.
   - Wobble — the axis of the Earth wobbles like a spinning top on a cycle of about 22 000 years.

2) These cycles affect how far the Earth is from the Sun, and the angle that the Sun's rays hit the Earth. This changes the amount of solar radiation (how much of the Sun's energy) the Earth receives. If the Earth receives more energy, it gets warmer.

3) Tilt and wobble also affect how much solar radiation is received at different latitudes at different times of year.

4) Orbital changes may have caused the glacial and interglacial cycles of the Quaternary period.

2 Solar Variation

1) The Sun's output of energy isn't constant — it changes in short cycles of about 11 years. This is known as solar variation.

2) Solar variation is caused by sunspots. Sunspots are cooler areas of the Sun's surface that are visible as dark patches. They increase the Sun's output of energy.

3) Periods when solar output is reduced and there are very few sunspots may cause the Earth's climate to become cooler in some areas.

3 Volcanic Activity

1) Major volcanic eruptions eject large quantities of material into the atmosphere.

2) Some of these particles reflect the Sun's rays back out to space, so the Earth's surface cools.

3) Volcanic activity may cause short-term changes in climate, e.g. the cooling that followed the eruption of Mount Pinatubo in 1991.

Volcanoes also release CO$_2$ (a greenhouse gas — see p.46), but not enough to cause warming.

Stretch, tilt and wobble — the Earth doing aerobics...

These ideas can seem a bit confusing, but don't panic — take your time and go through each one carefully. Basically, the more energy that the Earth receives, or that gets trapped here, the hotter it gets (and vice versa).

1) Explain two natural factors that can cause climate change. [4]

Climate Change — Human Activity

In the last 150 years or so <u>human activities</u> have begun to <u>change</u> the <u>climate</u>. We're slowly getting <u>warmer</u>...

The Greenhouse Effect Keeps the Planet Warm

1) The <u>temperature</u> of the Earth is a <u>balance</u> between the heat it <u>gets</u> from the <u>Sun</u> and the heat it <u>loses</u> to <u>space</u>.

2) The <u>incoming</u> energy from the Sun is <u>short-wave radiation</u>. The <u>outgoing</u> energy from the Earth is <u>long-wave radiation</u>.

3) <u>Gases</u> in the atmosphere naturally act like an <u>insulating layer</u> — they let short-wave radiation in, but <u>trap</u> long-wave radiation, helping to keep the Earth at the <u>right temperature</u>.

4) This is called the <u>greenhouse effect</u> ('cos it's a bit like a greenhouse trapping heat).

5) Gases that trap heat are called <u>greenhouse gases</u> — they include <u>carbon dioxide</u> (CO_2) and <u>methane</u> (CH_4).

- Some greenhouse gases are <u>stronger</u> than others, e.g. <u>CH_4</u> absorbs <u>more</u> heat than <u>CO_2</u>.
- Different greenhouse gases <u>stay</u> in the atmosphere for different lengths of time. For example, <u>CH_4</u> usually stays in the atmosphere for around <u>10 years</u> after it has been emitted.
- The <u>longer</u> the gases stay in the atmosphere, the more they'll contribute to <u>warming</u>.

Human Activities are Making the Greenhouse Effect Stronger

1) There's a <u>scientific consensus</u> (general agreement) that <u>human activities</u> are <u>causing</u> climate change by making the <u>greenhouse effect</u> stronger. This is called the <u>enhanced greenhouse effect</u>.

2) <u>Too much</u> greenhouse gas in the atmosphere means <u>too much</u> energy is trapped and the planet <u>warms up</u>.

3) <u>Humans</u> are increasing the <u>concentration</u> of greenhouse gases:

Industry
1) Most <u>industry</u> uses a lot of energy.
2) Some <u>industrial processes</u> also release greenhouse gases, e.g. <u>cement</u> is made from <u>limestone</u>, which contains <u>carbon</u>. When cement is produced, <u>lots of CO_2</u> is <u>released</u> into the atmosphere.
3) <u>Industrial waste</u> may end up in <u>landfill sites</u> where it decays, releasing <u>methane</u>.

Transport
1) Most <u>cars</u>, <u>lorries</u>, <u>ships</u> and <u>planes</u> run on fossil fuels, which release greenhouse gases when burnt.
2) <u>Car ownership</u> is rapidly <u>increasing</u> in some <u>emerging</u> countries, e.g. <u>China</u>.
3) This means there are <u>more</u> cars on the <u>roads</u>, so more greenhouse gases are being <u>released</u>.

Farming
1) <u>Rice paddies</u> and <u>livestock</u> produce a lot of <u>CH_4</u>.
2) Trees <u>absorb</u> and <u>store CO_2</u>. <u>Clearing</u> land of trees for <u>agriculture</u> reduces the <u>absorption</u> of CO_2, leaving <u>more</u> CO_2 in the atmosphere.

Energy
<u>CO_2</u> is <u>released</u> into the atmosphere when <u>fossil fuels</u> like coal, oil and natural gas are <u>burnt</u>, e.g. in power stations.

Climate Change Negatively Affects People and the Environment

Temperatures are <u>expected</u> to <u>rise</u> by <u>0.3-4.8 °C</u> between <u>2005</u> and <u>2100</u>. This is <u>already</u> causing some <u>major effects</u> on <u>people</u> and the <u>environment</u>, and will <u>continue</u> to do so:

1) Climate change makes the sea <u>warmer</u>. This causes the water to <u>expand</u>, and <u>sea levels</u> to <u>rise</u>.

2) <u>Warmer</u> temperatures are causing <u>glaciers</u> to <u>retreat</u> (shrink) and <u>ice sheets</u> like Greenland to <u>melt</u>. This means that water <u>stored on land</u> as ice <u>returns</u> to the <u>oceans</u>, which also contributes to <u>sea level rise</u>. Sea level rise <u>increases</u> rates of <u>coastal erosion</u> and increases the risk of <u>flooding</u> in <u>coastal areas</u>.

3) <u>Glaciers</u> provide water for important <u>rivers</u>, e.g. the <u>Ganges</u>, so glacier retreat could lead to <u>flooding</u> in the short-term, but might eventually cause these rivers to <u>dry up</u> and <u>ecosystems</u> to be <u>lost</u>.

4) <u>Warmer</u> temperatures and more frequent <u>droughts</u> could negatively affect <u>farming</u> — e.g. <u>yields</u> of <u>maize</u> have got <u>smaller</u> due to <u>warming</u> in recent years. <u>Lower crop yields</u> could lead to <u>food shortages</u>, especially in areas near the equator. This could <u>increase malnutrition</u>, <u>ill health</u> and <u>death by starvation</u>.

UK Climate

You may think it <u>rains</u> a lot in the <u>UK</u>... Well, now's your chance to find out just <u>how much</u> rain we get.

The UK has a Mild Climate — Cool, Wet Winters and Warm, Wet Summers...

Temperature

Follows a <u>seasonal</u> pattern.
<u>Highest</u>: Jul-Aug (average 19 °C).
<u>Lowest</u>: Jan-Feb (average 6 °C).
<u>Temperature range</u>: <u>13 °C</u>.

Precipitation

Follows a <u>seasonal</u> pattern.
<u>Highest</u>: Oct-Jan (120 mm per month).
<u>Lowest</u>: Apr-Jul (70 mm per month).
<u>Fluctuates</u>: Feb-Mar.

Sunshine Hours

Follows a <u>seasonal</u> pattern.
<u>Highest</u>: May-Aug (170-180 hours per month).
<u>Lowest</u>: Dec-Jan (40 hours per month).

...But the UK Climate Hasn't Always Been Like This

1) The <u>climate</u> of the UK has <u>varied a lot</u> over the <u>last 1000 years</u>.

2) This graph shows how <u>temperatures</u> have <u>changed</u> since the year 1000:

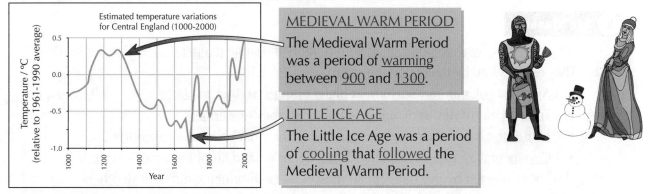

Estimated temperature variations for Central England (1000-2000)

MEDIEVAL WARM PERIOD
The Medieval Warm Period was a period of <u>warming</u> between <u>900</u> and <u>1300</u>.

LITTLE ICE AGE
The Little Ice Age was a period of <u>cooling</u> that <u>followed</u> the Medieval Warm Period.

There Are Regional Differences in Rainfall, Temperature and Winds

1) The <u>north</u> and <u>west</u> of the UK are generally <u>cooler</u> than the <u>south</u> and <u>east</u>.

2) The <u>sea</u> warms and cools <u>more slowly</u> than <u>land</u>, so <u>coastal</u> areas have <u>less temperature variation</u> through the <u>year</u> than <u>inland</u> areas.

3) In general, the <u>prevailing wind</u> in the UK comes from the <u>south west</u> (although there are <u>other</u> winds and <u>air masses</u> which affect the UK — see the next page). This brings <u>moist air</u> from the Atlantic, which means that the west of the UK tends to have <u>higher rainfall</u> than the east.

4) Temperatures tend to be lower and rainfall tends to be <u>higher</u> in areas of <u>higher elevation</u> — <u>mountainous</u> areas get <u>more</u> rainfall than <u>low-lying</u> areas.

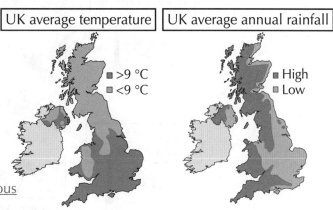

UK average temperature
■ >9 °C
■ <9 °C

UK average annual rainfall
■ High
■ Low

Warm and dry — I'm off to Norfolk...

You might not always need an umbrella in the sunny south east, but make sure you're covered for the exam — read the page again and check you know the main seasonal and regional patterns for climate in the UK.

UK Climate

The UK has the distinctly <u>mild</u>, <u>drizzly</u> climate that you know and love... time to find out <u>why</u>.

Continentality, the North Atlantic Drift and Air Masses Affect UK Weather

1) The <u>climate</u> of the UK is different to most other countries at a <u>similar latitude</u> — this is down to the UK's <u>location</u> on the edge of the Atlantic.

2) There are <u>three</u> reasons why this location gives the UK its <u>unique climate</u>:

1 Continentality

1) The UK is made up of <u>islands</u> so it is surrounded by the <u>sea</u>.

2) Areas <u>near</u> the sea are <u>warmer</u> than inland areas in <u>winter</u> because the <u>sea stores</u> up <u>heat</u> and <u>warms the land</u>.

3) Areas <u>near</u> the sea are <u>cooler</u> in <u>summer</u> because the <u>sea</u> takes a <u>long time</u> to <u>heat up</u> and so <u>cools the land down</u>.

4) This means that the UK is <u>milder</u> in <u>winter</u> and <u>cooler</u> in <u>summer</u> than countries on the <u>continent</u>, e.g. Germany.

Wish you were here!

2 The North Atlantic Drift

1) The North Atlantic Drift is an <u>ocean current</u> that brings <u>warm water</u> from the <u>Caribbean</u> across the <u>Atlantic</u> to the <u>west coast</u> of the UK.

2) This keeps the west coast of the UK <u>warmer</u> than other countries at <u>similar latitudes</u>.

The North Atlantic Drift is part of the Gulf Stream (see p.43).

3 Air Masses

1) Air masses are <u>large volumes of air</u> with roughly the same <u>temperature</u> and <u>water</u> content.

2) They're classified by the <u>region</u> they <u>form over</u>:

- <u>Arctic</u> or <u>Polar</u> air masses form at <u>high latitudes</u> (so they're <u>cooler</u>).
- <u>Tropical</u> air masses form at <u>low latitudes</u> (so they're <u>warmer</u>).
- <u>Maritime</u> air masses form over <u>oceans</u>, i.e. the Atlantic (so they're <u>wetter</u>).
- <u>Continental</u> air masses form over <u>land</u>, i.e. mainland Europe (so they're <u>drier</u>).

Lower latitudes are nearer the equator, while higher latitudes are nearer the poles.

3) The UK is affected by <u>five different air masses</u> — each bringing different <u>weather</u>:

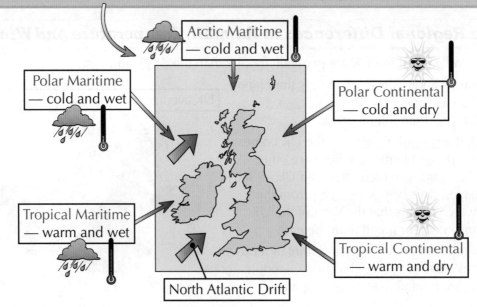

Arctic Maritime — cold and wet

Polar Maritime — cold and wet

Polar Continental — cold and dry

Tropical Maritime — warm and wet

Tropical Continental — warm and dry

North Atlantic Drift

Movement of air masses — caused by too many fizzy drinks...

You've probably guessed that the most common air mass for the UK is the good ol' tropical maritime. Anyhow, rain or no, have another read of how continentality, the North Atlantic Drift and air masses affect the UK climate.

Topic 2 — Weather Hazards and Climate Change

Tropical Cyclones

Tropical cyclones are <u>intense low pressure</u> weather systems with <u>heavy rain</u> and <u>strong winds</u> that spiral around the <u>centre</u>. They have a few other names (<u>hurricanes</u> and <u>typhoons</u>), but they're all the <u>same thing</u>.

Tropical Cyclones Develop over Warm Water

1) Most <u>tropical cyclones</u> occur in a band of <u>low pressure</u> and <u>warm temperatures</u> between <u>5°</u> and <u>30°</u> north and south of the equator. These conditions are created by <u>global atmospheric circulation</u> (see page 43).

2) Tropical cyclones develop when the <u>sea temperature</u> is <u>27 °C or higher</u> and when the <u>wind shear</u> (the <u>difference</u> in <u>windspeed</u>) between <u>higher</u> and <u>lower</u> parts of the atmosphere is <u>low</u>.

3) <u>Warm</u>, <u>moist</u> air <u>rises</u> and <u>condensation</u> occurs. This releases huge amounts of <u>energy</u>, which makes the storms <u>powerful</u>. The <u>rising air</u> creates an area of <u>low pressure</u>, which increases <u>surface winds</u>.

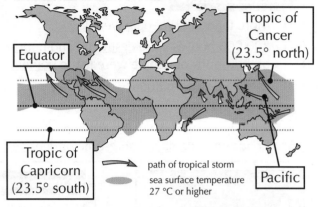

4) Tropical cyclones <u>move towards the west</u> because of <u>easterly winds</u> near the equator. The Earth's <u>rotation</u> deflects the winds, making the storms <u>spin</u>.

5) The cyclone <u>gets stronger</u> due to <u>energy</u> from the warm <u>water</u>, so <u>wind speeds increase</u>. They <u>lose strength</u> when they move over <u>land</u> or <u>cooler water</u> because the energy supply from the warm water is <u>cut off</u>.

6) The <u>majority</u> of storms occur in the <u>northern hemisphere</u> (especially over the <u>Pacific</u>), in <u>late summer</u> and <u>autumn</u>, when sea temperatures are <u>highest</u>. The <u>distribution</u> of tropical storms <u>doesn't change</u> over time, but the <u>number</u> of storms <u>varies</u> each year. In the <u>Atlantic</u>, the number of tropical storms has <u>increased</u> since <u>1984</u> — but there is <u>no overall trend</u> over the last <u>130 years</u>.

Learn the Features and Structure of a Tropical Cyclone

Tropical cyclones are <u>circular</u> in shape, <u>hundreds of kilometres wide</u> and usually last <u>7-14 days</u>. They spin <u>anticlockwise</u> in the <u>northern</u> hemisphere, and <u>clockwise</u> in the <u>southern</u> hemisphere.

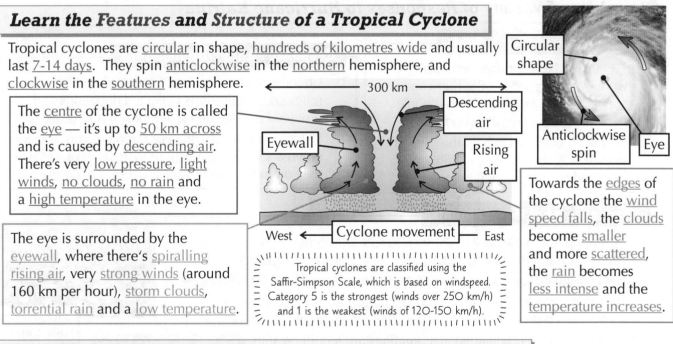

The <u>centre</u> of the cyclone is called the <u>eye</u> — it's up to <u>50 km across</u> and is caused by <u>descending air</u>. There's very <u>low pressure</u>, <u>light winds</u>, <u>no clouds</u>, <u>no rain</u> and a <u>high temperature</u> in the eye.

The eye is surrounded by the <u>eyewall</u>, where there's <u>spiralling rising air</u>, very <u>strong winds</u> (around 160 km per hour), <u>storm clouds</u>, <u>torrential rain</u> and a <u>low temperature</u>.

Towards the <u>edges</u> of the cyclone the <u>wind speed falls</u>, the <u>clouds</u> become <u>smaller</u> and more <u>scattered</u>, the <u>rain</u> becomes <u>less intense</u> and the <u>temperature increases</u>.

Tropical cyclones are classified using the Saffir-Simpson Scale, which is based on windspeed. Category 5 is the strongest (winds over 250 km/h) and 1 is the weakest (winds of 120-150 km/h).

Tropical Cyclones are Natural Hazards When They Hit Land

- HIGH WINDS — <u>windspeeds</u> in a tropical cyclone can reach <u>250 km/h</u>.
- INTENSE RAINFALL — tropical cyclones can release <u>trillions</u> of <u>litres</u> of water per day as rain. The rain gets <u>heavier</u> as you get <u>closer</u> to the <u>eye</u> of the cyclone.
- STORM SURGES — a <u>storm surge</u> is a large rise in <u>sea level</u> caused by <u>low pressure</u> and <u>high winds</u>. If the storm surge <u>coincides</u> with a high tide, flood <u>defences</u> can easily be <u>breached</u>.
- COASTAL FLOODING — <u>flooding</u> happens as a result of <u>storm surges</u> and <u>strong winds</u> driving <u>large waves</u> onto the shore.
- LANDSLIDES — <u>heavy rain</u> makes hills <u>unstable</u>, causing <u>landslides</u>.

Tropical Cyclone — Hurricane Katrina

EXAMPLE

Hurricane Katrina showed just how much <u>destruction</u> a cyclone can cause in a <u>developed</u> country.

Hurricane Katrina struck Mississippi and Louisiana, USA, in August 2005

<u>Hurricane Katrina</u>, a tropical cyclone, struck the <u>south-east USA</u> on <u>29th August 2005</u>.
The <u>impacts</u> of Hurricane Katrina were <u>severe</u>, particularly in <u>New Orleans</u> where flood defences <u>failed</u>.

Social Impacts

1) More than <u>1800 people</u> were <u>killed</u>.
2) <u>300 000 houses</u> were <u>destroyed</u> and <u>hundreds of thousands</u> of people were made <u>homeless</u>.
3) Large areas were <u>flooded</u>, including <u>80%</u> of <u>New Orleans</u>.
4) <u>3 million people</u> were left <u>without electricity</u>.
5) Roads were <u>damaged</u> and some <u>bridges collapsed</u>.

Economic Impacts

1) The total cost of the damage was estimated at <u>$150 billion</u>.
2) <u>Oil wells</u> and <u>pipelines</u> were <u>damaged</u> by the cyclone and had to <u>close</u>, affecting the <u>fuel supply</u> to other <u>industries</u>.
3) <u>230 000 jobs</u> were <u>lost</u> from damaged businesses.

Gulf of Mexico | Path of Katrina

Environmental Impacts

1) <u>Coastal habitats</u> such as sea turtle breeding beaches were <u>damaged</u>.
2) Some <u>coastal conservation areas</u> were destroyed, e.g. around <u>half</u> of <u>Breton National Wildlife Refuge</u> in Louisiana was <u>washed away</u>.
3) <u>Flooding</u> damaged oil refineries in Louisiana, causing massive <u>oil spills</u>.

There Were A Variety of Responses to Hurricane Katrina

Responses from Individuals

1) <u>70-80%</u> of New Orleans residents were <u>evacuated before</u> the hurricane <u>reached land</u>. However, some people decided <u>not to leave</u> their homes.
2) People <u>volunteered</u> to help the <u>relief effort</u> in their <u>neighbourhoods</u>, distributing food and helping rebuild homes.

Responses from Organisations

1) <u>Charities</u> such as the <u>Red Cross</u> and several <u>religious organisations</u> collected <u>donations</u> and provided <u>aid</u>, including millions of <u>hot meals</u>.
2) Volunteers from an <u>amateur radio network</u> provided emergency <u>communications systems</u> in places where the communications <u>infrastructure</u> was <u>destroyed</u>.

Responses from Governments

1) <u>Mississippi</u> and <u>Louisiana</u> declared <u>states of emergency</u> — they set up <u>control centres</u> and <u>emergency shelters</u>, and <u>stockpiled supplies</u>.
2) The <u>coastguard</u>, <u>police</u>, <u>fire service</u> and <u>army</u> rescued over <u>50 000 people</u>.
3) The US government provided over <u>$16 billion</u> for the <u>rebuilding</u> of homes, and provided funds to repair <u>other essential infrastructure</u>.
4) The US Army recommended that buildings are <u>rebuilt on stilts</u> or <u>not rebuilt at all</u> in <u>very low-lying areas</u>.
5) <u>Rescue</u> and <u>recovery</u> efforts were <u>hampered</u> by <u>disagreements</u> between <u>national</u>, <u>state</u> and <u>local officials</u>.
6) <u>Repaired</u> and <u>improved</u> flood defences for New Orleans costing <u>$14.5 billion</u> were completed in <u>2013</u>.

Flooding in New Orleans

The facts on Katrina make for grim reading, that's no joke.

Check you're clear on the impact and responses for your chosen example of a tropical cyclone in a developed country — try covering up the page and scribbling down a couple of points for each of the six boxes. No cheating...

Topic 2 — Weather Hazards and Climate Change

Tropical Cyclone — Cyclone Nargis

OK, one more example, this time looking at a developing country, then get ready for a change in the weather...

Cyclone Nargis hit Myanmar in May 2008

Cyclone Nargis hit the coast of Myanmar on 2nd May 2008. It had major impacts:

Environmental Impacts

1) The Irrawaddy Delta in Myanmar was the hardest hit area — a large proportion of it is only just above sea level and 14 000 km² of land was flooded.
2) 38 000 hectares of mangrove forests were destroyed.
3) The flooding caused erosion and salination (increased salt content) of the land.

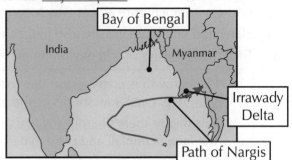

Social Impacts

1) More than 140 000 people were killed.
2) 450 000 houses were destroyed and 350 000 were damaged.
3) A lot of people suffered from diseases caused by poor sanitary conditions and contaminated water.

Economic Impacts

1) Around 65% of rice paddies in the Irrawaddy Delta were damaged, leading to a loss of livelihoods.
2) Fishing infrastructure such as ponds, boats and jetties were destroyed, damaging the local fishing and shrimp industries, which are important sources of income and food for local people.
3) The cyclone was estimated to have caused over US$4 billion of damage.

International Organisations' Responses were Blocked by the Government

Individuals, organisations and the government responded to the cyclone in different ways:

Responses from Individuals

1) Warnings were issued on the TV and radio, but they didn't reach people in poor rural communities. This meant more people were killed because they didn't know what to do or where to evacuate to.
2) Many people were left to cope and rebuild houses, boats and farms by themselves.

Responses from Organisations

1) The United Nations raised US$315 million to provide emergency food, shelter and medical staff by helicopter.
2) The World Food Programme distributed over 70 000 tons of food — and was still providing food assistance over one year later.

Responses from Governments

1) The government of Myanmar had been spending money on military resources rather than evacuation plans or emergency preparation — so it was unable to respond quickly or effectively to the cyclone.
2) The government also initially refused to accept foreign aid and wouldn't allow aid workers into the country.
3) Some of the aid sent by other countries was seized by the military, which delayed its delivery to the people who needed it.
4) The delays in accepting international aid increased the number of deaths because help for some people came too late.

The slow response to Cyclone Nargis made the consequences worse...

You need to know one example of a cyclone in a developed country and one in a developing or emerging country — it's fine if you studied different examples from Katrina and Nargis in class. Jot down a couple of examples of how the impacts and responses for each of your chosen cyclones were affected by the country's level of development.

Topic 2 — Weather Hazards and Climate Change

Arid Environments and Drought

You might want to grab a big bottle of <u>water</u> before you read this page, because it's all about <u>dry places</u> (<u>arid environments</u>) and times when conditions are <u>drier than normal</u> (<u>droughts</u>).

Arid Environments are Very Dry by Definition

There's more about deserts on page 58.

1) Arid environments are places which <u>normally</u> have <u>very low rainfall</u>, e.g. <u>deserts</u>.

2) Many arid environments are also <u>hot</u>, causing water to <u>evaporate faster</u> than it can be <u>replaced</u> by rain.

3) The <u>characteristics</u> of arid environments reflect the <u>lack of water</u> in these environments:

> 1) Plant growth is pretty <u>sparse</u> due to the <u>lack of rainfall</u>. The plants are usually quite <u>short</u> (e.g. cacti, low shrubs or short woody trees) and there are <u>few tall trees</u>.
>
> 2) This means there's <u>hardly any leaf fall</u>, so the <u>soil</u> is <u>shallow</u> and <u>not very fertile</u>. The lack of rainfall and plant material also means that the soil is often <u>dry</u> and <u>dusty</u>.
>
> 3) These are <u>challenging</u> conditions, but they are <u>normal</u> in an arid environment — the <u>plants</u>, <u>animals</u> and <u>people</u> living there are <u>used to dry conditions</u> and have <u>adapted to cope</u> with <u>limited water supplies</u>.

Drought is when Conditions are Drier than Normal

1) A <u>drought</u> is a <u>severe shortage</u> of <u>water</u> in a particular location. There are a few different causes of drought (see the next page), but droughts often happen when <u>rainfall</u> is <u>below average</u> for a <u>long period</u> (weeks, months or years).

2) <u>Water supplies</u>, e.g. lakes and rivers, become <u>depleted</u> during a drought because <u>people keep using them</u> but they <u>aren't replenished</u> by rainfall.

3) As well as low rainfall, droughts are often accompanied by <u>high temperatures</u>. This <u>increases</u> the <u>rate of evaporation</u> and the <u>demand</u> for water, <u>depleting</u> water supplies even <u>faster</u>.

4) Droughts can happen <u>anywhere</u>, and the <u>length</u> of a drought is <u>different</u> in <u>different places</u>. E.g. the <u>worst drought</u> in <u>Britain</u> since records began lasted <u>16 months</u>, whilst droughts in <u>East African countries</u> have lasted for <u>more than a decade</u>.

Droughts can be Hazardous

Droughts mean there is <u>less water than usual</u>. This can cause <u>hazards</u> for <u>people</u> and <u>ecosystems</u>, which both depend on water for <u>survival</u>.

> 1) <u>Depletion</u> of water supplies leads to <u>shortages</u> and <u>lower water levels</u> in rivers, lakes and reservoirs, causing <u>aquatic</u> plants and animals to <u>die</u>. Lakes and reservoirs become <u>stagnant</u> and there is less <u>fresh water</u> to <u>dilute</u> waste materials like <u>sewage</u>. This increases the risk of <u>contamination</u> of water supplies and can cause outbreaks of <u>diseases</u> like <u>cholera</u>.
>
> 2) A lack of water can also damage <u>crops</u> and harm <u>livestock</u>. This can lead to <u>food shortages</u>, which cause <u>hunger</u> and <u>malnutrition</u>. Farmers may also lose their <u>livelihoods</u>.
>
> 3) <u>Soil</u> dries out and <u>plants</u> die, which leaves the soil <u>vulnerable</u> to <u>erosion</u> by wind and rain. Erosion removes the <u>topsoil</u> — so even when rain returns, it can be <u>difficult</u> to grow crops again. If there are <u>already</u> food shortages, this can <u>make the situation worse</u>, causing <u>starvation</u>.
>
> 4) During a drought, soil <u>hardens</u> and <u>sewers</u> can become <u>blocked</u>. This can cause <u>flooding</u> when rain finally falls, as the water can't drain away quickly enough. Flooding can damage <u>homes</u>, <u>farmland</u> and <u>infrastructure</u>.
>
> 5) <u>Vegetation</u> becomes very <u>dry</u>, making <u>wildfires</u> more likely. Wildfires can <u>destroy houses</u>, <u>crops</u>, <u>forests</u> and <u>animals</u>.

EXAM QUESTION

Finally, a chance to show off my dry sense of humour...

1) *Explain one difference between the weather conditions of drought and the climate of an arid environment.* [2]

Topic 2 — Weather Hazards and Climate Change

Causes of Drought

Droughts can be caused by changes in the <u>weather</u>, the <u>depletion</u> of water <u>sources</u>, or by <u>human activities</u>.

Droughts are Caused by a Combination of Factors

Meteorological

1) <u>Meteorological</u> factors can cause an area to get <u>less rainfall</u> than <u>average</u>.

2) <u>Changes</u> in <u>atmospheric circulation</u> can mean it <u>doesn't rain much</u> in an area for <u>months</u> or <u>years</u>. E.g. the drought in <u>Australia</u> in the 2000s (see next page) was made <u>worse</u> by a change in the air and ocean currents in the Pacific.

"Meteorological" just means "relating to weather and climate".

3) Changes in atmospheric circulation can also make the <u>annual rains fail</u> — e.g. <u>monsoon rains don't come</u> when they normally do in places like <u>India</u>.

4) Low rainfall is also caused when <u>high pressure</u> weather systems <u>stop depressions</u> (weather systems that <u>cause rain</u>) from entering an area, e.g. the <u>UK</u>.

Hydrological

1) <u>Rivers</u>, <u>lakes</u>, <u>reservoirs</u> and <u>aquifers</u> (rocks that store water underground), are all part of the <u>hydrological system</u>. A <u>lack of water</u> in these <u>stores</u> can lead to a drought.

2) Drought is <u>more likely</u> in areas which <u>rely</u> on <u>rainfall</u> and stores of <u>surface water</u> (e.g. lakes and rivers). In <u>warm</u>, <u>dry</u> conditions, surface water <u>evaporates</u> quickly, so it gets depleted faster than in <u>aquifers</u> or <u>groundwater</u>.

3) Hydrological factors can <u>take a while</u> to have an effect, but can also have much <u>long-lasting impacts</u> — once depleted, water stores can take <u>months</u> or even <u>years</u> to be <u>replenished</u>.

Human

1) <u>Intensive farming</u> depletes water supplies by using large volumes of water for <u>irrigation</u>. Farming <u>livestock</u> also demands a lot of water, e.g. for <u>animals</u> to <u>drink</u>.

2) <u>Building dams</u> across rivers creates <u>reservoirs</u> which provide water for local people, but dams also <u>reduce</u> the <u>flow</u> of water <u>downstream</u>, which can <u>cause</u> droughts in other areas.

3) <u>Deforestation</u> reduces the amount of water that can be held in the soil, so land dries out more <u>quickly</u>. Trees release a lot of <u>moisture</u> into the <u>air</u> through their leaves — so deforestation can make the atmosphere of an area <u>drier</u>, contributing to the <u>meteorological</u> causes of drought.

Some Places are More Vulnerable to Drought than Others

1) This <u>map</u> shows the <u>distribution</u> of <u>severe droughts</u> around the <u>world</u>.

2) The areas which experience the <u>most severe</u> droughts are normally found at about <u>30° north</u> and <u>south</u> of the equator, e.g. <u>northern</u> and <u>southern Africa</u>, the <u>Middle East</u>, <u>Australia</u>, <u>western South America</u> and parts of <u>North America</u>.

3) The pattern of droughts can be explained by <u>global atmospheric circulation</u> (p.43). <u>Cool</u>, <u>dry</u> air <u>sinks</u> at 30° north and south of the equator. This creates a belt of <u>high pressure</u> where there is very <u>little rainfall</u>.

4) The locations affected by drought <u>vary</u> over <u>time</u>. Since 1950, there have been <u>more droughts</u> in <u>Africa</u>, <u>Asia</u> and the <u>Mediterranean</u> and <u>fewer droughts</u> in the <u>Americas</u> and <u>Russia</u>.

5) Some scientists have <u>suggested</u> that climate change might cause droughts to become <u>more frequent</u> and <u>more severe</u> in the future.

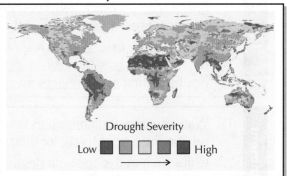

Drought Severity

Low ▮▮▮▮▮ High

Better not to give weather hazards the benefit of the drought...

You'll need to be able to talk about the different causes of droughts in the exam, so give the page another read and make sure the key points are as firmly embedded in your brain as a turnip stuck in a dried-up field.

Drought — Australia

I'm going to spoil you with another page on <u>drought</u> — and we're heading down under for this one.

There was a Drought in Australia in the Early 21st Century

1) <u>South-east Australia</u> suffered from a <u>severe</u>, <u>long-term drought</u> from roughly <u>2001 to 2009</u>, although scientists don't agree on exactly when it started and finished. It's known as the <u>Millennium Drought</u> or the "<u>Big Dry</u>".

2) The <u>worst-hit area</u> was the <u>Murray-Darling Basin</u>, an important <u>agricultural region</u>.

AUSTRALIA
Murray-Darling Basin
30° S

Impacts on People

1) <u>Water levels</u> in <u>lakes</u> and <u>rivers</u> (particularly the Murray and Darling) <u>fell</u>, so water supplies ran <u>low</u>.

2) The largest impacts were on <u>farming</u>:
- <u>Crop yields fell</u>, and crops that rely on <u>irrigation</u> (watering) were particularly badly affected, e.g. <u>rice production</u> fell to just <u>2%</u> of pre-drought totals. This <u>increased food prices</u>.
- Livestock <u>died</u> — the number of <u>sheep</u> in Australia <u>fell</u> by around <u>8 million</u> during 2002-2003.
- <u>Farmers' incomes</u> fell, and over <u>100 000</u> people employed in farming <u>lost their jobs</u>.

3) <u>Dust storms</u> caused by the drought affected <u>inland Australia</u> and some <u>coastal cities</u>.

4) The drought created the right conditions for <u>wildfires</u>. Over <u>30 000 km^2</u> of land <u>burned</u>, and <u>hundreds</u> of <u>houses</u> were <u>destroyed</u>. <u>8 people</u> were <u>killed</u>.

Impacts on Ecosystems

1) The drought caused <u>vegetation loss</u> and <u>soil erosion</u>, and rivers and lakes suffered from outbreaks of <u>toxic algae</u>.

2) <u>Rivers</u> and <u>marshland</u> ecosystems <u>dried up</u> and water <u>temperatures</u> rose, causing plants and animals to die and <u>populations</u> to <u>decrease</u>. Some <u>invertebrates</u> need <u>floods</u> to be able to <u>breed</u> — these species nearly became <u>extinct</u>.

3) Wildfires destroyed or damaged <u>habitats</u>, which will take decades to recover. E.g. <u>Stromlo Forest</u> was completely destroyed by <u>wildfires</u> in <u>2003</u>.

Responses to the Drought Focused on Reducing Water Use

<u>Individuals</u>, <u>organisations</u> and the Australian <u>government</u> responded to the drought in a few different ways.

Individuals

1) People started using <u>water-saving</u> measures, such as re-using <u>grey water</u> (e.g. watering plants with dishwater) and using <u>water-efficient</u> showers.

2) Farmers also used water-saving <u>techniques</u> such as <u>drip irrigation</u>, which delivers water <u>directly</u> to the <u>roots</u> of crops, preventing water <u>loss</u> through <u>evaporation</u>.

3) Some people in <u>rural</u> areas responded to the loss of <u>farming income</u> by <u>diversifying</u> their incomes — e.g. by getting <u>part-time jobs</u> away from the farm.

Organisations

1) <u>Schools</u> and <u>media</u> organisations ran campaigns <u>encouraging</u> people to <u>reduce</u> their water use.

2) An Australian research institute, <u>CSIRO</u>, teamed up with <u>businesses</u> to breed new, <u>drought-tolerant</u> varieties of <u>wheat</u>.

Government

1) <u>Water conservation measures</u> were introduced. E.g. the <u>3 million people</u> who rely on the <u>River Murray</u> for their water supply had their allocation <u>reduced</u>.

2) Cities such as <u>Sydney</u> built <u>desalination plants</u> to turn sea water into drinking water.

3) The Australian government provided more than <u>23 000</u> rural families and <u>1500</u> small businesses with <u>income support</u> to help them <u>survive</u>.

4) The government has also <u>invested</u> in <u>improving forecasting</u>, to help farmers <u>prepare</u> for drought.

Ex-stream temperatures — making Australia's rivers run dry...

After the Big Dry comes the Big Learn. You'll need to know all the impacts and responses for the Millennium Drought — unless you've got a different drought case study for a developed country up your sleeve, that is.

Drought — Ethiopia

Droughts in developed countries like Australia are pretty serious, but the impacts can be even <u>worse</u> in <u>developing</u> or <u>emerging</u> countries — people and governments often don't have enough <u>resources</u> to cope.

There was a Drought in Ethiopia in 2016

1) Ethiopia is a <u>developing</u> country in the <u>Horn of Africa</u>. Large areas of Ethiopia have a <u>semi-arid</u> climate, and the country is extremely <u>vulnerable</u> to droughts.

2) In <u>2016</u>, south and south-eastern Ethiopia were hit by one of the most <u>intense</u>, <u>widespread</u> and <u>longest-lasting</u> droughts for over 30 years.

3) The drought was caused by a <u>change</u> in the <u>pattern</u> of <u>global atmospheric circulation</u>, which made the region even <u>hotter</u> and <u>drier</u> than normal.

4) The <u>impacts</u> of the drought were <u>severe</u>, and were <u>still</u> being felt over a year later:

Impacts on People

1) <u>85%</u> of people in Ethiopia depend on <u>agriculture</u> as their main livelihood, with many farmers relying on <u>rain-fed agriculture</u>. Without rain, crops did not grow. Farmers in some regions lost <u>50-90%</u> of their crops.

2) There was a lack of <u>pasture</u> (grass) for <u>livestock</u> (cattle, goats and camels) to graze on. <u>Milk production</u> slowed down, and by 2017 up to <u>2 million</u> animals had <u>died</u>.

3) Many people lost their <u>jobs</u> in farming and had to <u>move</u> to cities to try to find work.

4) The lack of food and employment caused widespread <u>food insecurity</u> and <u>malnutrition</u> — aid organisations estimated that <u>70 000 people</u> were at risk of <u>starvation</u>. In 2017, <u>7.8 million</u> people needed <u>emergency assistance</u> to meet their <u>basic food needs</u>.

Rain-fed agriculture is a type of farming where the only water supply is from rainfall — there's no irrigation.

Impacts on Ecosystems

1) Water sources started to <u>dry up</u> and plants <u>died</u>, meaning there was also <u>less food</u> and <u>water</u> available for <u>wildlife</u>.

2) The <u>loss</u> of vegetation damaged important <u>habitats</u> for wildlife, threatening <u>endangered species</u>, such as the <u>Ethiopian Wolf</u>.

3) Drought also made areas vulnerable to <u>wildfires</u>, <u>flooding</u>, <u>wind erosion</u> and <u>desertification</u>.

Desertification is a process where vegetated land in arid environments is degraded and becomes dry and infertile.

Responses to the Drought Provided Emergency Relief to Farmers

Governments

1) The Ethiopian government distributed food from its <u>national food reserve</u> through the <u>Productive Safety Net Program</u>, in which people work on <u>public building projects</u> in return for <u>food</u> or <u>money</u>.

2) The government also helped people who had to leave their homes, providing them with <u>permanent housing</u> near to <u>sources of water</u>.

Individuals

1) People <u>migrated</u> away from drought-affected areas to search for <u>new livelihoods</u> or to work on the Productive Safety Net Program.

2) Farmers in some areas have switched from growing <u>cereal crops</u> to a more <u>resilient</u> crop called <u>chat</u>.

Organisations

1) <u>Charities</u> and <u>international organisations</u> provided <u>humanitarian aid</u> to fund <u>emergency food</u>, <u>water</u> and <u>medicine</u>.

2) The <u>Food and Agriculture Organisation</u> (FAO) of the United Nations requested <u>US$20 million</u> for programmes such as <u>distributing seeds</u> and preventing the spread of <u>pests</u> in key crops like <u>maize</u>. The FAO also <u>co-ordinated</u> responses to make sure help <u>reached</u> people in the <u>worst-affected</u> areas.

3) The FAO also helped to <u>treat livestock</u> that <u>became ill</u> during the drought. Animals that would not make it through the drought were <u>slaughtered safely</u> to <u>prevent</u> the spread of <u>disease</u>.

People in Ethiopia are still experiencing impacts of the drought...

Now you know about what happened during the Ethiopian drought of 2016, have a crack at this question:

1) Explain two impacts of drought on people in a named emerging or developing country. [4]

Topic 2 — Weather Hazards and Climate Change

Revision Summary

Wow, that was quite a whirlwind — climate change, cyclones and droughts. You've made it through the topic though, so I thought I'd reward you with this — a beautiful page of revision questions. It looks like a lot, but you'll be surprised at how much you just learned. Try answering a few questions at a time, and check the answers on the pages. Once you can answer the questions while spinning anticlockwise (clockwise if you're in the southern hemisphere) and juggling three kangaroos, the next topic awaits you...

Global Atmospheric Circulation and Heat Transfer (p.43) ☑

1) How does global atmospheric circulation lead to high and low pressure belts?
2) Describe how ocean currents transfer heat around the Earth.

Climate Change (p.44-46) ☑

3) What is the Quaternary period?
4) Give three sources of evidence for climate change over the Quaternary period.
5) Explain how Milankovitch cycles can cause climate change.
6) What is the greenhouse effect?
7) How can human activities increase the concentration of greenhouse gases in the atmosphere?
8) Give one negative effect that climate change has on the environment.

UK Climate (p.47-48) ☑

9) Describe the seasonal pattern of rainfall in the UK.
10) What was the Little Ice Age?
11) How does the climate vary as you move from west to east across the UK?
12) Describe how continentality influences weather in the UK.
13) a) What is the North Atlantic Drift?
    b) How does it affect the UK's climate?
14) Name two air masses that influence weather in the UK.

Tropical Cyclones (p.49-51) ☑

15) True or false — tropical cyclones develop when the sea temperature is 25 °C or higher.
16) Do tropical cyclones move east or west across the ocean?
17) What can cause a tropical cyclone to lose strength?
18) Which way does a tropical cyclone rotate in the southern hemisphere?
19) Describe two characteristics of the eye of a tropical cyclone.
20) Give five natural hazards which are caused by tropical cyclones.
21) a) Give an example of a tropical cyclone that occurred in an emerging or developing country.
    b) What were the economic impacts of the cyclone?
    c) How did organisations respond to the cyclone?

Arid Environments and Droughts (p.52-55) ☑

22) Give three characteristics of arid environments.
23) What is a drought?
24) Give two hazards that can be caused by drought.
25) Give three ways that human activities can contribute to drought.
26) Explain why some places are more vulnerable to drought than others.
27) a) Give an example of a drought that occurred in a developed country.
    b) What were the impacts of the drought on ecosystems?
    c) How did governments respond to the drought?

Global Ecosystems

Time for a whistle-stop tour of the <u>world's ecosystems</u>. All aboard...

You Need to Know the Global Distribution of Large-Scale Ecosystems

1) This map shows the location of the world's main <u>large-scale ecosystems</u>.

2) An <u>ecosystem</u> is a community of <u>living</u> organisms and their <u>non-living</u> environment.

3) The <u>climate</u> in an area determines what <u>type of ecosystem</u> forms. So different parts of the world have <u>different ecosystems</u> because they have <u>different climates</u>.

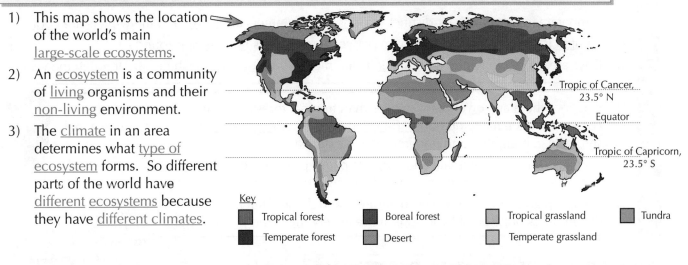

Tropic of Cancer, 23.5° N

Equator

Tropic of Capricorn, 23.5° S

<u>Key</u>

▮ Tropical forest   ▮ Boreal forest   ▮ Tropical grassland   ▮ Tundra

▮ Temperate forest   ▮ Desert   ▮ Temperate grassland

The Distribution of Ecosystems is Affected by Local Factors

<u>Climate</u> (i.e. <u>temperature</u>, <u>rainfall</u> and <u>sunshine hours</u>) is the main factor influencing the <u>distribution of ecosystems</u>, but there are other factors that alter distribution at a <u>smaller scale</u>:

1) <u>Altitude</u> (height above sea level) — <u>higher</u> altitudes are <u>colder</u>, so <u>fewer</u> plants grow there, which also <u>limits</u> the number of animal species. This means there's not much <u>organic matter</u>, so soils are <u>thin</u> or <u>non-existent</u>.

Generally, as altitude increases, biodiversity decreases.

2) <u>Soil type</u> — more <u>nutrient-rich</u> soils can support <u>more</u> plants. The <u>acidity</u>, <u>drainage</u> and <u>thickness</u> of soils also <u>varies</u>, affecting the <u>plants</u> that can <u>grow</u>. For example:

Yes, it's a bit chilly.

Welcome to the 27th floor

- <u>Peat soils</u> are very <u>acidic</u>, so only <u>acid-tolerant</u> plants such as <u>conifers</u> can grow in these soils.

- <u>Clay soils</u> are <u>sticky</u>, so <u>water can't</u> flow through very <u>easily</u>, making it hard for plants that need <u>well-drained soils</u> to grow.

- <u>Thin soils</u> (e.g. on <u>mountain tops</u>) do not have enough <u>nutrients</u> for <u>large trees</u> to grow.

Tropical Forests Have a Hot, Wet Climate

Tropical forests are found in <u>low-lying areas</u> near the <u>equator</u>.
These areas have the hot, wet climate needed for <u>tropical</u> plants to <u>grow well</u>:

Climate

1) The <u>climate</u> in tropical forests <u>doesn't change</u> throughout the year — it's always <u>hot</u> and <u>rainy</u> (see page 63).

2) <u>Day length</u> is the same (about <u>12 hours</u>) <u>all year</u> round, so the forests get plenty of <u>sunshine</u>.

See pages 63-67 for more on tropical forests.

Characteristics

1) <u>Plants</u> — almost all of the trees are <u>evergreen</u> (they don't <u>drop</u> their <u>leaves</u> in a particular <u>season</u>). Plants grow <u>quickly</u> and are <u>adapted</u> to take in <u>maximum light</u>.

2) <u>Animals</u> — the <u>dense</u> vegetation provides lots of <u>food</u> and different <u>habitats</u> for <u>animals</u>, so there are lots of <u>different species</u> of animal, e.g. <u>sloths</u>, <u>pythons</u>, <u>beetles</u> and <u>macaws</u>.

3) <u>Soils</u> — plants shed leaves all year round. These <u>decompose</u> quickly, so there's a constant supply of <u>nutrients</u> in the <u>soil</u>, and these nutrients are <u>cycled quickly</u>.

Global Ecosystems

Temperate Forests *Have a Mild, Wet Climate*

Head to p.118 for more on latitude.

Temperate forests are found in places with high rainfall and mild temperatures, in the mid-latitudes.

Climate

1) Temperate forests have four distinct seasons. The summers are warm and the winters are cool.
2) Rainfall is very high (up to 1500 mm per year) and there's rain all year round.
3) Days are shorter in winter and longer in summer — the hours of sunshine vary through the year.

Characteristics

1) Plants — there are fewer plant species than tropical forests, but more than boreal forests. Forests are often made up of broad-leaved trees that drop their leaves in autumn (e.g. oak), shrubs (e.g. brambles) and undergrowth (e.g. ferns).
2) Animals — the mild climate and range of plants provides food and habitats for mammals (e.g. foxes, squirrels), birds (e.g. woodpeckers, cuckoos) and insects (e.g. beetles, moths).
3) Soils — plants lose their leaves in autumn, and the leaf litter decomposes quite quickly, so soils are relatively thick and nutrient-rich.

Deciduous woodlands are an example of a temperate forest ecosystem — there's more about them on pages 68-72.

Boreal Forests *Have a Cold, Dry Climate*

Boreal forests are located in the high latitudes, where plants and animals are adapted to the cold climate.

Climate

1) Boreal forests have short summers and long winters. In winter, average temperatures are below –20 °C and can drop much lower. In summer, average temperatures are about 10 °C.
2) Precipitation is low — generally less than 500 mm per year. A lot of this falls as snow.
3) Boreal forests get lots of daylight during the summer months, but little or none during the winter. Skies tend to be clear, so during daylight hours there's plenty of sunshine.

Characteristics

1) Plants — most trees are evergreen, so they can grow whenever there's enough light. Coniferous trees such as pine and fir are common, as are low-growing mosses and lichen.
2) Animals — there are relatively few animal species in boreal forests compared to other forests, because there is less food available. Animals that do live there include black bears, wolves, elk and eagles.
3) Soils — the cool, dry climate means that needles from the trees decompose slowly, so soils are quite thin, nutrient-poor and acidic. In some areas the ground is frozen for most of the year.

Deserts *Have Low Rainfall*

Most deserts are found in a belt of high pressure and low rainfall between 15° and 35° north and south of the equator. Deserts generally have hot, dry climates.

Not all deserts are hot — some are mild (e.g. the Atacama desert, which is at high altitude) and some are cold (e.g. the Gobi desert, which is at a higher latitude).

Climate

1) Rainfall is very low — less than 250 mm per year. It might only rain once every two or three years.
2) Hot desert temperatures range from very hot in the day (e.g. 45 °C) to cold at night (below 0 °C).
3) Hot deserts get more daylight during the summer than the winter. Because there is little cloud cover, they get lots of hours of sunshine every day.

Characteristics

1) Plants — plant growth is sparse due to lack of rainfall. Plants that do grow include cacti and thornbushes. Many plants have a short life cycle, only appearing when it rains.
2) Animals — relatively few animal species live in hot deserts. Those that do are adapted to cope with the harsh climate. Animals that live there include lizards, snakes, insects and scorpions.
3) Soil — the sparse vegetation means that there is little leaf litter, and the dry climate means that organic matter is slow to decompose. As a result, soils are mostly thin and nutrient-poor.

Global Ecosystems

Tropical Grasslands **Have a Mostly Dry Climate**

Tropical grasslands are found near the equator, in places where there isn't enough rain to support many trees.

Climate

1) Tropical grasslands have quite low rainfall (800-900 mm per year) and distinct wet and dry seasons. Fires are common during the dry season.

2) Temperatures are highest (around 35 °C) just before the wet season and lowest (about 15 °C) just after it. Tropical grasslands are near the equator, so they get lots of sunshine all year round.

Characteristics

1) Plants — tropical grasslands consist mostly of grass, scrub and small plants, with a few scattered trees, e.g. acacia. These plants have adapted to recover quickly after a fire.

2) Animals — there are lots of insects, including grasshoppers, beetles and termites. Larger animals include lions, elephants, giraffes, zebras and antelope.

3) Soils — grass dies back or is burned during the dry season, forming a thin, nutrient-rich soil, but nutrients are washed out of the soil during the wet season.

Temperate Grasslands **Have Distinct Hot and Cold Seasons**

Temperate grasslands are found at higher altitudes and higher latitudes than tropical grasslands.

Climate

1) Temperate grasslands have hot summers (up to 40 °C) and cold winters (down to −40 °C).

2) They receive 250-500 mm precipitation each year, mostly in the late spring and early summer.

3) Because they're found at mid-latitudes, the amount of light they receive varies through the year.

Characteristics

1) Plants — temperate grasslands are also dominated by grasses and small plants. Rainfall is too low to support large plants, so there are very few trees.

2) Animals — they are home to fewer animal species than tropical grasslands — mammals include bison and wild horses, and rodents such as mole rats.

3) Soils — the high temperatures in summer mean that decomposition happens quickly, so soils are relatively thick and nutrient-rich.

Tundra **Has a Cold, Dry Climate**

Tundra is found at high latitudes (above 60° N) in northern Europe, Alaska and northern Canada.

Climate

1) Temperatures are low — around 5-10 °C during the summer and lower than −30 °C in the winter.

2) Precipitation is also very low — less than 250 mm per year. Most of this falls as snow.

3) Tundra is found at high latitudes, so it gets near-continuous daylight in the summer and little or no daylight in the winter. There is more cloud cover in the summer.

Characteristics

1) Plants — the cold climate and lack of light in winter make it hard for plants to grow, and there are hardly any trees. Vegetation includes mosses, grasses and low shrubs.

2) Animals — the cold climate and lack of vegetation means that relatively few animal species live in the tundra. Those that do include Arctic hares, Arctic foxes, mosquitoes and lots of birds. Some animals migrate south for the winter.

3) Soil — the sparse vegetation produces little leaf litter, and organic matter decomposes slowly in the cold, dry climate, so soil is thin and nutrient-poor. There is a layer of permafrost (permanently frozen ground) below the soil surface, which can stop water from draining away.

Global echo-systems — they go round and round and round...

Make sure you know where these ecosystems are found, what they're like and the factors affecting their distribution.

Humans and the Biosphere

Resources are just all the things we use — and it turns out we use an awful lot of them and get pretty much everything from the biosphere. I know, I thought everything came from Santa too...

The Biosphere *Provides Lots of Resources*

1) The biosphere includes all parts of the Earth that are occupied by living organisms — it's the plants, animals, bacteria and fungi as well as the soil and water that they live in.

2) Living organisms provide loads of goods that people need to survive. For example:

FOOD — Most people get their food from the biosphere indirectly — e.g. from farmed cereals, fruit, vegetables and livestock. Some people get food directly from the biosphere — e.g. picking wild fruit, vegetables and nuts and hunting and trapping animals. People also eat fish which are caught from rivers, lakes and the sea. Fish can also be farmed in tanks or pens.

MEDICINE — Lots of plants have medicinal properties and are used to cure illnesses and keep people healthy. Plant species in tropical forests have been used to create over 7000 drugs, e.g. quinine from the cinchona tree is used to treat malaria.

BUILDING MATERIALS — People get materials from the biosphere which are used for construction — e.g. trees are used for timber. Clay can be quarried directly from soil and made into bricks or tiles.

FUEL — Many people rely on plants and animals for fuel for cooking and keeping warm. Wood, dried grass and dried animal dung are burnt as fuel. People who live in areas with little vegetation (like the tundra), use animal fat, e.g. blubber from seals, as fuel for oil lamps. Fossil fuels are also extracted from parts of the biosphere (see below).

Humans *Exploit the Biosphere*

The biosphere is also exploited by companies for commercial gain (to make a profit). Increasing demand and improving technology is increasing the scale of commercial exploitation. For example:

Energy

Demand for energy is increasing as the world population increases and becomes wealthier. There are more people who have more electronic devices, e.g. laptops and phones (see p.101):

- Large areas of forest are cut down to clear land for the growing of crops that can be used to make biofuels, or to make way for coal mines or power stations.
- Drilling for oil and gas in the tundra is damaging the biosphere because pipelines are melting the permafrost.
- Some areas of tropical forest have been flooded by the building of hydroelectric dams.
- Fracking (see p.102) can pollute the air and contaminate groundwater.

Biofuels are fuels that are made from processing plants or animal products.

Water

Demand for water is also increasing because of increases in global population — people use water for washing, irrigating farmland etc. Water resources, e.g. lakes, rivers and aquifers (underground water stores), can be over-exploited — this is happening in arid areas like the Sahara desert. This can cause damage to the biosphere, as plants and animals no longer have enough water to survive.

Minerals

Minerals such as gold and iron are used in building, scientific instruments, electrical appliances and lots of other things — and demand for them is increasing. Minerals are often extracted by mining. Mines in tropical forests are responsible for lots of deforestation and toxic chemicals are washed into streams and rivers, killing wildlife. Open pit mining removes large areas of the land surface, which reduces habitat for plants and animals.

Fridges — vital for all your re-sauce needs...

The biosphere has it all, so you've got to know it all. Cover the page and jot down some examples of the resources that the biosphere provides. Make sure you know the different ways in which humans are exploiting the biosphere, too.

UK Ecosystems

You need to know about the main <u>ecosystems</u> in the <u>UK</u>. There aren't any rainforests, but there is rain...

The UK Has its Own Distinctive Ecosystems

The UK has <u>four</u> main <u>terrestrial</u> (land-based) ecosystems — <u>heaths</u>, <u>moorlands</u>, <u>wetlands</u> and <u>woodlands</u>.

1) <u>Heaths</u> are found in <u>lowland</u> areas, <u>below 1000 m</u>. There are <u>large areas</u> of heath in the <u>south</u> of England — e.g. the <u>Dorset Heaths</u> and the <u>New Forest</u>.

2) <u>Moorland</u> is found in <u>upland</u> areas — e.g. in <u>Scotland</u>, <u>northern England</u> and <u>Wales</u>.

3) <u>Wetlands</u> are often found on <u>floodplains</u>, e.g. the <u>Somerset Levels</u>, or near <u>rivers</u> and <u>lakes</u>, e.g. the <u>Norfolk Broads</u> in East Anglia. Wetlands can also be found in some <u>upland areas</u>.

4) <u>Woodlands</u> used to cover <u>most of the UK</u>, and there are still small areas of woodland throughout the UK's lowlands. Large areas of woodland include the <u>Forest of Dean</u> in <u>southern England</u> and <u>Kielder Forest</u> in <u>northern England</u>.

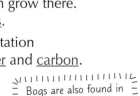
Approx. distribution of UK ecosystems

Heaths
Moorlands & bogs
Lowland wetlands
Woodlands

Much of the UK is covered by farmland, which isn't a natural ecosystem.

Heaths and Moorlands are Similar Ecosystems

1) Heaths and moorlands are <u>open landscapes</u> with <u>poor soils</u> and <u>few trees</u>.

2) They have <u>acidic soils</u> and <u>high rainfall</u>, which affects the kind of plants which can grow there. In the UK the <u>main plants</u> on moorlands and heaths are <u>heather</u>, <u>gorse</u> and <u>grasses</u>.

3) On flatter ground the soil can become <u>waterlogged</u>, creating a <u>bog</u>. In bogs, vegetation <u>decomposes slowly</u> to form a layer of <u>peat</u>, which can store large amounts of <u>water</u> and <u>carbon</u>.

4) The main difference between heaths and moorlands is the <u>altitude</u> at which they are found — moorlands are <u>upland</u> ecosystems and heaths are found in <u>lowland</u> areas. This leads to <u>differences</u> in the <u>species</u> that can survive there.

Bogs are also found in wetlands (see below).

Heaths

1) Heaths can have <u>dry</u> and <u>sandy</u> soils (especially in the <u>south</u> and <u>east</u> of the UK) or <u>wet</u> and <u>peaty</u> soils (in the <u>north</u> and <u>west</u>).

2) They provide habitats for some rare <u>plants</u> e.g. <u>yellow centaury</u>.

3) These plants provide <u>habitats</u> for lots of <u>insects</u>, which in turn provide <u>food</u> for birds (e.g. <u>nightjars</u>) and rare <u>reptiles</u> like <u>sand lizards</u>.

Coastal heath in Cornwall

Moorlands

1) Moorlands provide <u>habitats</u> for important <u>animals</u> and <u>birds</u>, such as <u>mountain hares</u> (in Scotland and the Peak District), <u>golden plover</u> and <u>hen harriers</u>.

2) Many moorland areas are used for <u>grazing animals</u> such as <u>sheep</u>, and to raise <u>grouse</u>, a wild bird that is shot for <u>sport</u>. The grouse eat the <u>shoots</u> of the <u>heather</u> and nest in the plants. Areas of heather moorland are <u>burnt</u> each year to encourage <u>new growth</u> of heather for the grouse to eat.

Wetlands are Home to Many Insects

1) Wetlands are found in places where soils are <u>waterlogged</u> for <u>most</u> or <u>all</u> of the <u>year</u> — e.g. <u>marshes</u>, <u>fens</u> and <u>bogs</u>. Wetlands also include places which <u>flood seasonally</u>, e.g. the <u>Somerset Levels</u>.

2) This means they have <u>anaerobic</u> soils (the water stops oxygen from getting into the soil).

3) Vegetation in bogs decomposes very <u>slowly</u>, forming <u>peat</u>. <u>Bogs</u> have <u>acidic</u> soils, but <u>marshes</u> tend to have <u>neutral</u> or <u>alkaline</u> soils.

4) Only <u>certain plants</u> can grow in these wet, anaerobic conditions — e.g. <u>reeds</u> and <u>mosses</u>.

5) Wetlands provide habitats for <u>mammals</u>, e.g. <u>otters</u> and <u>water voles</u>, and birds, e.g. <u>bittern</u> and <u>snipe</u>.

6) Wetlands have the ideal <u>breeding conditions</u> for <u>flying insects</u>, e.g. <u>dragonflies</u> and <u>damselflies</u>. These insects are a <u>source of food</u> for other animals, e.g. <u>bats</u>.

Topic 3 — Ecosystems, Biodiversity and Management

UK Ecosystems

Just one more terrestrial ecosystem to look at, and then it's time for a quick look at marine ecosystems.

Woodlands *Provide Important Habitats for Wildlife*

There's more about deciduous woodlands on pages 68-72.

1) Most of the native woodland in the UK is deciduous (the trees lose their leaves in the autumn). Common native trees include oak, ash and beech, but there are many others.

2) Deciduous woodlands often have fertile soils. Fallen leaves from the trees decompose and mix with the existing soil to form a thick soil called brown earth. This fertile soil and the shelter of the trees provides the right conditions for smaller plants — e.g. lichens and bluebells.

3) Coniferous woodlands are also found in many areas of the UK. Most of the trees in coniferous woodlands (e.g. Scots Pine) are evergreen — they keep their leaves all year round. Most coniferous woodlands are commercial plantations, where trees are grown for timber.

4) Many animals live in UK woodlands, including badgers, foxes and grey squirrels. Woodlands are also important habitats for birds such as owls and woodpeckers.

Marine Ecosystems *Provide Resources — but are Being Degraded*

1) The UK has a range of important ecosystems around its coast, including salt marshes, estuaries, cold-water coral reefs and deep sea habitats. These marine ecosystems provide us with many resources:

> 1) Recreation — people use estuaries and other coastal marine ecosystems for leisure activities such as swimming, fishing and boating. Income from tourism provides livelihoods in coastal areas.
>
> 2) Energy — deep sea platforms are used to drill for oil, which is used as fuel for transport and industry. Natural gas is also extracted from under the seabed. Marine ecosystems also provide sites for renewable energy generation (e.g. tidal, wave and wind energy).
>
> 3) Fishing — people catch fish from marine ecosystems as a source of food. The fishing industry also provides jobs. Coastal marine ecosystems provide feeding grounds and good breeding conditions for the main fish species which are caught and sold for food.

Mine!

2) However, human activities are degrading (damaging) these ecosystems. For example:

Pollution
> 1) Marine animals eat plastic waste, mistaking it for food. The plastic collects in the animals' bodies and can kill them.
>
> 2) Industrial waste (e.g. from manufacturing medicines) can affect the health of marine organisms.
>
> 3) Run-off from farmland can cause eutrophication. Excess fertilisers run into estuaries, causing algae to grow very rapidly. The algae reduce the supply of oxygen and light to the seabed, killing organisms living in seabed habitats.

Damage to the Seabed
> 1) Dredging (clearing out mud and other material from the sea floor) to create shipping routes removes important nutrients from the seabed. Dredging also damages seabed plants and reduces the supply of food to marine organisms.
>
> 2) Fishing with trawl nets damages seabed habitats, e.g. coral reefs, which recover very slowly.
>
> 3) Building marine infrastructure such as offshore wind farms and oil platforms can physically damage the sea floor and can harm organisms living on the seabed.

Fishing
> 1) The demand for fish in the UK is greater than the supply of wild fish. This leads to overfishing — popular fish species are caught faster than they can be replaced through breeding. This causes fish numbers to decline.
>
> 2) Overfishing can have knock-on impacts on populations of birds, seals and other marine organisms, as there are fewer fish for them to eat and they can get trapped in fishing nets.

We really had to trawl the bottom to find a joke about this...

Make sure you've got the characteristics of the UK's main ecosystems properly stuck in your head before you move on.

Tropical Rainforests

If you want to set the scene for this page, I recommend a <u>hot shower</u> and a CD of <u>shrieking monkey noises</u>...

Tropical Rainforests are Hot and Wet All Year Round

Tropical rainforests are made up of a whole set of <u>abiotic</u> (non-living) and <u>biotic</u> (living) components:

Climate
- The climate is <u>the same all year</u> round — there are <u>no definite seasons</u>.
- It's <u>hot</u> (the temperature is generally between <u>20-28 °C</u> and only varies by a few degrees over the year). This is because near the <u>equator</u>, the <u>sun is overhead</u> all year round.
- <u>Rainfall</u> is very high, around 2000 mm per year. It <u>rains every day</u>, usually in the <u>afternoon</u>.

Soil
The soil <u>isn't very fertile</u> as heavy rain <u>washes nutrients away</u>. Decaying fallen leaves provide a layer of nutrients on the soil <u>surface</u>, but this layer is <u>very thin</u> as decay is <u>fast</u> in the <u>warm</u>, <u>moist</u> conditions.

Water
A lot of the <u>rain</u> is <u>intercepted</u> (stopped) by the tree <u>canopy</u>. Some water is <u>absorbed</u> by plants and <u>stored</u> inside them. Water also <u>runs off</u> the soil into <u>streams</u>, which feed into some of the <u>largest rivers</u> in the <u>world</u>, e.g. the Amazon and the Congo.

Plants
Most trees are <u>evergreen</u> to take advantage of the <u>continual growing season</u>. Many trees are really <u>tall</u> and the vegetation cover is <u>dense</u> — very <u>little light</u> reaches the forest floor. There are lots of <u>epiphytes</u> (plants that grow on other living plants and take <u>nutrients</u> and <u>moisture</u> from the air), e.g. orchids and ferns.

Animals
Rainforests are home to <u>more animal species</u> than any other ecosystem. Gorillas, jaguars, anacondas, tree frogs and chimps are all <u>examples</u> of rainforest animals. There are also loads of species of <u>insects</u> and <u>birds</u>. Many animals are <u>brightly coloured</u> and make a lot of <u>noise</u>.

Humans
The rainforests are home to many people, who have <u>adapted</u> to life there over many <u>generations</u>. They make a living by <u>hunting</u> and <u>fishing</u>, <u>gathering nuts</u> and <u>berries</u> and <u>growing vegetables</u> in small garden plots.

Rainforests are Interdependent Ecosystems

The <u>biotic</u> components of rainforests (plants, animals and people) and the <u>abiotic</u> components (climate, soils, water) are <u>closely related</u> — if one of them <u>changes</u>, the others are <u>affected</u>. For example:

1) The warm and wet <u>climate</u> means that <u>plants</u> grow <u>quickly</u> — the <u>dense leaf cover</u> offers some protection from wind and heavy rainfall, while <u>root systems</u> hold the soil together — this stops it being <u>eroded</u>.

2) The <u>lack of wind</u> near the forest floor means that many <u>plants</u> there have to rely on <u>bees</u>, <u>butterflies</u>, or other animals for <u>pollination</u>. <u>Symbiotic relationships</u> between <u>plants</u> and <u>animals</u> (where they each <u>depend</u> on the other for <u>survival</u>) are <u>very common</u> in tropical rainforests. For example:

> <u>Agouti</u> (a rodent) are one of the <u>only</u> animals who can <u>crack open</u> the hard seed pod of the <u>Brazil nut</u> to eat the nut inside. Sometimes, the agouti <u>bury</u> the nuts — these can <u>sprout</u> into <u>new seedlings</u>. If the agouti became <u>extinct</u>, the Brazil nut trees would <u>decline</u> and so could all the other <u>animals</u> who <u>live in</u> or <u>feed on</u> the Brazil nut trees. <u>People</u> who <u>sell</u> Brazil nuts to make a living may also be affected.

3) <u>Epiphytes</u> get access to <u>light</u> by growing high up on other plants, but they don't have access to the <u>nutrients</u> in the soil — they are <u>dependent</u> on <u>rainfall</u> to provide <u>water</u> and <u>nutrients</u>.

4) <u>Changes</u> to the rainforest ecosystem can have <u>knock-on effects</u> on the whole ecosystem. For example, <u>deforestation</u> reduces the amount of <u>CO_2</u> being absorbed from the atmosphere, which adds to the <u>greenhouse effect</u> and changes the <u>climate</u> (see p.46).

EXAM QUESTION

Just like an agouti and a Brazil nut tree...

...your revision and exam results are interdependent. So make sure you can answer this question:

1) Explain one reason why the climate of tropical rainforests leads to a high density of vegetation. [2]

Tropical Rainforests — Plants and Animals

If you've ever been locked in a sauna full of shrubs and giant insects (who hasn't?), then you'll know that it's no easy task living in the rainforest. Plants and animals are specially adapted for the conditions.

Plants are Adapted to the Hot, Wet Climate

1) Tropical rainforests have a layered structure — they are stratified. This affects how much sunlight can reach the different levels of vegetation. Plants are adapted to the conditions found in each layer.

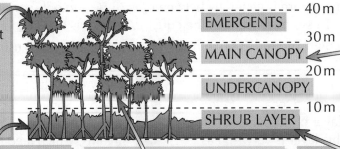

The emergents are the tallest trees, which poke out of the main canopy layer. They have straight trunks and only have branches and leaves at the top where they can get light.

The main canopy is a continuous layer of trees. Like emergents, they only have leaves at the top. The dense layer of leaves shades the rest of the forest.

Tall trees also have big roots called buttress roots. These support the trees, keeping them stable as they grow taller. The roots are above the ground, so they can get nutrients from the rich layer on the soil surface.

The undercanopy is made up of younger trees that have yet to reach their full height. They can only survive where there are breaks in the canopy to let a little bit of light through.

The shrub layer is nearest the ground where it's quite dark. Shrubs have large, broad leaves to absorb as much of the available light as they can.

2) Plants also have thick, waxy leaves with pointed tips (called drip-tips). The tips channel the water to a point so it runs off — that way the weight of the water doesn't damage the plant, and there's no standing water for fungi and bacteria to grow in.

Animals have Also Adapted to the Environment

Animals are adapted in different ways so that they can find food, escape predators and move around easily:

1) Strong limbs — Many animals spend their entire lives high up in the canopy. They have strong limbs so that they can spend all day climbing and leaping from tree to tree, e.g. howler monkeys.

2) Camouflage — Some animals are camouflaged, e.g. leaf insects look like leaves so they can hide from predators.

3) Modified beaks — Birds have beaks which are specially adapted to their diet, e.g:
   - Macaws have short, strong beaks for breaking open nuts.
   - Toucans have long, light beaks to help them reach fruits and insects.

4) Modified wings — Birds have wings that are adapted for flying in the undercanopy. Some birds have short, pointy wings so that they can easily manoeuvre between the dense tangle of branches in the trees, e.g. the harpy eagle has a short wingspan.

Are you in there, Frank?

Food Chains show the Relationships Between Plants and Animals

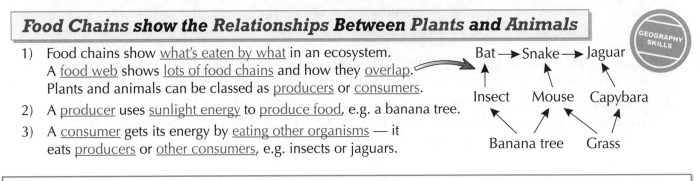

1) Food chains show what's eaten by what in an ecosystem. A food web shows lots of food chains and how they overlap. Plants and animals can be classed as producers or consumers.

2) A producer uses sunlight energy to produce food, e.g. a banana tree.

3) A consumer gets its energy by eating other organisms — it eats producers or other consumers, e.g. insects or jaguars.

Bat → Snake → Jaguar
Insect   Mouse   Capybara
Banana tree   Grass

GEOGRAPHY SKILLS

I thought we were going on a visit to the leaky tap factory...

...turns out that it was drip tip not trip. Now I've got that terrible joke out of the way, you can concentrate on learning about how plants and animals have adapted to tropical rainforest — make sure you know what each adaptation is for.

Tropical Rainforests — Nutrients & Biodiversity

Tropical rainforests are packed with more <u>nutrients</u> than an extra-large double super kale salad with extra kale.

Nutrients are Cycled Quickly in Tropical Rainforests

1) The <u>nutrient cycle</u> is the way that nutrients move through an ecosystem.

2) It can be shown using the <u>Gersmehl model</u> of nutrient cycling. The model shows that there are <u>three stores</u> in an ecosystem:
   - living organisms (<u>biomass</u>),
   - dead organic material, e.g. fallen leaves (<u>litter</u>),
   - the <u>soil</u>.

3) In the cycle, nutrients are <u>transferred</u> between these three <u>stores</u>.

4) The <u>size</u> of the circles and arrows is <u>proportional</u> to the <u>amount</u> of <u>nutrients</u>.

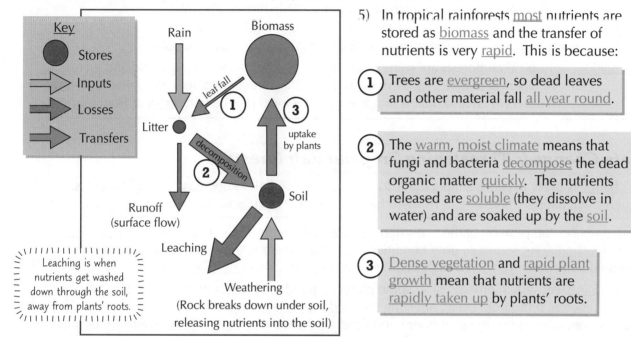

Leaching is when nutrients get washed down through the soil, away from plants' roots.

5) In tropical rainforests <u>most</u> nutrients are stored as <u>biomass</u> and the transfer of nutrients is very <u>rapid</u>. This is because:

1) Trees are <u>evergreen</u>, so dead leaves and other material fall <u>all year round</u>.

2) The <u>warm</u>, <u>moist climate</u> means that fungi and bacteria <u>decompose</u> the dead organic matter <u>quickly</u>. The nutrients released are <u>soluble</u> (they dissolve in water) and are soaked up by the <u>soil</u>.

3) <u>Dense vegetation</u> and <u>rapid plant growth</u> mean that nutrients are <u>rapidly taken up</u> by plants' roots.

Rainforests Have Very High Biodiversity

1) <u>Biodiversity</u> is the <u>variety</u> of organisms living in a particular area — both <u>plants</u> and <u>animals</u>.

2) Rainforests have extremely <u>high biodiversity</u> — they contain around <u>50%</u> of the world's <u>plant</u>, <u>animal</u> and <u>insect species</u>, and may contain <u>around half</u> of <u>all life</u> on Earth. This is because:

- Rainforests have been around for a <u>very long time</u> (10s of millions of years) <u>without</u> the <u>climate changing</u> very much, so there has been lots of time for <u>plants</u> and <u>animals</u> to <u>evolve</u> to form <u>new species</u>.

- The <u>layered structure</u> of the rainforest provides lots of different <u>habitats</u> — plants and animals <u>adapt</u> to become highly <u>specialised</u> to their particular <u>environment</u> and <u>food source</u> (their 'ecological niche') so lots of <u>different species</u> develop.

- Rainforests are <u>stable</u> environments — it's <u>hot</u> and <u>wet all year</u> round. They are also very <u>productive</u> (the plants grow <u>quickly</u> and <u>all year round</u>, which produces lots of <u>biomass</u>) because of the high rate of nutrient cycling (see above). This means that plants and animals don't have to cope with <u>changing conditions</u> and there is always <u>plenty</u> to <u>eat</u>. This means they are able to <u>specialise</u>.

Just thinking about all that cycling has me exhausted...

There's lots to think about with nutrient cycling in tropical rainforests, but understanding the Gersmehl model is a great place to start. If you can remember the stores and key transfers, then you're well on your way to nailing nutrients.

Tropical Rainforests — Human Uses and Impacts

We get loads of good and services from <u>rainforests</u> — if we didn't have rainforests, I might not be having <u>chocolate</u> brownies for tea. But rainforests are <u>under threat</u>, and it's mostly our fault...

Tropical Rainforests *Provide Lots of Goods* and *Services*

<u>High biodiversity</u> (the range of <u>plants</u> and <u>animals</u> found there)
means rainforests are a <u>rich source</u> of <u>goods</u> and <u>services</u>. E.g.:

1) <u>Food</u> — Rainforests provide food, e.g. <u>meat</u> from wild animals, for people who live there.
   Some of the plants that provide <u>everyday foods</u> that we eat in the <u>UK</u>, like
   <u>cocoa</u>, <u>coffee</u>, <u>bananas</u> and <u>sugar</u>, originally came from rainforest ecosystems.

2) <u>Medicines</u> — Many human <u>medicines</u> are adapted from chemicals found in rainforest plants
   — e.g. the Madagascar periwinkle is used to make medicines that fight cancer.
   <u>Undiscovered</u> species might give us <u>new</u> medicines in the <u>future</u>.

3) <u>Timber</u> — Rainforest trees provide some of the most <u>popular</u> kinds of wood,
   e.g. <u>mahogany</u>. The timber industry also creates <u>jobs</u> for local people.

4) <u>Recreation</u> — Tropical rainforests are some of the most <u>beautiful</u> places in the world and increasing
   numbers of people <u>visit</u> them every year. They are great places to <u>admire</u> and <u>study</u>
   nature, which also means that they provide local people with <u>income</u> from <u>tourism</u>.

Climate Change *is Threatening Tropical Rainforests*

<u>Climate change</u> is likely to cause temperatures to <u>increase</u> and rainfall to <u>decrease</u> in tropical areas,
and <u>droughts</u> will happen more <u>often</u>. This will have a <u>severely negative impact</u> on <u>tropical rainforests</u>:

1) <u>Structure</u> (the composition of the ecosystem) — plants living in tropical rainforests are <u>adapted</u>
   to <u>moist conditions</u>, so hotter, drier conditions can cause them to grow more slowly or <u>die</u>, and
   eventually become <u>extinct</u>. Droughts can lead to <u>fires</u>, which can <u>destroy</u> large areas of forest.

2) <u>Functioning</u> (ecosystem processes) — some plants respond to changes in the climate by <u>producing</u>
   <u>fruit</u> at <u>different times</u> from usual, affecting the <u>food supply</u> of animals which <u>eat</u> the fruit. Leaf
   litter decomposes more <u>slowly</u> in drier conditions, so there are <u>fewer nutrients</u> available for plants.

3) <u>Biodiversity</u> — climate change will reduce the <u>productivity</u> of rainforests,
   meaning that they can't <u>support</u> as many <u>specialised</u> plants and animals.
   Rainforests are highly <u>interdependent</u> ecosystems (see p.63), so the loss
   of the most <u>vulnerable</u> species will have <u>knock-on effects</u> on other species.

Productive ecosystems have lots of plant growth — they produce a lot of biomass.

Deforestation *is Another Threat to Tropical Rainforests*

There are several <u>economic</u> and <u>social</u> reasons why tropical rainforests are <u>chopped down</u>:

Economic

1) <u>Agriculture</u> — some forest is cleared by <u>small</u> farmers in order to
   grow food for <u>themselves</u> and their <u>families</u> (<u>subsistence</u> farming).
   Most forest clearance is to make way for huge <u>commercial</u>
   farms like <u>cattle ranches</u> or <u>palm oil</u> and <u>soya plantations</u>.

2) <u>Resource extraction</u> — trees are <u>felled</u> to make <u>furniture</u> and for
   <u>construction</u>. <u>Road building</u> for logging also requires more <u>tree</u>
   <u>clearance</u>. Precious <u>minerals</u> like <u>gold</u>, <u>copper</u> and <u>iron</u> can also
   be found in the rainforest, so <u>mining</u> activities clear vast areas too.

Social

<u>Population pressure</u> —
as the population in the
area <u>increases</u>, <u>trees</u>
are <u>cleared</u> to <u>make land</u>
for <u>new settlements</u>.
Trees are also used as
fuel for <u>cooking</u> or to
burn to make <u>charcoal</u>.

Chocolate doesn't just grow on trees you know — oh wait...

Time to see if you really know this page as well as (deep down inside) you know you should:

1) Explain how agriculture can lead to deforestation in tropical rainforests. [2]

Topic 3 — Ecosystems, Biodiversity and Management

Management in the Amazon

Cor blimey, rainforests do face a lot of threats. It's not all doom and gloom for them though. In fact, this page is all about ways people are trying to manage the biggest rainforest of them all — the mighty Amazon.

People are Trying to Use and Manage the Amazon Sustainably

1) The Amazon rainforest is the north of South America and covers an area of around 8 million km², including parts of Brazil, Peru, Colombia, Venezuela, Ecuador, Bolivia, Guyana, Suriname and French Guiana.

2) Some management strategies aim to use the Amazon rainforest in a way that's sustainable — allowing people today to get the things that they need, without stopping people in the future getting what they need.

3) These sustainable management strategies are affected by political factors (e.g. governance) and economic factors (e.g. commodity value and ecotourism).

Governance

Governance is about the control of rainforests and who has a say in how rainforests are used. Some areas of rainforest are protected by national and international laws, e.g.:

- The Central Amazon Conservation Complex (CACC) in Brazil is the largest protected area in the rainforest, covering around 60 000 km². The CACC has been classified as a World Heritage Site by the United Nations, which means it's protected by international treaties. Access to the CACC is restricted, and there are strict limits on hunting, logging and fishing.

In other areas, local communities are involved in rainforest governance with support from NGOs:

- Natütama is an organisation in Puerto Nariño in Colombia that is working with the local community to protect river species, e.g. the Amazon river dolphin. It employs local people to teach other people in the community how they can protect endangered river animals and their habitats. Local fishermen collect information about the number and distribution of species, and report any illegal hunting or fishing that is taking place.

Commodity Value

Commodity value means how much different goods and services from rainforests are worth. Sustainable management strategies make sure that healthy rainforests are worth more than the timber and other resources that can be extracted from them — e.g. by promoting sustainable forestry, which balances the removal of trees to sell with the conservation of the forest as a whole.

1) Selective logging involves only felling some trees so that the forest is able to regenerate. This can save the logging company money in the long term as they don't need to replant so many trees.

2) International agreements try to reduce illegal logging, and promote wood from sustainably managed forests. For example, the Forest Stewardship Council® (FSC) marks sustainably sourced timber products with its logo so that consumers can choose sustainable products.

3) Precious Woods Amazon is a logging company operating in Brazil. They place limits on the number of trees that can be cut down, to make sure the forest can regenerate. They also use a variety of species, so that no species is over-exploited. They are FSC®-certified.

Ecotourism

Ecotourism is tourism that minimises damage to the environment and benefits the local people.

1) Yachana Lodge is an ecotourism project in Ecuador, in a remote area of the Amazon rainforest where local people rely on subsistence farming to provide a living.

2) The project employs local people, giving them a more reliable income and a better quality of life. It also encourages the conservation of the rainforest so that visitors continue to want to visit.

3) Tourists visit in small groups so that harm to the environment is minimised, and take part in activities to raise awareness of conservation issues.

4) Tourists have to pay entrance fees — this brings in more money for rainforest conservation. Profits are invested in education projects to promote conservation in the local community.

If only we could order a few billion trees with next day delivery...

And that's about it for rainforests. Make sure you understand the different ways of managing rainforests sustainably and learn plenty of case study facts — you'll need them in the exam. Now make like a tree and get out of here...

Deciduous Woodlands

Ah, the <u>woods</u> in autumn — the crunch of leaves, birdsong, and the sound of <u>revision notes</u> being scribbled...

Deciduous Woodlands have Distinct Seasons

1) Deciduous woodlands are made up of <u>broad-leaved trees</u> that lose their <u>leaves</u> in the <u>autumn</u>.

2) They are mostly found in the <u>mid-latitudes</u>, between <u>40°</u> and <u>60° north</u> and <u>south</u> of the Equator, e.g. in <u>Europe</u>, the <u>USA</u>, <u>New Zealand</u> and <u>Japan</u>.

3) Like all ecosystems, deciduous woodlands have distinctive <u>abiotic</u> (non-living) and <u>biotic</u> (living) features:

Climate

1) The climate is <u>temperate</u> — there are <u>no extremes</u> of temperature or rainfall.

2) There are usually <u>four seasons</u> — spring, summer, autumn and winter. <u>Summer</u> is the <u>warmest</u> season, with <u>long daylight hours</u> and average temperatures of <u>15-17 °C</u>. <u>Winter</u> is the <u>coolest</u> season, but temperatures usually stay <u>above freezing</u>.

3) <u>Rainfall</u> is quite <u>high</u> — about <u>1000 mm</u> a year. It rains <u>throughout the year</u>.

Soil

1) The <u>fallen leaves</u> decompose quite <u>quickly</u> in the <u>mild</u>, <u>wet</u> climate, forming a <u>thick layer</u> of organic matter (<u>humus</u>) which <u>enriches</u> the soil.

2) <u>Earthworms</u> and other organisms in the <u>soil</u> mix the humus with <u>minerals</u> from weathered <u>rock</u> to form a <u>rich</u>, <u>fertile</u> soil called <u>brown earth</u>.

Water

It <u>rains</u> all year round, supplying water to <u>streams</u>, <u>rivers</u> and <u>lakes</u>. Pools and lakes sometimes <u>freeze</u> in the <u>winter</u> months.

HUMUS

Plants

Deciduous woodlands are usually dominated by <u>tall</u>, <u>broad-leaved trees</u>. Most of the trees are <u>deciduous</u> — they <u>lose</u> their <u>leaves</u> in the <u>autumn</u>. The plants are <u>stratified</u> in three main layers (see next page), with <u>smaller</u>, <u>shade-tolerant</u> plants growing under the <u>main canopy</u> of trees.

Animals

The <u>different layers</u> of trees and plants provide <u>habitats</u> for <u>different animals</u>. For example:

1) <u>Birds</u>, <u>insects</u> and small <u>mammals</u> (e.g. <u>squirrels</u> and <u>dormice</u>) live in <u>trees</u>.

2) <u>Larger</u> mammals like <u>foxes</u> and <u>rabbits</u> make their homes by burrowing in the <u>ground</u> under the trees.

Humans

1) Deciduous woodlands have <u>historically</u> been home to people who make a livelihood by getting <u>goods</u> from the woodland, e.g. <u>wood</u> for <u>fuel</u>, and <u>nuts</u> and tree <u>sap</u> for <u>food</u>.

2) People also exploit deciduous woodlands for commercial purposes (e.g. <u>timber</u>) and use woodlands as places for <u>recreation</u>.

Abiotic and Biotic Components of Deciduous Woodlands are Interdependent

1) The climate, soil, water, plants, animals and people in deciduous woodlands are all <u>interdependent</u> — changes to <u>one</u> factor causes <u>changes</u> to the <u>others</u>.

2) These components are all <u>connected</u> by <u>nutrient cycles</u> (see p.70) and the <u>water cycle</u>. Trees get <u>water</u> and <u>nutrients</u> from the <u>soil</u>. When they <u>photosynthesise</u>, they release <u>oxygen</u>, which <u>humans</u> and <u>animals</u> need to <u>breathe</u>. When <u>leaves</u> fall from the trees these <u>decompose</u>, <u>returning</u> nutrients to the <u>soil</u>.

3) Woodlands are often <u>sheltered</u>, so trees can't <u>rely</u> on the <u>wind</u> to <u>disperse</u> their seeds by <u>blowing</u> them away. Instead, many trees depend on <u>animals</u> to do this for them:

- Animals rely on trees as <u>habitats</u>. The animals eat <u>fruits</u> from the trees and release <u>seeds</u> in their <u>excrement</u> (poo). These seeds grow into <u>new plants</u>.

- Some species of <u>ant</u> carry <u>seeds</u> from plants on the <u>woodland floor</u> to their <u>nests</u> and feed the seed casing to their <u>young</u>. This <u>disperses</u> the seeds <u>away</u> from the parent plant, helping the plant species to <u>spread</u>.

Humans can cause deforestation in deciduous woodlands. This has similar effects as in tropical rainforests (p.66).

You can revise all this — I beleaf in you...

Get the main biotic and abiotic characteristics of deciduous woodlands in your head and the job's a good 'un.

Deciduous Woodlands — Plants and Animals

For <u>half the year</u>, deciduous woodlands have all the charm of a seaside resort in January — <u>cold</u>, <u>wet</u>, <u>dark</u> and <u>nothing to eat</u>. Not all plants and animals can put up with this — they need special <u>adaptations</u> to survive.

Plants are Adapted to Make the Most of Sunlight

1) Like in tropical rainforests (p.64), the <u>plants</u> in deciduous woodlands are <u>stratified</u> in <u>layers</u>. The plants in each layer have <u>adapted</u> to make the most of the <u>varying levels</u> of <u>sunlight</u> that reach each layer.

Deciduous trees have <u>broad</u>, <u>flat</u> leaves and <u>spread</u> their <u>branches</u> wide. This forms a <u>dense canopy</u> which <u>captures sunlight</u>.

Some plants get sunlight by <u>climbing</u> trees, e.g. <u>honeysuckle</u> and <u>ivy</u>.

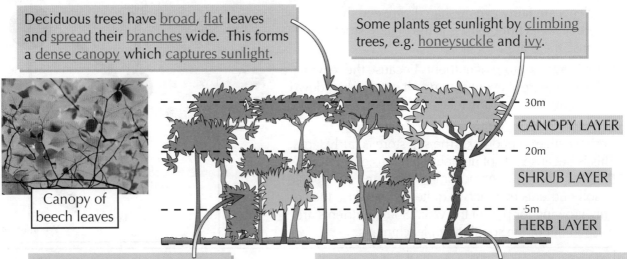

Canopy of beech leaves

30m

CANOPY LAYER

20m

SHRUB LAYER

5m

HERB LAYER

The <u>shrub layer</u> is dominated by plants which are <u>adapted</u> to the <u>lack</u> of sunlight. E.g. <u>hazel</u> has very <u>wide</u> leaves to get as <u>much</u> sunlight as <u>possible</u>.

Only <u>some</u> sunlight can get <u>through</u> the canopy, so the plants that grow on the woodland <u>floor</u> are <u>shade-tolerant</u>. Some plants grow in the <u>spring</u> when the canopy is still growing so there is <u>more</u> sunlight reaching the woodland floor, e.g. <u>bluebells</u>.

2) As the weather gets <u>cooler</u> in the <u>autumn</u>, deciduous trees start to <u>conserve</u> (save) their resources by drawing <u>food</u> and <u>nutrients</u> back from the <u>leaves</u> into the <u>stems</u>. The leaves <u>stop</u> capturing sunlight, and eventually dry up and <u>fall</u> off the tree.

3) This helps the tree to conserve <u>water</u>, which is usually <u>lost</u> through openings in the surfaces of leaves. It also means that the tree doesn't have to use energy to <u>protect</u> the leaves from <u>freezing</u>.

4) When the temperatures get <u>warmer</u> again in the spring, this sends <u>signals</u> to the tree that it can begin producing <u>new</u> leaves. These leaves capture sunlight throughout the <u>spring</u> and <u>summer</u>, which helps the tree <u>grow</u> until the cycle starts again in the <u>autumn</u>.

Animals are Adapted to the Changing Seasons

1) Animals have adapted to the <u>changing seasons</u> and <u>conditions</u> in deciduous woodlands. They have to be able to cope with <u>warm summers</u> and <u>cold winters</u>.

2) Many birds (e.g. <u>flycatchers</u> and <u>nightingales</u>) avoid the cold weather by <u>migrating</u> in the autumn. They fly to <u>warmer climates</u> nearer the equator where they can find <u>food</u> more <u>easily</u>, and <u>return</u> to deciduous woodlands in the <u>spring</u>.

3) Some mammals (e.g. <u>hedgehogs</u> and <u>brown bears</u>) <u>hibernate</u> during the winter months. Hibernating allows animals to <u>protect</u> themselves from the <u>cold</u> and <u>reduce</u> their need for <u>food</u>. Their <u>heartbeat</u> and <u>breathing</u> rate <u>slow down</u> so they can survive on the <u>fat</u> stored in their body.

4) Some animals <u>store</u> food in the autumn, when it is <u>easily available</u> — e.g. <u>squirrels</u> store <u>nuts</u> in the <u>ground</u> and under bushes. They use these stores to <u>survive</u> through the winter when there is <u>less food</u> available.

I think hibernation would be unbearable...

Make sure you know how plants and animals in deciduous woodlands are adapted to their environment.

1) Explain why some animals in deciduous woodlands migrate. [2]

Deciduous Woodlands — Nutrients & Biodiversity

The movement of tasty <u>nutrients</u> around deciduous woodland ecosystems <u>feeds</u> the <u>plants</u> and <u>animals</u>...

Nutrients are Cycled more Slowly than in Tropical Rainforests

1) In deciduous woodlands, <u>nutrients</u> are <u>cycled</u> between three stores:
<u>biomass</u> (living organisms), <u>litter</u> (dead organisms, e.g. fallen leaves) and the <u>soil</u>.

2) This can be shown with a <u>Gersmehl model</u> (p.65).

3) Nutrients are fairly <u>evenly shared</u> between the
different stores but <u>biomass</u> is the <u>biggest</u> store,
because there are a <u>lot</u> of <u>trees</u>.

4) <u>Litter</u> is a <u>large store</u> of nutrients because the leaves
fall from the trees <u>every autumn</u>. It gets broken down
by <u>decomposers</u> to form a layer of <u>humus</u>.

5) <u>Soil</u> is formed of <u>humus</u> combined with <u>minerals</u>
from weathered <u>bedrock</u>. The soil store is fairly <u>large</u>.
This is because lots of nutrients get <u>transferred</u> from
the litter store through <u>decomposition</u>, and the <u>uptake</u>
of soil nutrients by plants is quite <u>low</u> because they're
only growing for <u>part</u> of the year. Some nutrients are
<u>washed out</u> of the soil through <u>leaching</u>.

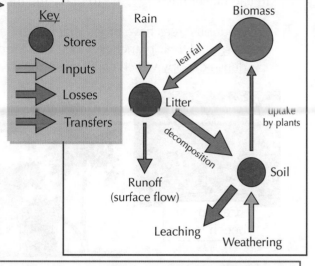

The transfers in deciduous woodlands are <u>smaller</u> and <u>slower</u> than in tropical rainforests (p.65). This
is because there is <u>lower rainfall</u> (and so less <u>runoff</u> and <u>leaching</u>) and litter <u>decomposes</u> more <u>slowly</u>
in the <u>cooler climate</u>. Deciduous woodlands are <u>less productive</u> and have a much <u>shorter growing
season</u> than tropical rainforests, so there is <u>less biomass</u> and <u>lower rates</u> of <u>nutrient uptake</u> by plants.

Deciduous Woodlands have Moderate Biodiversity

Deciduous woodlands have <u>moderate biodiversity</u> — they are home
to a <u>fairly wide variety</u> of <u>fungi</u>, <u>plants</u> and <u>animals</u>. This is because:

1) Deciduous woodlands have a <u>temperate</u> climate — there are no <u>temperature extremes</u>
and there's <u>plenty of rainfall</u> through the year. This means that <u>lots</u> of plants and animals
can survive in the climate — though not as many as would thrive in a <u>tropical</u> climate.

2) The <u>different plant layers</u> in deciduous woodlands provide <u>several</u> different <u>habitats</u> —
plants and animals <u>adapt</u> to become <u>specialised</u> to the particular conditions of their habitat,
so <u>different organisms</u> are found in each layer. <u>Oak</u> trees can support <u>350</u> different
<u>insect</u> species, which live in different parts of the trees, from the <u>canopy</u> to the <u>roots</u>.

3) Deciduous woodlands are very <u>seasonal</u> environments. In the summer they are <u>productive</u>
with <u>high rates</u> of <u>nutrient cycling</u>, but in the <u>winter</u> there is <u>not much growth</u>, many species
are <u>dormant</u>, and there <u>isn't much</u> for animals to <u>eat</u>. This means that plants and animals
have to cope with these <u>changing conditions</u> and it's difficult for <u>specialist</u> organisms
(e.g. animals with only a <u>few</u> possible <u>food</u> sources) to <u>survive</u>.

4) Many deciduous woodlands have experienced a lot of <u>disturbance</u> by <u>human activities</u>,
e.g. deforestation. This has <u>prevented</u> the <u>vegetation</u> from becoming <u>established</u> enough
to <u>support</u> a lot of <u>different species</u>.

You say Gers-meal, I say Gers-mail...

*Don't worry — you don't really have to know how to pronounce Gersmehl for the exam, but you might be asked to
explain the difference between the nutrient cycles in deciduous woodlands and tropical rainforests. So get learnin'.*

Topic 3 — Ecosystems, Biodiversity and Management

Deciduous Woodlands — Human Uses & Impacts

This is Geography, so this section wouldn't be complete without something about how <u>humans</u> are <u>exploiting</u> deciduous woodland <u>ecosystems</u>. Not the most cheerful subject, but you'll need to know it for the exam...

Deciduous Woodlands Provide Lots of Goods and Services

Humans have been getting <u>goods</u> and <u>services</u> from deciduous woodlands for <u>hundreds</u> of years:

- <u>Timber</u> — deciduous trees provide <u>hardwood</u> which is well-suited for constructing things, e.g. <u>furniture</u>.
- <u>Fuel</u> — humans use <u>wood</u> or make <u>charcoal</u> for <u>fuel</u> to heat their <u>homes</u> and for <u>cooking</u>.
- <u>Conservation</u> — some deciduous woodlands, especially <u>ancient</u> woodlands, are home to <u>rare</u> or <u>endangered</u> species of plants and animals. People make sure these woodlands are <u>conserved</u> and <u>cared for</u> so that they can <u>continue</u> to be <u>enjoyed</u> and to provide <u>services</u> to us.
- <u>Recreation</u> — woodlands are used by humans for many recreational activities such as <u>mountain-biking</u>, <u>walking</u>, <u>zip wires</u> and <u>horse-riding</u>.

Deciduous Woodlands are Threatened by Climate Change

1) Deciduous woodlands are <u>less vulnerable</u> to <u>climate change</u> than other ecosystems because they are found in regions with <u>temperate</u> climates, so changes to the climate will be <u>less extreme</u> than in other areas.

2) Many of the species living in deciduous woodlands are <u>generalists</u> (they have several sources of food and can survive in different habitats), so they are able to <u>adapt</u> to some changes in the climate.

3) However, if climate change <u>continues</u>, it could have <u>negative</u> effects on deciduous woodland ecosystems:

- <u>Structure</u> — <u>temperate</u> areas where deciduous woodlands are found are likely to have <u>more extreme weather events</u>, e.g. droughts and storms. Some tree species may grow more <u>slowly</u> or <u>die</u> if they do not have <u>enough water</u>. <u>Strong winds</u> in <u>storms</u> can <u>knock trees down</u>, especially <u>more mature</u> (older) trees which are important <u>habitats</u> for <u>wildlife</u>.
- <u>Functioning</u> — changes in temperature may <u>encourage</u> animals to <u>come out</u> of hibernation <u>too early</u>, before there are enough sources of <u>food</u>. This could cause some of the animals to <u>starve</u>. <u>Higher rainfall</u> in the winter can cause <u>leaching</u>, which decreases the amount of <u>nutrients</u> in the <u>soil</u>, meaning that trees grow <u>more slowly</u>.
- <u>Biodiversity</u> — <u>insects</u> that <u>damage trees</u> could <u>increase</u> in number with climate change. <u>Currently</u>, many of these insects <u>die</u> during the <u>winter</u>, but with warmer winters <u>more pests</u> will be able to <u>survive</u> until the next summer. <u>Higher temperatures</u> will also allow new <u>invasive species</u> to move into deciduous woodlands, which could lead to a <u>loss</u> of <u>existing species</u> and a <u>decline</u> in <u>biodiversity</u>. The loss of <u>mature trees</u> due to <u>storms</u>, <u>drought</u> and <u>pests</u> will <u>reduce</u> the amount of <u>habitat</u> available, so some <u>rare</u> and <u>endangered</u> animal species may become extinct.

Deforestation is also a Threat to Deciduous Woodlands

Deciduous woodlands are threatened by <u>deforestation</u>, which has <u>economic</u> and <u>social</u> causes:

Economic

1) <u>Timber extraction</u> — deciduous trees are <u>slow-growing</u>, so they are often cut down <u>more quickly</u> than they can be replaced. In many places deciduous woodlands are being <u>replaced</u> with <u>plantations</u> of cheaper, faster-growing <u>coniferous</u> trees to use for <u>timber</u>.

2) <u>Agricultural change</u> — woodlands are also cleared to make <u>bigger fields</u> which are more <u>efficient</u> to farm using <u>modern farming methods</u>, e.g. using large-scale <u>machinery</u>.

Social

<u>Urbanisation</u> and <u>population growth</u> — there's an increasing number of people living in <u>towns</u> and <u>cities</u>, so woodlands are <u>cleared</u> to make space for <u>building houses</u> and <u>roads</u>. <u>Population growth</u> is also increasing <u>demand</u> for timber, e.g. for use in <u>construction</u>.

Why can't people just leaf woodlands alone...

It looks like a lot to learn, but test yourself on this page and you'll have human impacts on deciduous woodlands down.

Management in the Forest of Dean

You wooden believe how <u>important</u> it is to make sure we <u>manage</u> deciduous woodlands <u>sustainably</u>...

The Forest of Dean is an Area of Deciduous Woodland in England

Forest of Dean

1) The Forest of Dean is an area of <u>110 km²</u> of <u>ancient</u>, mostly <u>deciduous</u> woodland in <u>Gloucestershire</u>, southern England.

2) It is <u>managed</u> by the <u>Forestry Commission</u>, which is a <u>government</u> department.

3) The Forest of Dean has a <u>long history</u> of <u>exploitation</u> and <u>management</u> by humans. Some areas of forest were <u>cleared</u> in the 1800s and 1900s to mine <u>iron ore</u> and <u>coal</u>. The forest's <u>oak trees</u> have been <u>harvested</u> for timber since the <u>1600s</u>.

4) The area around the Forest of Dean is now home to over <u>80 000 people</u>. Parts of the forest are used to produce <u>timber</u>, but local people and communities mostly use the forest for <u>recreation</u> and <u>conservation</u>.

Different Groups are Helping to Manage the Forest of Dean Sustainably

The Forest of Dean provides important <u>goods</u> and <u>services</u>. <u>Stakeholders</u> (groups of people with an interest in how the forest is managed) have come up with ways of <u>managing</u> the forest more <u>sustainably</u>, so that it <u>continues</u> to provide these goods and services <u>now</u> and for <u>future generations</u>.

Coppicing

1) Coppicing is a <u>traditional</u> woodland management <u>technique</u>. It involves cutting trees at the <u>base</u>, above the roots. The tree puts out new <u>shoots</u>, which can then be <u>harvested</u>. This is more <u>sustainable</u> than <u>chopping down</u> trees and <u>replanting</u> them, as coppiced trees keep their <u>root</u> system and <u>recover quickly</u>.

2) Coppicing takes a lot of <u>time</u> and <u>effort</u>, so most people use <u>cheaper</u>, <u>faster</u> methods like <u>felling</u> the whole tree. However, a project called <u>New Leaf</u> is training <u>young people</u> to coppice trees in the Forest of Dean to help tackle youth <u>unemployment</u> and make sure wood is <u>harvested sustainably</u>.

Outreach and Education

1) Several <u>local</u> and <u>national organisations</u> have <u>joined together</u> in a programme called <u>Foresters' Forest</u>.

2) Foresters' Forest focuses on <u>outreach</u> — raising <u>awareness</u> about the woodlands. The programme <u>encourages</u> people to <u>participate</u> in forest <u>management</u>, e.g. by holding events where people can help with <u>litter picking</u> or <u>wildlife surveys</u>.

3) The programme also works with <u>local schools</u> to <u>educate</u> young people about the forest.

Recreation

The Forest of Dean is a popular <u>tourist destination</u> for <u>outdoor activities</u>. The Forestry Commission has made <u>cycle</u> and <u>walking trails</u> in the forest. These stop people <u>damaging</u> the <u>forest floor</u> and keep <u>disruptive</u> activities like mountain biking away from <u>sensitive</u> habitats.

Wildlife Management

1) There's been a big <u>debate</u> about the management of the forest's <u>wild boar</u> population. The wild boar probably <u>escaped</u> from a farm and then <u>bred</u> — there are now around <u>1500</u> wild boar in the forest.

2) Some local people say the wild boar make the forest more <u>interesting</u> to tourists. But the boar can be a <u>nuisance</u> — they <u>damage</u> parks and gardens and some people find them <u>threatening</u>.

3) As the boar population <u>grows</u>, their impact on the forest ecosystem is becoming <u>unsustainable</u> — e.g. the boar root around in the <u>undergrowth</u>, which may damage the <u>habitats</u> of rare <u>butterflies</u>. In response, the Forestry Commission have been <u>culling</u> (systematically killing) the wild boar.

Dean there, done that...

You might have studied a different case study of a deciduous woodland — whichever it is, make sure you can write about some specific examples of sustainable management strategies that have been used there.

1) Explain how deciduous woodlands are managed sustainably in a named location. [8]

Revision Summary

Well I thought that section was a real tree-t and I bet it has left you wanting more. Luckily for you, here's a page full of revision questions. Threats to your exam grade include not being able to answer these questions, so I suggest you manage the situation by leafing back through anything you can't answer first time.

Global Ecosystems (p.57-60) ☑

1) What is an ecosystem?
2) Why do different parts of the world have different ecosystems?
3) Where are boreal forests found?
4) Give one ecosystem that is mostly found between the Tropics of Cancer and Capricorn.
5) a) Give two local factors which affect the distribution of ecosystems.
   b) Explain the effect these factors have on the distribution of ecosystems.
6) True or false: tropical forests have a distinct summer and winter.
7) Describe the soil in the temperate forest ecosystem.
8) What kinds of plants are found in boreal forests?
9) What is the soil like in deserts?
10) What is the main difference between temperate grasslands and tropical grasslands?
11) What sorts of animals are found in the tundra ecosystem?
12) Give four goods which humans get from the biosphere.
13) Explain how human exploitation of minerals can damage the biosphere.

UK Ecosystems (p.61-62) ☑

14) Describe the distribution of wetlands in the UK.
15) Give two differences between moorlands and heaths.
16) Give two resources that the UK's marine ecosystems provide.
17) How is fishing degrading the UK's marine ecosystems?

Tropical Rainforests (p.63-67) ☑

18) Describe the climate of tropical rainforests.
19) Give an example of an interdependent relationship in the tropical rainforest ecosystem.
20) Why do some trees in the rainforest have buttress roots?
21) Why are nutrients cycled quickly in tropical rainforests?
22) Why does the layered structure of tropical rainforests increase biodiversity there?
23) Give four goods or services which humans get from tropical rainforests.
24) How is climate change threatening biodiversity in tropical rainforests?
25) Give three causes of deforestation in tropical rainforests.
26) Explain how ecotourism is helping people to manage a named tropical rainforest sustainably.

Deciduous Woodlands (p.68-72) ☑

27) Describe the soils found in deciduous woodlands.
28) Why do deciduous trees lose their leaves in the autumn?
29) What are the three nutrient stores found in deciduous woodlands?
30) Explain why deciduous woodlands have moderate biodiversity compared to tropical rainforests.
31) How does population growth lead to deforestation in deciduous woodlands?
32) Describe two different approaches to sustainable management that are being used in a named deciduous woodland.

Urbanisation

Urban areas (towns and cities) are popular places to be and getting ever more so — some faster than others...

Urbanisation is Happening Fastest in Poorer Countries

1) Urbanisation is the growth in the proportion of a country's population living in urban areas.

2) It's happening in countries all over the world — more than 50% of the world's population currently live in urban areas (3.9 billion people) and this is increasing every day.

3) Most of the population (about 79%) of developed countries already live in urban areas. Since the 1960s, the rate of urbanisation has fallen — the rate of urban growth in developed countries is now very slow.

4) A smaller proportion (35%) of the population in developing countries currently live in urban areas. In general, the fastest rates of urbanisation in the world are in developing countries, mainly in Africa. However, the overall rate has decreased since the 1960s.

5) The percentage of the population living in urban areas varies in emerging countries. Some, such as Thailand, South Africa and China, are experiencing rapid urban growth. In general, the rate of urbanisation has been high (1960-1990) but is slowing down in some countries, e.g. in the Caribbean.

Urbanisation is Caused by Rural-Urban Migration and Natural Increase

1) The rate of urbanisation varies in countries at different levels of development because of economic change. This leads to rural-urban migration — the movement of people from the countryside to the cities.

2) Urbanisation is also caused by natural increase. Natural increase is when the birth rate is higher than the death rate, i.e. more people are being born than are dying, so the population grows.

3) It's normally young people that move to cities to find work. These people then have children in the cities, which increases the proportion of the population living in urban areas. Also, better health care in urban areas means people live longer, again increasing the proportion of people in urban areas.

4) A combination of rural-urban migration and natural increase has meant that urbanisation has occurred at different times and different rates in developed, emerging and developing countries:

Developed

1) The highest rates of urbanisation in developed countries happened during the Industrial Revolution (in the 18th and 19th centuries) as people moved to cities to work in the factories.

2) Since the 1960s the proportion of people living in urban areas has increased very slowly — lots of people already live in urban areas. De-industrialisation in the 1960-70s (see p.80) meant fewer jobs were available in manufacturing industries — some people moved away as city centres became run-down. Many people now prefer to live in rural areas — counter-urbanisation (see p.78).

3) Natural increase doesn't increase urbanisation much — many countries have low or falling birth rates, e.g. Japan. Even during the Industrial Revolution high death rates kept population growth low.

Emerging and Developing

1) In emerging and developing countries birth rates are high and death rates are falling — natural increase is causing the rate of urbanisation to increase rapidly.

2) A combination of pull factors (things drawing people into cities) and push factors (things driving people out of rural areas) is leading to high rates of urbanisation as people leave the countryside in search of better jobs and a higher standard of living.

- Pull factors — over the last 50 years a lot of manufacturing moved to emerging countries, where labour costs were lower and there are less strict environmental, labour and planning laws. This is creating urban industrial areas with lots of manufacturing and service jobs.

- Push factors — many rural areas are very poor and have limited access to resources, e.g. electricity and clean water. High population growth puts pressure on farmland making it less productive and increased mechanisation can reduce the number of jobs available.

My natural increase comes from my love of cream cakes...

What better way to start a new section than learning the page and then having a crack at an exam question:

1)   Describe how global trends of urbanisation vary between different parts of the world.   *[2]*

Urbanisation

The lure of the <u>city lights</u> can be strong, but many dreams have been crushed by the <u>challenges</u> of <u>urban growth</u>. I'm not trying to be cruel, it's just that the streets <u>aren't always</u> paved with gold...

Urbanisation *Causes Problems in Developed Countries...*

There are lots of <u>good</u> things about urban areas in <u>developed</u> countries — there are often better <u>employment opportunities</u> than in rural areas, and they have a better variety of <u>entertainment facilities</u>. However, urbanisation has put <u>pressure</u> on cities:

Housing — <u>huge demand</u> for houses and <u>lack of space</u> means that <u>house prices</u> and <u>rents</u> can be very <u>high</u>. As a result, workers on <u>lower incomes</u> often can't afford to live <u>near</u> to where they work and many people can't afford to <u>buy</u> homes.

Overcrowding — <u>high populations</u> and a <u>shortage of housing</u> can lead to <u>overcrowding</u>. Adults <u>house-sharing</u> is becoming <u>more common</u>.

Transport — urban areas often have <u>good transport systems</u> but <u>high populations</u> and increasing numbers of <u>commuters</u> can <u>stress</u> the transport networks. Roads are frequently <u>congested</u> and overcrowding can lead to <u>delays</u> on buses and trains.

Services — cities provide some of the best <u>education</u> and <u>health care</u>. However, <u>high populations</u> can mean that <u>access</u> is <u>difficult</u>, especially for <u>poorer people</u>. <u>Waiting times</u> for health care can be long and emergency vehicles can be <u>delayed</u> by <u>traffic</u>. Schools may <u>struggle</u> with <u>large class sizes</u> and there can be <u>long waiting lists</u> for the best performing schools.

... and in Developing and Emerging Countries

Cities offer <u>lots</u> of <u>opportunities</u> for the people migrating there — e.g. better access to education, health care and employment. The <u>growing population</u> can also help increase the <u>wealth</u> and <u>economic development</u> of the city, as well as the <u>country</u> it's in. However, <u>very rapid growth</u> puts <u>pressure</u> on cities, causing <u>problems</u>:

Economic Consequences

1) There may not be <u>enough jobs</u> for everyone, leading to high levels of <u>unemployment</u>.

2) Lots of people work in the <u>informal sector</u>, where the jobs aren't <u>taxed</u> or <u>regulated</u> by the government. People often work <u>long hours</u> in <u>dangerous conditions</u> for <u>little pay</u>.

3) People may <u>not</u> have access to <u>education</u> so they are unable to develop the skills needed to get better <u>jobs</u>.

Social Consequences

1) There <u>aren't enough houses</u> for everyone — many people end up in <u>squatter settlements</u> that are <u>badly built</u> and <u>overcrowded</u>.

2) <u>Infrastructure</u> can't be built fast enough — people often <u>don't</u> have access to <u>basic services</u>, e.g. clean water, proper sewers or electricity. This can cause <u>poor health</u>.

3) There can be high levels of <u>crime</u>.

Environmental Consequences

If cities grow <u>rapidly</u>, waste disposal services, sewage systems and environmental regulations for factories <u>can't keep pace</u> with the growth.

1) Rubbish often isn't <u>collected</u> or it may end up in big <u>rubbish heaps</u>. This can damage the <u>environment</u>, especially if it's <u>toxic</u>.

2) <u>Sewage</u> and <u>toxic chemicals</u> can get into rivers, <u>harming wildlife</u>.

3) The <u>road system</u> may not be able to <u>cope</u> with all the <u>vehicles</u>. <u>Congestion</u> causes increased <u>greenhouse gas</u> emissions and <u>air pollution</u>.

Urban problems — when your hip hop flops...

Countries at different stages of development face some similar pressures but the impacts are a bit different. The effects of urbanisation come up again in the case studies later in this topic so it's worth getting to grips with them now.

Urbanisation in the UK

Urban centres don't just spring up in any old place — most of them are where they are for a reason.

The Urban Population of the UK is Unevenly Distributed

The population distribution in the UK is very uneven — the major urban centres have the highest population densities. The degree of urbanisation in the UK is affected by a range of factors:

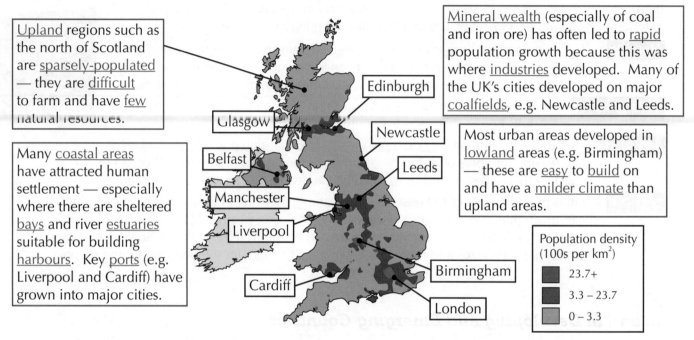

Upland regions such as the north of Scotland are sparsely-populated — they are difficult to farm and have few natural resources.

Many coastal areas have attracted human settlement — especially where there are sheltered bays and river estuaries suitable for building harbours. Key ports (e.g. Liverpool and Cardiff) have grown into major cities.

Mineral wealth (especially of coal and iron ore) has often led to rapid population growth because this was where industries developed. Many of the UK's cities developed on major coalfields, e.g. Newcastle and Leeds.

Most urban areas developed in lowland areas (e.g. Birmingham) — these are easy to build on and have a milder climate than upland areas.

Population density (100s per km²)
- 23.7+
- 3.3 – 23.7
- 0 – 3.3

The Rate of Urbanisation Varies Across the UK

The rate of urbanisation is highest in areas where the economy is growing. People mostly move to urban centres to find work or to take a job with higher wages.

Slow Growth

- In general, urban areas in the north and west of the UK are growing slowly and some have a declining population, e.g. Blackpool.

  One exception is Edinburgh, which has a strong financial sector.

- The decline of manufacturing industry (see p.80) has had a greater negative impact on cities in the north and west, causing high job losses.

- Average wages are lower and there are fewer employment opportunities, e.g. average weekly earnings in 2017 were just £501 in Newcastle compared to £727 in London.

- This means that many people move away to find work elsewhere and few people are attracted there.

Fast Growth

- Urban areas in the south and east of the UK are growing more rapidly. Two of the fastest growing urban areas are Milton Keynes and Cambridge.

- The growth of service and high-tech industries has mostly benefited the south. As wealth increases, people have more money to spend on services, creating more jobs which attracts workers. Slough, a large town near London, has one of the highest rates of business start-ups in the country. Thriving urban areas with lots of services, e.g. cafés and music venues, are also more attractive places to live.

- Around half of all international migrants move to London or the South East. This increases the rate of urbanisation there.

Slough down, you're growing too fast...

If you think anywhere north of Birmingham is Scotland then I'd advise you to take a look at the map again. You need to know where the major urban centres in the UK are and why some are growing faster than others.

Topic 4 — Changing Cities

Urban Change — London

London — where the streets are paved with gold and everyone has tea with the Queen on a Friday afternoon.

London is a Global City in South East England

1) London is sited on the flat floodplain of the River Thames near where it meets the sea.

2) It is the UK's capital city and is an essential part of the UK's economy. Over 20% of the UK's income comes from London.

3) London is culturally important to the UK — it has major museums and galleries, a thriving music scene and is a centre for fashion and theatre.

4) London's sprawl outwards has been partly stopped by a 'green belt' — land that isn't allowed to be built on. It also has lots of large parks, e.g. Hyde Park.

5) It is the centre of the UK's transport system. It was a major port until 1981 and still has shipping links. There are two major international airports (Heathrow and Gatwick) plus three smaller ones, e.g. London City Airport. There is easy access to mainland Europe via the Channel Tunnel.

6) It has a major influence on its surrounding area. Companies are attracted to the region by the proximity to London, which increases jobs and wealth. The South East and East of England are the two biggest regional economies in the UK outside London.

7) London's important globally too — it's a world city and, along with New York, one of the two most important financial centres in the world. There are more foreign banks in London than anywhere else.

London

France

You Need to Know the City's Structure

Different types of land use are found in particular areas of London because they have similar requirements. This creates distinct zones within the city, which have different functions — commercial, industrial and residential. Function and building age vary across London.

Chelsea · City · Newham · Thurrock

Surbiton · Crockenhill

	Area (example)	Main Function	Description
CBD (Central Business District)	City of London	Commercial	Mix of new high-rise office blocks and historical buildings. Land is expensive so building density is high. There are a few small parks.
Inner city	Newham	Low-class residential	High-density, old terraced housing, 1960s-70s high-rise flats and modern apartment buildings. Poor environmental quality, some green space.
	Chelsea	High-class residential	80% houses built before 1919. Land is expensive so building density is high. Lots of large terraced houses, some converted into flats. High quality green space — most houses have gardens.
Suburbs	Surbiton, Kingston upon Thames	Middle-class residential	Good quality 20th century semi-detached housing, along with shops and restaurants. Most houses have gardens and there are large areas of good quality green space.
Urban-Rural fringe	Crockenhill, Sevenoaks	High-class residential	Large, detached and semi-detached houses (pre-1900) with gardens — the area is surrounded by countryside.
	Thurrock	Industrial, commercial	Industry includes oil refineries, manufacturing and a container port. Lakeside retail park opened in 1990.

A week at the Ritz — now that would be a high-class residential...

...but it's probably not going to be your next geography field trip. You might have studied a different case study in class so feel free to learn that one instead. Whichever you choose, make sure you know its four major functional zones.

Urban Change — London

London is changing due to movements of <u>people</u>, <u>jobs</u> and <u>services</u>. It's all in, out, in, out, shake it all about...

London has Gone Through Four Distinct Urban Processes

Urbanisation

Urbanisation is the <u>increase</u> in the <u>proportion</u> of the population living in built-up <u>urban areas</u>. Urban areas <u>spread</u> into the <u>surrounding countryside</u> as the population increases.

- London grew rapidly during the <u>Industrial Revolution</u>, from around three quarters of a million people in 1760 to over 3 million by 1860 as people <u>moved</u> from surrounding areas to <u>work</u> in the factories.
- Major industries in London included the <u>Docklands</u> shipyards and <u>Woolwich Royal Arsenal</u>, which manufactured guns and ammunition.
- Workers lived in <u>small terraced houses</u> around the <u>factories</u>, e.g. in Poplar and Deptford. Lots of houses around the centre of London were built <u>before 1900</u>.

Suburbanisation

Suburbanisation is the movement of people from the <u>middle</u> of the city to the <u>edges</u> — urban areas <u>expand rapidly</u> (<u>sprawl</u>) as <u>housing</u> is <u>built</u> in the <u>outskirts</u>.

- Lots of suburbanisation occurred in London from the <u>1930s</u> to <u>60s</u>.
- Urbanisation caused the centre of London to become <u>overcrowded</u> and <u>polluted</u>, with <u>little</u> 'natural' space. Suburban areas, e.g. Surbiton in south west London, offered more open <u>green spaces</u> and seemed more <u>family-friendly</u>. In Surbiton, there is a variety of good quality housing along with shops, restaurants, schools and parks.
- Improvements in <u>transport networks</u> meant that people could live in the suburbs and <u>commute</u> in to the city to work. <u>Trains</u> from Surbiton reach London Waterloo in about <u>20 minutes</u> and it is close to the A3, one of the <u>main routes</u> into London.

Counter-urbanisation

<u>Counter-urbanisation</u> is the movement of people <u>away</u> from large <u>urban areas</u> to smaller settlements and <u>rural areas</u>. This process began in London in the <u>1970s</u> and is still continuing today.

- Rural areas on the outskirts of London, e.g. Sevenoaks District in Kent, are attracting people from London who want a <u>better quality of life</u>.
- Increased <u>car ownership</u> and improved <u>public transport</u> mean that people can live <u>further</u> from the city and <u>commute</u> to work — Sevenoaks is just over 20 minutes on the train to London Bridge. By 2007, London commuters made up nearly 40% of the population of Sevenoaks District.
- Improved <u>communication services</u> (e.g. high-speed internet connections) make it easier for people to live in rural areas and <u>work from home</u>. This also means that some companies <u>no longer</u> need to be in a city centre and can move to <u>rural areas</u> where land is <u>cheaper</u>, e.g. Bluewater Shopping Centre was built in an old chalk quarry in Greenhithe, Kent.

Re-urbanisation

<u>Re-urbanisation</u> is the movement of people <u>back into</u> urban areas. <u>Regeneration</u> of the city centre and run-down inner city areas can encourage people to return.

- The London Docklands area was <u>regenerated</u> in 1980s-90s as a centre for <u>finance</u> and <u>business</u>, with <u>new office space</u> in Canary Wharf as well as <u>shopping centres</u> and <u>housing</u> developments. This has attracted people back to the area.
- Once re-urbanisation has <u>started</u> it tends to <u>continue</u> — as soon as a few businesses had invested and people started to return, it encouraged <u>other businesses</u> to invest. Canary Wharf is now home to many media organisations and global banks, e.g. Barclays.
- Smaller <u>businesses</u> have also thrived — people have <u>more money</u> to spend in local shops and cafés.
- <u>Young</u>, <u>single people</u> often want to live <u>close to their work</u> in areas with good <u>entertainment</u> <u>services</u> (e.g. bars and nightclubs). Over <u>80%</u> of people living in Canary Wharf are aged <u>16-64</u> and nearly <u>40%</u> of households are occupied by a <u>single adult under 65</u>.

Urban Change — London

The Population of London is Young, Ethnically Diverse and Growing

1) The population of London is relatively <u>young</u>. London has a <u>higher</u> proportion of <u>working age people</u> and a <u>lower</u> proportion of <u>over 65s</u> than the national average.

2) London's population is also <u>ethnically diverse</u> — around 37% of people in London were born in another country. Ethnic diversity in London <u>increased</u> between the 2001 and 2011 censuses — in 2001, 60% of the population were white British, but by 2011 this had fallen to 45%.

3) The population of London is <u>large</u> and <u>growing</u> — at the 2011 census it was 8.17 million. This is an increase of 14% since the last census in 2001. There are two main <u>reasons</u> why the population is growing:

International migration — e.g. around <u>100 000</u> more people <u>arrived</u> in London from <u>abroad</u> than <u>left</u> in 2014.

Natural increase — there are <u>more births</u> than <u>deaths</u> in the city. This is partially because many people <u>migrating</u> into the city are of the <u>age</u> when they're likely to start having children (see below). <u>More than half</u> of <u>new babies</u> each year are born to <u>international</u> immigrants.

4) <u>National</u> migration (people moving within the UK) is slowing population growth as <u>more</u> people <u>leave</u> London than move to it from <u>other parts of the UK</u>. In 2011 there was a <u>net outflow</u> from London of <u>all age groups</u>, except the 20-24 age group.

People Migrate for Work, Study or to be with Family

1) 35% of all <u>international migrants</u> to the UK live in <u>London</u>.

2) Many immigrants in London have come from the <u>EU</u> to <u>work</u>. There was a demand for both <u>high skilled</u>, <u>specialist labour</u> and <u>low-skilled workers</u>, and the EU allows free movement of people within its member countries to find work. Lots of people have come from <u>Germany</u>, <u>Hungary</u> and <u>Poland</u>. In 2016, the UK voted to leave the EU, which is changing the patterns of migration to the UK.

3) Most <u>non-EU</u> migrants come to London to <u>study</u> or to be with <u>family</u>. After the Second World War many people migrated to the UK from <u>Commonwealth</u> countries, e.g. the Caribbean, India and Pakistan.

4) Lots of young people (aged 20-24) move from other areas of the UK to London to <u>study</u> or <u>work</u>. There are several top-class <u>universities</u>, e.g. UCL, LSE and Imperial College. London also has the highest average wages of any city in the UK. <u>Families</u> and <u>older</u> people tend to move <u>out</u> of the city to other parts of the UK to avoid high house prices and find a more pleasant, peaceful environment (see previous page).

Migration Influences the Character of Different Parts of the City

Age Structure — most <u>immigrants</u> are of <u>working age</u>. There is now a <u>high percentage</u> of people aged <u>25-34</u> in <u>inner city</u> London and a <u>lower proportion</u> of people <u>over 65</u>. Most national immigrants to London are aged <u>20-34</u> and international immigrants are aged <u>16-34</u>.

Ethnicity — ethnic diversity is <u>higher</u> in <u>inner city areas</u>, e.g. <u>52%</u> of people in <u>Newham</u> are foreign-born compared to <u>29%</u> in <u>Kingston upon Thames</u>, but it's increasing in some suburbs, e.g. Bexley.

Housing — the high rate of immigration is leading to <u>overcrowding</u>. Poorer immigrants often live in <u>older terraces</u> and 1960s-70s <u>council tower blocks</u> in the <u>inner city</u>, which are more <u>affordable</u>. Some areas, e.g. Islington, have been <u>gentrified</u> — wealthier people have moved in and regenerated them by improving their houses.

Services — in <u>inner city</u> areas where immigration rates are <u>high</u>, there is an increasing <u>demand</u> for <u>services</u> such as <u>education</u> and <u>health care</u> (e.g. for school places and maternity care). However, these areas are often amongst the <u>poorest</u> parts of the city, so it's <u>difficult</u> to provide what's needed. Other areas, e.g. Camden, have been <u>studentified</u> — a high student population has led to thriving services and entertainment venues.

Posh chicken restaurants — they've been gentrifried...

You're not done with this case study yet, not by a long way, but why not have a crack at this lovely question:

1) Explain the impact that international migration has had on ethnicity in a named UK city. [2]

Urban Change — London

CASE STUDY

Turns out the streets aren't paved with gold after all — who knew. London has a load of <u>challenges</u> to face...

De-industrialisation Caused Decline in parts of the Inner City and CBD

<u>De-industrialisation</u> is when <u>manufacturing industries</u> move out of an area.
De-industrialisation in London began in the 1960s and was caused by <u>four</u> main factors:

1) <u>Globalisation</u> — this is the process of countries becoming more <u>interdependent</u>. A lot of manufacturing moved <u>overseas</u>, where <u>labour costs</u> are <u>lower</u>, e.g. Marks and Spencer now make clothes in India.

2) <u>De-centralisation</u> — many <u>shops</u> and <u>businesses</u> moved out of the CBD to locations on the edge of town and along the M4 corridor, where land is <u>cheaper</u> and there are <u>better transport links</u> and <u>easier access</u>.

3) <u>Technological advances</u> — <u>new machinery</u> made manufacturing processes more efficient so fewer people were needed. There is also a growing demand for <u>high-tech products</u> — the new technology is often made in factories outside the city centre and has also meant more businesses no longer need to be in the CBD.

4) <u>Developments in transport</u> — the invention of <u>large shipping containers</u> meant that the bigger ships could no longer travel up the river to London's docks — the <u>shipping trade</u> and all the <u>associated industries</u> in the Docklands area were lost. <u>Improvements</u> in transport have made it <u>easier</u> for companies to locate part of their business (e.g. manufacturing) in <u>other countries</u> and keep the <u>headquarters</u> in London.

De-industrialisation has had both <u>negative</u> and <u>positive</u> impacts on London:

Negative

1) The <u>decline</u> of the <u>docks</u> and <u>manufacturing</u> industries in London's <u>East End</u> led to mass <u>unemployment</u> — 20% of jobs were lost between 1966 and 1976 in the dockland areas. This led to <u>poverty</u> and lower living standards. Many families <u>moved away</u> from the area.

2) As people moved away, many buildings were left <u>empty</u>. Derelict buildings were targets for graffiti and <u>vandalism</u>. Many areas in London's Docklands became <u>run down</u>.

3) There was also a <u>decrease</u> in local <u>services</u>, e.g. shops, schools and health care facilities, as there weren't enough <u>people</u> or <u>money</u> to support them.

Positive

1) Many <u>TNCs</u> (transnational corporations), e.g. HSBC and BP, locate their <u>sales</u> and <u>marketing</u> departments and <u>headquarters</u> in London because of its <u>importance</u> as a <u>financial centre</u>.

2) New <u>high-tech</u> industries have located in <u>business parks</u>, e.g. North London Business Park. New industrial areas, e.g. Crossways Business Park by the QEII bridge, have been developed on the outskirts of London, providing <u>jobs</u> there.

Economic Change is Increasing Inequality in London

1) <u>De-industrialisation</u> has led to many areas of the <u>inner city</u> becoming <u>deprived</u>, e.g. Hackney.

2) However, the growth of <u>financial industries</u>, e.g. in the City of London, has created many very <u>high-paying jobs</u>, with salaries averaging around £70 000.

3) The map shows how deprivation <u>varies</u> across London.

4) The inequality means there are differences in <u>quality of life</u>:

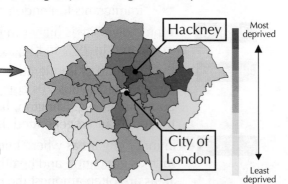

- There are <u>fewer manufacturing jobs</u> in the inner city — <u>new industries</u> locate on the <u>outskirts</u>, so it's <u>harder</u> for people in the inner city to find <u>suitable work</u>. More than <u>25%</u> of London's population are living in <u>poverty</u>, due to <u>unemployment</u> or <u>low wages</u>.

- Rapid population growth puts <u>pressure</u> on services, e.g. health and education. Funding services is also harder in <u>deprived areas</u>, where councils get <u>less money</u> from <u>taxes</u> and <u>businesses</u>.

- Many children from <u>poorer families</u> end up in under-performing schools. This can lead to a cycle of poverty, e.g. where a <u>lack of education</u> leads to a <u>limited</u> range of <u>jobs</u>, and <u>lower incomes</u>.

- <u>Unhealthy lifestyles</u>, e.g. drinking, smoking and poor diets, are more common in <u>deprived areas</u> — <u>life expectancy</u> is about <u>5 years lower</u> in <u>poorer</u> areas of the city than in wealthier areas.

Urban Change — London

Changes in Retailing Have Affected the CBD and Edge of London

London is experiencing changes in shopping patterns similar to the rest of the UK. People are becoming less likely to shop in the city centre and more likely to buy things online or go to shopping centres on the edge of London (or other less central locations). This has affected retail businesses in London:

1) The CBD has declined — falling shopper numbers and high rents mean many smaller independent shops can no longer afford to remain in the centre of London. Larger retail chains have also struggled — the BHS store on Oxford Street had to close when the company shut down in 2016.

2) The number of edge- and out-of-town shopping centres has increased — large shopping centres, e.g. Bluewater and Lakeside, have been built on the edge of the city where land is cheaper and there is less congestion and more parking space.

3) Internet shopping has increased — this has put further pressure on high street shops. Some firms have moved to distribution centres on the edge of the city where they can distribute goods to online shoppers more easily. Others have been forced to close down, e.g. Marks & Spencer has had to close a number of stores due to declining visitor numbers.

Strategies are Needed to Make Urban Living More Sustainable

Sustainable strategies are about improving things for people today without negatively affecting future generations. They need to consider the environment, the economy and people's social well-being.

Big cities need so many resources that it's unlikely they'd ever be truly sustainable. But things can be done to make a city (and the way people live there) more sustainable and to improve people's quality of life.

Employment — increasing employment opportunities reduces poverty and improves economic sustainability. The London Living Wage encourages businesses to pay a fair wage that takes into account the high cost of living in London. Skills programmes, e.g. En-route to Sustainable Employment, mean that people can progress to higher paid jobs.

Recycling — more recycling means fewer resources are used, e.g. metal cans can be melted down and used to make more cans. Waste recycling schemes include the collection of household recycling boxes and recycling facilities for larger items, e.g. fridges. However, only 33% of rubbish in London is recycled — the lowest level in the whole of England.

Transport — noise and air pollution can be reduced, for example:
- congestion charging discourages drivers from entering the city centre at peak times.
- self-service bicycles and bike lanes make it easier and safer for people to cycle instead of drive.
- electric buses and zero-emission taxis are helping to reduce emissions from public transport.

Housing — the BedZED development is a large-scale sustainable community in south London. The houses have thick insulation, solar heating systems and water-saving appliances, all of which help to reduce energy consumption and conserve resources. The houses are built from locally-sourced materials, giving them a smaller carbon footprint, and many properties on the development have subsidised rents (making them more affordable).

Health — improving access to health care, reducing air pollution and providing green spaces makes cities healthier places to live, which reduces inequalities in health (see previous page). Barts Health NHS Trust is creating green spaces for community use, including allotments where fruit and vegetables can be grown. They are also working with local communities to encourage healthy eating and regular exercise.

Education — achieving good exam results helps to break the cycle of poverty and under-achievement in deprived areas. Strategies to close the gap between the best and worst performing schools include taking pupils to university open days and working closely with individual pupils to support them through difficulties at home. Some schools are also increasing contact with parents to encourage them to help their children learn.

Strategies are needed to make revision more sustainable — tea anyone?

And there you have it, that's the last of this enormous case study. You need to know all the problems economic change had caused for your chosen city and some of the long-term solutions for making it more sustainable. OK, crack on.

Urban Growth — Lagos

CASE STUDY

Strap in, buckle up and generally prepare yourself mentally and physically for a tour of Lagos...

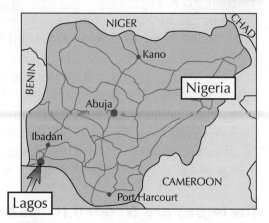
Nigeria
Lagos

Lagos is the Biggest City in Africa

Lagos is a city in Nigeria — a developing country, but the richest country in Africa. The city's population is over 21 million, and it's one of the fastest-growing urban areas in the world.

1) Lagos is located at the outlet of the massive Lagos Lagoon (see map below) on the Atlantic western coast of Nigeria.

2) This location is ideal for its port, which is one of the biggest in Africa. The city has spread outwards from its origin on Lagos Island around the lagoon and along the coast.

3) Lagos is well connected by road to the other major towns in Nigeria, e.g. Abuja (the national capital). It has an international port and airport, making it an important centre for regional and global trade.

4) Lagos is Nigeria's biggest city for population and business. It was the national capital until 1991 and remains the main financial centre for the whole of West Africa. The city contains 80% of Nigeria's industry and lots of global companies are located there.

5) It is the centre of the Nigerian film industry 'Nollywood' and has a thriving music scene, which has introduced music styles such as Afrobeat and Afro hip-hop — this gives it cultural importance in Nigeria.

Different Areas of Lagos have Different Functions

1) The development of Lagos means that land use and building age varies across the city.

2) The oldest parts of the city are on Lagos Island, which is now the CBD. Many of the old buildings have been redeveloped as high rise office blocks and luxury shops. Land is very expensive.

3) By 1960 the city had spread north and east along the main road and rail links, e.g. creating the suburb of Mushin. Industries developed near major transport links, e.g. Ikeja industrial estate near the airport.

4) Rapid expansion meant that by 1990 Lagos had merged with the smaller surrounding towns to form a continuous urban area. The city has continued to sprawl into the surrounding countryside.

5) It has mainly spread north as it is hemmed in by the lagoon to the east and major rivers to the west. It has also expanded west along the Lagos-Badagry express-way, e.g. in Ojo.

6) Slums have developed on less desirable land on the outskirts of Lagos throughout its history. However, as the city has sprawled outwards, many of the slums have become part of the main urban area of Lagos.

	Area	Age and function
CBD	Lagos Island	Modern high-rise office buildings, local government headquarters and banks, plus old lower-class housing.
Inner city	Mushin	Older, high-density, low-quality houses.
	Ikeja	Large industrial estate built in the 1960s, with factories making e.g. plastics and textiles.
Suburbs	Victoria Island	Modern, high-class residential and commercial — lots of businesses and shops.
Urban-rural fringe	Ojo	Sprawling, low-density new housing on the outskirts of the city.
	Lekki	New industrial zone and port being built.

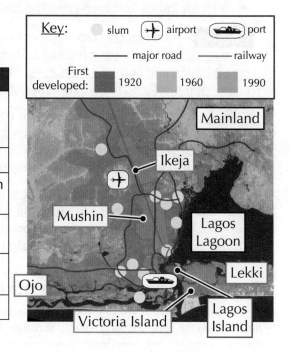

Key: ● slum ✈ airport ⛴ port
— major road — railway
First developed: ■ 1920 ■ 1960 ■ 1990

Mainland
Ikeja
Mushin
Lagos Lagoon
Lekki
Ojo
Victoria Island
Lagos Island

Urban Growth — Lagos

Lagos's Population is Growing Rapidly

Lagos's population has <u>grown</u> for <u>different reasons</u> at different <u>times</u>:

Historic

1) The city was under <u>British rule</u> during <u>colonial</u> times and was a centre of <u>trade</u>. This attracted <u>traders</u> and <u>merchants</u> to the city.

2) Many <u>ex-slaves</u> also came to Lagos, e.g. from <u>Sierra Leone</u>, <u>Brazil</u> and the <u>West Indies</u>.

1960s-1990s

1) After Lagos gained <u>independence</u> there was <u>rapid economic development</u> — the <u>export</u> of <u>oil</u> made some people very <u>wealthy</u>.

2) The government financed lots of <u>construction projects</u>, e.g. building <u>sea ports</u>, <u>oil refineries</u> and <u>factories</u>. The <u>jobs</u> created led to <u>rapid urbanisation</u> — lots of people moved <u>to</u> Lagos from <u>rural Nigeria</u>. This is called <u>rural-urban migration</u>.

3) <u>Birth rates</u> were <u>high</u> and <u>death rates</u> were <u>lower</u> leading to <u>high rates</u> of <u>natural increase</u> — a rapidly <u>growing</u> population.

Recent

1) <u>Most</u> of the population growth in Lagos is due to <u>rural-urban migration</u>.

2) The countries <u>bordering</u> Nigeria, e.g. Chad and Niger, are <u>poor</u> and <u>involved</u> in conflict — many people leave these countries for a <u>better life</u> in Lagos.

3) There are also lots of <u>national migrants</u> from the <u>northern states</u> of Nigeria where there is lots of <u>ethnic</u> and <u>religious conflict</u> and high levels of <u>poverty</u>.

4) There is some international migration from the <u>USA</u>, the <u>UK</u> and <u>China</u>. This is mainly people who are employed by <u>foreign businesses</u> operating in <u>Lagos</u>.

5) The rate of <u>natural increase</u> is still <u>high</u> — <u>birth</u> rates are still higher than <u>death</u> rates though <u>both</u> are slowly falling.

Migration has Affected Different Parts of Lagos

Age structure — migration of <u>young people</u> seeking <u>work</u> has affected the age structure of Lagos. About <u>two thirds</u> of the population of Lagos are aged <u>29 or under</u> and just <u>2%</u> are <u>over 65</u>. The highest proportions of <u>over 65s</u> are found in <u>central areas</u>, e.g. Lagos Island, where families have been in the same properties that they have owned for generations and there are <u>fewer migrants</u>. The highest proportions of <u>working age people</u> are found in <u>inner city areas</u>, e.g. Ikeja, near industrial areas and factories where they can find <u>work</u>.

Ethnicity — <u>wealthier</u> areas tend to have more <u>mixed ethnicities</u> than poorer areas. <u>Poor migrants</u> seek out relatives or friends of the <u>same ethnicity</u>. The <u>Yoruba</u> ethnic group is the most dominant in Lagos, and these Nigerians are more concentrated in older parts of the city, e.g. Lagos Island, where they have lived since Lagos was just a fishing village. <u>Westerners</u> and other <u>foreigners</u>, e.g. Chinese, mainly live on <u>Victoria Island</u> or in <u>Ikoyi</u> in higher-class residential areas close to the <u>CBD</u> where most foreign firms are located.

Housing — migration into Lagos has meant that previously empty areas are now <u>built on</u>, e.g. slums are built on areas of <u>wasteland</u>. In other <u>undesirable locations</u> people have built <u>wooden huts</u> on <u>stilts</u> in the <u>lagoon</u>, e.g. Makoko. As wealthy Nigerians and foreigners have moved in, some of the old middle-class residential areas have become <u>high-class luxury housing</u>, e.g. the old middle-class area of <u>Ikoyi</u> is now one of the <u>richest</u> neighbourhoods in Lagos with <u>redeveloped apartments</u>.

Services — <u>migration</u> into Lagos has meant service provision hasn't been able to keep up with <u>demand</u>. Most poor migrants end up living in <u>slums</u> with <u>no formal services</u>, e.g. schools and health care facilities. In contrast, migration of <u>Westerners</u> to the wealthiest parts of the city has led to a high concentration of elite and <u>international schools</u>, e.g. the British International School on Victoria Island, and some of the <u>best health care facilities</u> in Lagos, as the rich can afford to pay for them.

Lagos — growing brick by brick...

Plenty to learn on these two pages about the growth of Lagos. Make sure you've got it sorted before you move on.

Urban Growth — Lagos

Lagos has massive <u>inequality</u> issues and <u>challenges</u> in just about every area. Yep, this page is a gloomy one...

There are Big Inequalities in Lagos

Lagos's <u>economic growth</u> has attracted both <u>wealthy</u> and <u>poorer</u> migrants, who have settled in <u>different parts</u> of Lagos. This has led to areas of <u>extreme wealth</u> and <u>extreme poverty</u>, with big differences in <u>quality of life</u>:

Wealthy Areas

1) Wealthy people have settled in <u>central areas</u> of Lagos near to the <u>main financial</u> and <u>leisure</u> districts, where they can afford the <u>higher house prices</u> and get to avoid long <u>commutes</u>.

2) The very rich live in luxurious and very expensive <u>gated communities</u>, e.g. on <u>Banana Island</u>, with their own leisure facilities, health centres, schools and police stations.

3) Lagos does not have enough electricity-generating <u>capacity</u> to satisfy the <u>whole</u> city, so neighbourhoods have to <u>take it in turns</u> to have electricity. The very wealthy improve their quality of life by running their own <u>powerful generators</u>.

Poor Areas

The poor can't afford <u>high quality housing</u> — they end up living in <u>slums</u> on land that regularly <u>floods</u> or is close to <u>polluting factories</u>. Electricity is not available to the <u>poorest</u> people in slums, meaning they are reliant on small petrol <u>generators</u>, which cause air pollution and <u>reduce quality of life</u>. Lack of <u>waste disposal</u> leads to <u>high health risks</u>. <u>Food</u> and <u>water</u> are often <u>contaminated</u> with industrial waste.

Lagos faces Challenges in Housing, Pollution, Services and Jobs

1 Housing Shortages & Squatter Settlements

Housing can't be built <u>fast enough</u> to keep pace with population growth. This causes house prices to <u>rise</u>, making them <u>unaffordable</u> for many people. Over <u>60%</u> of the city's population live in <u>slums</u>.

1) Houses are often <u>flimsy</u>, <u>wooden huts</u>. These are <u>illegally</u> built — people face <u>eviction</u> if slums are <u>demolished</u> to <u>clean up</u> the city.

2) The only <u>electricity</u> comes from <u>illegal connections</u> that often <u>cut out</u>.

3) There are high levels of <u>crime</u> — many slums are <u>patrolled</u> by gangs called 'area boys' who both <u>commit crimes</u> and act as <u>informal</u> 'police' in the slum.

2 Pollution

1) Most of the city doesn't have access to proper <u>sewers</u>, e.g. in Makoko <u>communal toilets</u> are shared by <u>15 households</u> and most of the waste goes <u>straight</u> into the <u>lagoon</u> below — it's always full of <u>rubbish</u> and <u>raw sewage</u>. This <u>causes health problems</u>, e.g. cholera.

2) The <u>huge</u> population produces <u>lots</u> of waste — approximately <u>9000 tonnes per day</u>.

3) Only about <u>40% of rubbish</u> is officially collected and there are <u>large rubbish dumps</u>, e.g. Olususun, which contain <u>toxic waste</u>. <u>Waste disposal</u> and <u>emissions</u> from factories are <u>not controlled</u>, leading to <u>air</u> and <u>water pollution</u>.

4) Lagos also has some of the <u>worst traffic congestion</u> in the <u>world</u>, leading to further air pollution.

3 Limited Service Provision

1) There aren't enough schools for the population (e.g. there is only <u>one primary school</u> in Makoko) and many families <u>can't afford</u> to send their children to school.

2) There aren't enough <u>health care facilities</u> and many people can't <u>afford</u> to pay for treatment.

3) Only about <u>40%</u> of the city is <u>connected</u> to the <u>state water supply</u>. The pipes are <u>old</u> and <u>rusty</u> — the water often gets <u>contaminated</u> with <u>sewage</u>.

4) The state water company <u>supplies less than half</u> of what is <u>needed</u>. Water is in such short supply that people pay <u>hugely inflated prices</u> to get water from <u>informal sellers</u>.

4 Under-employment

1) There aren't enough <u>formal jobs</u> for the <u>growing population</u> — people have to make money <u>any way they can</u>, e.g. by <u>scavenging</u> in the Olususun rubbish dump for items to sell.

2) About <u>60%</u> of the population work in <u>informal</u> (unofficial) jobs, e.g. street sellers, barbers.

3) There's <u>no protection</u> for informal workers. <u>Street-sellers'</u> stalls are <u>bulldozed</u> to make way for <u>new developments</u> and <u>road widening</u>.

4) Lots of people live on less than <u>$1.25 per day</u>.

Topic 4 — Changing Cities

Urban Growth — Lagos

The Government is Trying to Improve People's Quality of Life

Social
- The government has begun work on a US $2.5 billion plan which includes new water treatment plants and distribution networks so more people have access to clean, piped water.
- Two light rail lines are under construction to relieve road congestion along major commuter routes.
- The Lagos Affordable Public Housing (LAPH) programme is planning to build 20 000 new homes with their own community facilities. The Rent-to-Own scheme makes houses more affordable for young buyers by reducing the size of the deposit.

Economic
- The government is investing in training and education programmes, e.g. ReadySetWork, to ensure young people are employable when they leave school or university, and hundreds of Coding Centres have been set up to improve people's ICT skills.
- Almost US $14 million has been loaned to help set up 6000 small and medium-sized businesses to provide more employment opportunities.

Environmental
- Recycling banks are being put in every estate to limit the amount of waste that ends up in the huge rubbish dumps.
- Small electricity generators (used by households when the power goes out) are a big source of air pollution. To improve air quality the government banned the import of small generators — instead communities are encouraged to get together to run one larger generator, which will produce less emissions overall.

Strategies to Solve Lagos's Problems can be Top-Down or Bottom-Up

Top-down approaches involve large-scale organisations, e.g. governments, carrying out large-scale projects, whereas bottom-up approaches are led by communities or NGOs (non-governmental organisations) working with local people. Top-down and bottom-up approaches are being used to improve quality of life for the people of Lagos — but they both have advantages and disadvantages:

See p.91 for more on top-down and bottom-up strategies.

	Advantages	Disadvantages
Top-down	• Can achieve large improvements that affect the whole city, e.g. the improved water supply should provide enough water for everyone at a low cost by 2020. • Can carry out higher-cost projects that communities or NGOs would struggle to fund. • Can address economic, social and environmental sustainability.	• Often very expensive, e.g. Nigeria had to borrow almost US $1 billion from the World Bank to fund construction of its light rail line. • Top-down approaches don't always have the support of communities, who may decide to ignore or undermine the strategy. For example the bus rapid transit is often delayed due to cars and stalls blocking the bus lane. • May not help those most in need, e.g. the ban on small generators affects the poor more than the rich as they are less able to afford cleaner alternatives.
Bottom-up	• Planned with the local community, so it has their support and can target issues that most concern local people. • Often funded by donations from more developed countries or wealthy people, so there's low cost to the people they help or the Nigerian government.	• Smaller scale so projects reach fewer people. • Funds may be limited — especially during economic recessions (periods of economic decline) when the need may be greatest. Schemes often rely on donations from people in more developed countries but people can't afford to give as much during a recession. • Can lack coordination — there may be several NGOs with the same aims working separately.

La-gosh, that's a lot of case study to learn...

You might have studied a different city in a developing or emerging country. That's fine, just make sure you have enough information to cover the key points on these pages. You're almost done now — just a few revision questions...

Revision Summary

Well, that was a whole load of fun. I bet you're dying to go and tell someone about rural-urban migration and de-industrialisation now — but if you can hold it in just a little bit longer, have a go at these questions to check you really know your suburbanisation from your counter-urbanisation. Once you can answer them all in your sleep, feel free to go and share the joy with as many people you like. Although you should probably crack on with the next topic instead.

Urbanisation (p.74-76) ☐

1) What is urbanisation?
2) Where is urbanisation taking place most rapidly?
3) Give two reasons why urbanisation takes place.
4) Give an example of an economic change that is leading to migration in developed countries.
5) Outline why many cities in developing countries are growing.
6) Which areas of the UK have a high population density?
7) Give one reason for the location of an urban centre in the UK.
8) Give one region of the UK with a relatively low rate of urbanisation.
9) Outline why some areas of the UK have relatively high rates of urbanisation.

Urban Change — Case Study (p.77-81) ☑

For a major city in the UK that you have studied:
10) How is the city connected to the country it is located in?
11) Describe the main land use in the inner city.
12) Describe the variations in building age in the city.
13) What is suburbanisation?
14) Give two reasons why counter-urbanisation is taking place.
15) Give two characteristics of the population.
16) How has migration affected the age structure in different parts of the city?
17) List four causes of de-industrialisation.
18) Describe two differences in quality of life in the city.
19) Outline three recent changes in retailing patterns.
20) Outline two strategies that are improving sustainability in the city.

Urban Growth — Case Study (p.82-85) ☐

For a city in a developing or emerging country that you have studied:
21) Where are the oldest buildings found?
22) Describe the main functions of the urban-rural fringe.
23) Give one reason why the population has grown rapidly in recent years.
24) Describe how migration has affected housing in different parts of the city.
25) Give two reasons for the differences in the quality of life within the city.
26) Outline three challenges that the people in the city face.
27) Outline one government initiative that is trying to improve quality of life in the city.
28) Give two advantages of top-down approaches to improving quality of life in the city.
29) Give two disadvantages of bottom-up strategies to improving quality of life in the city.

Measuring Development

This topic might seem a little <u>tricky</u> — but take a <u>deep breath</u> and <u>believe in yourself</u> and you'll be <u>just fine</u>.

Development *is when a* Country *is Improving*

1) When a country <u>develops</u>, it gets <u>better</u> for the people there. People <u>define</u> development in different ways:

> **Economic** — progress in <u>economic growth</u>, e.g. how <u>wealthy</u> a country is, its level of <u>industrialisation</u> and use of <u>technology</u>.

> **Social** — improvement in people's <u>standard of living</u>, e.g. <u>better health care</u> and access to <u>clean water</u>.

> **Political** — having a <u>stable</u> political system with <u>institutions</u> that can <u>meet the needs</u> of society.

2) <u>Human development</u> is about improving people's quality of life — it includes economic, social and political aspects of development. There are many <u>factors</u> which affect the <u>level</u> of human development in a country:

- <u>Economic</u> — having <u>enough money</u> to provide <u>shelter</u>, <u>food</u> and <u>clothing</u>.
- <u>Social</u> — e.g. <u>education</u> improves people's <u>job</u> choices and good <u>sanitation</u> increases life expectancy.
- <u>Technological</u> — new technology can help <u>other</u> aspects of development, e.g. by improving education, health care and food security (see below). Increasing access to <u>mobile phones</u> and the <u>internet</u> means people are more <u>connected</u> and have more <u>information</u> available, giving them more <u>choices</u>.
- <u>Cultural</u> — e.g. in some cultures it is <u>traditional</u> for women to stay at home and not work. This can hold back development as there is <u>less household income</u> and <u>more inequality</u> between men and women.
- <u>Food security</u> — whether people are able to eat <u>enough nutritious food</u> to stay healthy and active.
- <u>Water security</u> — whether there is a reliable and sustainable source of <u>good quality water</u> to meet everyone's needs — for industry, agriculture and personal health.

I make this development about 25 m.

There Are Loads of Measures of Development

1) Development is <u>pretty hard to measure</u> because it <u>includes so many things</u>. But you can <u>compare</u> the development of different countries using 'measures of development'.

Name	What it is	A measure of...	As a country develops, it gets...
<u>Gross Domestic Product (GDP)</u>	The <u>total value</u> of <u>goods</u> and <u>services</u> a <u>country produces</u> in a <u>year</u>. It's often given in US$.	Wealth	Higher
<u>GDP per capita</u>	The GDP <u>divided</u> by the <u>population</u> of a <u>country</u>. It's often given in <u>US$</u> and is sometimes called <u>GDP per head</u>.	Wealth	Higher
<u>Gini coefficient</u>	A measure of <u>economic inequality</u>. Countries are given a score between <u>0</u> (<u>equal</u>) and <u>100</u> (total <u>inequality</u>).	Inequality	Lower
<u>Gender Inequality Index</u>	A number that's calculated using data on e.g. <u>women's education</u>, access to <u>jobs</u>, <u>political rights</u> and <u>health</u> during <u>pregnancy</u>. The <u>higher</u> the score, the <u>more inequality</u>.	Women's rights	Lower
<u>Human Development Index (HDI)</u>	This is a number that's calculated using <u>life expectancy</u>, <u>education level</u> (e.g. average number of years of schooling) and <u>income per head</u>. Every country has an HDI value between <u>0</u> (<u>least developed</u>) and <u>1</u> (<u>most developed</u>).	Lots of things	Higher
<u>Corruption Perceptions Index (CPI)</u>	A measure of the level of <u>corruption</u> that is believed to exist in the public sector on a scale of <u>1-100</u>. The <u>lower</u> the score, the <u>more corruption</u>.	Corruption	Higher

2) <u>Single</u> indicators can be <u>misleading</u> if they are used <u>on their own</u> because, as a country develops, some aspects <u>develop before others</u>. So it might seem that a country's <u>more developed</u> than it <u>actually is</u>.

3) Using a composite indicator of development, where <u>more than one measure</u> is used (i.e. wealth and something else) avoids these problems. The <u>Human Development Index</u> is a composite indicator.

Measures of revision — they're called exams...

...so you'd best get learnin' the measures of development listed above. You'll need 'em later in the topic too.

1) *Name one measure of inequality.*   [1]

Global Development

Now you know what <u>development</u> is all <u>about</u>, it's time to find out which countries <u>top the list</u>...

Levels of Development Vary across the World

1) Countries can be <u>classified</u> based on their <u>level of development</u>.

2) <u>Developed</u> countries, e.g. the UK, have <u>very high</u> human development. <u>Emerging</u> countries, e.g. India, have <u>medium</u> to <u>high</u> human development. <u>Developing</u> countries, e.g. Chad, have <u>low</u> human development.

3) The <u>most developed</u> countries are in <u>north America</u>, <u>Europe</u> and <u>Australasia</u>, and the <u>least developed</u> countries are in <u>central Africa</u> and parts of <u>Asia</u>.

- ■ Developed
- ■ Emerging
- ■ Developing

increasing inequality
- ■ 25-32.9
- ■ 33-40.9
- ☐ 41-48.9
- ■ 49-56.9
- ■ 57-64.9

4) The level of development also varies <u>within</u> countries — some countries have <u>very rich</u> and <u>very poor</u> people, but in others wealth is more <u>evenly distributed</u>.

5) This map shows the <u>Gini coefficient</u> (see previous page) for countries across the world.

6) Generally, <u>inequality</u> is <u>highest</u> in <u>southern</u> and <u>central Africa</u>, and <u>South</u> and <u>Central America</u>.

Global Uneven Development is Caused by Lots of Factors

Physical

1) If a country has a poor climate (<u>really hot</u> or <u>really cold</u> or <u>really dry</u>) not much will grow. This <u>reduces</u> the amount of <u>food produced</u>, which can lead to <u>malnutrition</u> and a poorer <u>quality of life</u>. People also have fewer crops to <u>sell</u>, so <u>less money</u> to spend on <u>goods</u> and <u>services</u>.

2) Countries <u>with</u> few <u>raw materials</u> tend to <u>make less money</u> because they've got <u>fewer products to sell</u>. This means there is <u>less</u> to spend on <u>development</u>.

3) Countries that have a lot of <u>natural disasters</u> (e.g. Bangladesh, which floods regularly) have to <u>spend a lot of money rebuilding</u> after disasters occur so there's <u>less money</u> to spend on <u>development</u>.

Historic

1) Countries that were <u>colonised</u> (<u>ruled</u> by a <u>foreign country</u>) are often at a <u>lower</u> level of development when they gain <u>independence</u> than they <u>would be</u> if they had <u>not</u> been <u>colonised</u>.

2) <u>European countries</u> colonised much of Africa in the 19th century. They controlled the economies of their colonies, removed <u>raw materials</u> and <u>slaves</u>, and sold back expensive <u>manufactured goods</u>. This was <u>bad</u> for African <u>development</u> as it made parts of Africa <u>dependent</u> on Europe, and led to <u>famine</u>.

Economic

1) Trade is the <u>exchange</u> of <u>goods</u> and <u>services</u> between countries. If a country has <u>poor trade links</u> it won't make a lot of money, so there'll be <u>less</u> to spend on development.

2) Very poor countries <u>borrow money</u> from <u>other countries</u> and <u>international organisations</u>, which leads to <u>debt</u>. Any <u>money</u> a country makes is used to <u>pay back</u> the debt, so isn't used to develop.

3) Countries that mostly export <u>primary products</u> (raw materials like wood, metal and stone) tend to be <u>less developed</u>. This is because you don't make much <u>profit</u> by selling primary products. Their <u>prices</u> also <u>fluctuate</u> — sometimes the <u>price falls below</u> the <u>cost of production</u>. This means people <u>don't make much money</u>, so the government has <u>less</u> to spend on <u>development</u>.

Hot and dry — good for holidays, bad for development...

So, global development is pretty uneven and there are loads of things that can hinder it. Make sure you learn them all.

UK Development

The UK is very developed but there is also <u>inequality</u>. Like how I can't get a <u>decent pie</u> south of <u>Sheffield</u>...

Levels of Development Within the UK are Uneven

1) <u>Wealth</u> is <u>unevenly distributed</u> in the UK. In 2015, the UK had a Gini coefficient of <u>33.2</u>. Over <u>25%</u> of income is held by the <u>richest 10%</u> of people and just <u>2.9%</u> of income is held by the <u>poorest 10%</u>.

2) Most of the wealthiest people live in <u>southern</u> and <u>eastern</u> England. In general, <u>wages</u> are <u>lower</u> in the <u>north</u> than the south, e.g. the 2014 <u>average weekly wage</u> was <u>40% lower</u> in <u>Huddersfield</u> than <u>London</u>.

3) <u>Uneven development</u> leads to differences in <u>quality of life</u> across the UK. For example:

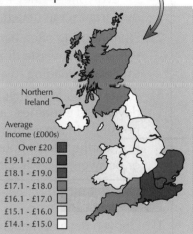

Northern Ireland

Average Income (£000s)

Over £20	■
£19.1 - £20.0	■
£18.1 - £19.0	■
£17.1 - £18.0	■
£16.1 - £17.0	■
£15.1 - £16.0	□
£14.1 - £15.0	□

<u>Unemployment</u> — Unemployment is <u>highest</u> in <u>North East</u> England (<u>5.0%</u>), and <u>lowest</u> in the <u>South West</u> (<u>2.9%</u>).

<u>Life Expectancy</u> — Generally, people living in <u>southern</u> England are <u>healthier</u> than people In <u>northern</u> England and <u>Scotland</u>. The <u>highest</u> life expectancy at birth for <u>males</u> (2011-2013) was in South East England (<u>80.4 years</u>) and the <u>lowest</u> was in <u>Scotland</u> (<u>76.8 years</u>).

<u>Education</u> — <u>GCSE results</u> are generally <u>better</u> in the <u>south</u> of England than the <u>Midlands</u> or the <u>north</u>. There is also a strong <u>link</u> between <u>educational attainment</u> and <u>household income</u> — students from <u>wealthier</u> families tend to get <u>better grades</u>.

4) <u>Not everywhere</u> in the <u>south</u> is <u>perfect</u> though — there is lots of <u>inequality</u> there too.

Physical, Historic and Economic Factors Have Affected UK Development

Physical

1) The <u>north</u> and <u>west</u> of the UK are more <u>mountainous</u> and have a <u>colder</u>, <u>wetter climate</u> than the south. This makes farming <u>less productive</u>.

2) It also makes it more difficult to develop <u>infrastructure</u> such as roads and railways. This means it is more <u>expensive</u> and <u>time-consuming</u> to transport goods and people to these locations, so there are fewer <u>industries</u> and fewer <u>jobs</u> available.

3) As people tend to have less money, <u>local councils</u> have <u>less</u> to spend on <u>development</u>.

Historic

1) London gets <u>lots of investment</u> in <u>infrastructure</u> and <u>services</u> because it is the UK's capital city. This has had a <u>positive knock-on effect</u> on the surrounding regions, e.g. the South East.

2) The <u>decline</u> of <u>heavy industry</u> (known as de-industrialisation — see p.80) has had a <u>greater negative impact</u> on the <u>north</u> of the UK, but the <u>growth</u> of the <u>post-industrial service industry</u> has mostly benefited the <u>south</u>.

3) Some areas, e.g. the North East, have struggled to develop <u>alternative industries</u>, so <u>unemployment</u> is <u>high</u> and <u>wages</u> are <u>low</u>.

Economic

1) Southern regions of the UK have <u>better transport links</u> to mainland Europe and the rest of the world. For example, the <u>Channel Tunnel</u> links South East England with France and 4 of the top 5 <u>busiest airports</u> in the UK are in <u>London</u>. This means that there are <u>better trade opportunities</u> in the south.

2) London has become a <u>global financial centre</u>. It has about <u>4 times</u> as many <u>jobs</u> as any other city in the UK and the <u>highest average income</u> in the country — mostly due to high-paying <u>finance</u> jobs.

3) Government policies such as <u>investment</u> in new <u>infrastructure</u> and <u>technology</u> and support for <u>businesses</u> (e.g. tax breaks) have increased <u>economic growth</u> in some areas, e.g. South Wales.

Inequalities affect all of us — just some more than others...

Uneven development is everywhere, even right here in the UK. It's not fair, I know, but it's still gotta be learnt.

Effects of Uneven Development

Trying to <u>develop</u> is a pretty tough ask. And things ain't great if you can't make it off the <u>bottom</u> of the pile...

Uneven Development *Affects People's Quality of Life*

<u>Lack of development</u> can make life <u>difficult</u> for people in <u>poorer countries</u>:

Housing

1) People may not be able to <u>afford</u> to buy a house or there may not be <u>enough</u> houses for everyone — they may have to build their own from <u>scrap materials</u>, e.g. in slums.

2) Slum housing often has no formal access to <u>services</u>, e.g. waste disposal, electricity or safe water, leading to a <u>poor quality of life</u>.

3) A lack of <u>building regulations</u> in less developed countries can lead to <u>poor quality housing</u>. In areas prone to natural disasters (e.g. earthquakes), houses may <u>collapse</u> or be <u>swept away</u> in landslides or floods.

Technology

1) <u>Uneven</u> development means that <u>some</u> countries have <u>better access</u> to <u>new technology</u> than others. For example, in <u>Chad</u> only about <u>2.5%</u> of people can <u>access</u> the <u>internet</u>, whereas in the <u>UK</u> it's about <u>90%</u> of people.

2) People in poorer countries may not be able to afford new <u>farm machinery</u> or <u>fertilisers</u>. This can lead to <u>lower yields</u> and <u>food insecurity</u>.

Employment

1) Conditions for workers in developing countries are often <u>poor</u>. Pay is <u>low</u>, hours are <u>long</u> and conditions can be <u>dangerous</u>.

2) For example, a high percentage of people in developing countries are employed in the <u>primary sector</u> (e.g. in agriculture).

3) In urban areas lots of poorer people work in <u>low-skilled service jobs</u>, e.g. on market stalls. They may also work in <u>factories</u>, e.g. manufacturing clothing.

Health

1) In some less developed countries, <u>lack</u> of <u>clean water</u> and <u>poor health care</u> mean that many people suffer from <u>diseases</u> such as malaria and cholera. This leads to <u>lower life expectancies</u>.

2) It is also easier for wealthier people to get access to <u>quality health care</u> and <u>healthy food</u>.

3) <u>Infant mortality</u> is also much <u>higher</u> in less developed countries, e.g. <u>85.4</u> deaths per 1000 babies born in <u>Chad</u> compared to <u>4.3</u> in the <u>UK</u>.

Water Security

1) There may be <u>limited</u> formal provision of <u>water</u> (e.g. wells or piped water) in developing countries. For example, <u>52%</u> of people in the <u>Democratic Republic of the Congo</u> (DRC) don't have access to <u>safe drinking water</u>.

2) Where water is scarce, supplies of drinking water can become <u>polluted</u> by sewage, industrial chemicals or nitrogen from fertilisers.

3) Some <u>diseases</u>, e.g. cholera and typhoid, are passed on through <u>contaminated</u> water.

4) Poorer people may have to <u>walk a long way</u> to collect water every day.

Food Security

1) People in poorer countries may not get enough to eat, which can lead to <u>undernutrition</u> (an imbalance of nutrients in the diet), <u>starvation</u> and <u>death</u> — <u>66%</u> of people in the DRC are <u>undernourished</u>.

2) Pressure to grow enough to eat can also lead to <u>soil erosion</u>, so the land becomes less and less fertile and it's <u>harder</u> to produce <u>food</u>.

3) A shortage of food can lead to <u>rising prices</u> so the poorest people can't feed themselves properly.

Education

1) <u>Less developed</u> countries <u>can't afford</u> to invest as much in <u>education</u> as <u>developed</u> countries.

2) <u>Poorer</u> people may not be able to afford <u>school fees</u> or <u>children</u> may have to <u>work</u> to support their families instead of attending <u>school</u> — only <u>72%</u> of children complete primary education in the <u>DRC</u> compared to <u>100%</u> in the <u>UK</u>.

3) Lack of <u>education</u> means people can't get <u>better-paid</u>, <u>skilled jobs</u> in the future.

Uneven development — what happens if you do one-armed push ups...

...or so I heard, anyway. The impacts of uneven development may not be cheerful reading but that won't stop the examiners grilling you on it. So read the page, cover it, scribble down the main points, then check you've got 'em all.

Increasing Development

Time to look at how to <u>increase</u> development — from grand <u>international</u> efforts to humble <u>local</u> projects.

International *Strategies Aim to Reduce Uneven Development*

Inter-governmental Agreements

1) The governments of several <u>different countries</u> can <u>work together</u> to help to increase development. This is known as an <u>inter-governmental agreement</u>.

2) They often involve <u>inter-governmental organisations</u> (IGOs), e.g. the World Bank and the United Nations (UN).

3) For example, the <u>The Millennium Development Goals</u> aimed to improve life in developing countries. All <u>UN member states</u> agreed to try to achieve the goals by 2015.

International Aid

1) International aid is <u>money</u> or <u>resources</u> (e.g. food, doctors) <u>given</u> by one country to another country. Aid can also be provided by an <u>organisation</u> (e.g. a charity or IGO).

2) Aid is spent on development projects, e.g. constructing <u>schools</u> to <u>improve literacy</u> rates, building <u>dams</u> and <u>wells</u> to <u>improve clean water supplies</u> and providing <u>farming knowledge</u> and <u>equipment</u> to <u>improve agriculture</u>.

3) <u>Short-term aid</u> can also be given to help countries cope with <u>emergencies</u>, e.g. natural disasters.

Strategies to Increase Development *are either Top-Down or Bottom-Up*

1) Top-down development projects — a <u>government</u> or <u>large organisation</u>, e.g. an inter-governmental organisation or transnational corporation (TNC), makes <u>decisions</u> about how to <u>direct</u> the project.

2) Bottom-up development projects — <u>local people</u> and <u>communities</u> decide on ways to improve things for their own community. <u>Non-governmental organisations</u> (NGOs) can also be involved.

	Top-down approaches	Bottom-up approaches
Advantages	• Often used for <u>large projects</u>, e.g. <u>dams</u> for hydroelectric power (HEP) or <u>irrigation schemes</u>. These aim to solve <u>large scale</u> problems and improve the lives of <u>lots</u> of people. • Projects can improve the country's <u>economy</u>, helping with <u>long-term development</u>.	• They often aim to <u>improve</u> the <u>quality of life</u> for the <u>poorest</u> and <u>most vulnerable</u> people in society. • <u>Local people</u> have a <u>say</u> in how the money will be <u>used</u>, so they get what they <u>need</u>. • Projects often <u>employ</u> local people, so they <u>earn money</u> and <u>learn new skills</u>. • They often have a low <u>environmental impact</u>. • Projects are usually much <u>cheaper</u>. • <u>Intermediate</u> technology is used.
Limitations	• If the aid takes the form of a <u>loan</u>, the country may have to <u>pay back</u> the money. • Large projects are often <u>expensive</u>. • They <u>may not benefit everyone</u> — e.g. HEP may not supply power to remote areas. • If governments are <u>corrupt</u>, they may use the <u>money</u> for their <u>own purposes</u>, so it doesn't help development. • The projects are often <u>high-tech</u> and <u>energy intensive</u>. The <u>recipient</u> country may become <u>dependent</u> on <u>technology</u> and <u>workers</u> from the <u>donor</u> country for <u>operation</u> and <u>maintenance</u>.	*Intermediate technology is simple, affordable and cheap to maintain.* • Most <u>money</u> comes from <u>charities</u>, which often rely on <u>donations</u> from people in richer countries. • Projects are usually <u>small-scale</u>, e.g. building or maintaining a well in a village, so they <u>don't benefit everyone</u>. • Different organisations (e.g. charities) may <u>not work together</u>, so projects may be <u>inefficient</u>.

Still or sparkling?

Clean drinking water? Bottoms up...

Development is a complicated matter with no easy solutions. Luckily revision is more straightforward.

1) *Explain one way in which top-down approaches to development differ from bottom-up approaches.* [2]

Development — India

India is an <u>emerging</u> country with a <u>huge population</u> and <u>lots of potential</u>. Time for a whirlwind tour...

India is an Emerging Country in Southern Asia

1) <u>India</u> is an <u>emerging</u> country with a rapidly <u>growing economy</u>. It has the <u>second largest</u> population in the world (approx. 1.3 billion) and is <u>still growing</u>.

2) India was a <u>British colony</u> until <u>1947</u>, but now has its own <u>democratically elected</u> government.

3) India has a <u>rich</u> and <u>diverse cultural</u> background. It's renowned for its production of '<u>Bollywood</u>' films, which are exported <u>worldwide</u>.

4) India has a beautiful and <u>varied landscape</u>, including areas of <u>mountains</u>, <u>desert</u>, <u>great plains</u> and a large <u>coastline</u>, making it an attractive <u>tourist destination</u>.

5) The large <u>coastline</u> also allows the development of <u>ports</u>, such as Mumbai, increasing trade opportunities.

Some Regions of India are Developing Faster than Others

1) Development across India is very <u>uneven</u>. The <u>core-periphery model</u> can be used to describe this uneven development. <u>Core</u> areas are highly <u>industrialised</u>, <u>urbanised</u> and centres for <u>economic growth</u>. The <u>periphery</u> is mainly <u>rural</u> with <u>few jobs</u> and <u>little economic development</u>.

2) Core areas have developed where there are <u>raw materials</u>, e.g. after the discovery of coal and iron ore, the <u>Damodar valley</u> became a centre for <u>heavy engineering</u> and has three major <u>steelworks</u>. Access to large rivers and <u>ports</u> allows transport of goods and people.

3) Once industries move in to an area there is a <u>multiplier effect</u> — people have <u>better jobs</u>, so more money to spend on <u>local services</u>. This generates <u>wealth</u> in the area so there is investment in <u>infrastructure</u>, which attracts <u>more industries</u> and so on.

	Maharashtra	Bihar
Urban population (%)	45	11
GDP per capita ($)	2561	682
HDI	0.572	0.367

4) <u>GDP</u> per capita is <u>highest</u> in the <u>south</u> and <u>west states</u>, e.g. Maharashtra, which have the <u>highest</u> proportion of people living in <u>urban</u> areas. <u>More money</u> means these areas are able to spend more on <u>health care</u>, <u>housing</u> and <u>education</u> which improves people's <u>quality of life</u>.

5) <u>Peripheral rural</u> states, e.g. Bihar, have higher rates of <u>poverty</u>. Bihar is still dependent on <u>agriculture</u> for much of its <u>income</u> but <u>crop yields</u> and <u>prices</u> are very <u>variable</u>. Infrastructure is <u>poor</u>, e.g. there are very few bridges crossing the River Ganges, making it difficult for industries to transport their <u>goods</u>.

Changes in Economic Sectors have had Positive and Negative Effects

1) <u>Agriculture</u> (the main <u>primary industry</u> in India) employs <u>43%</u> of the working population, but is becoming a <u>smaller</u> part of India's economy. Investment has been <u>decreasing</u> so there aren't many <u>new jobs</u> or <u>new techniques</u> being introduced. <u>Population growth</u> has increased pressure on jobs, and workers tend to be <u>unskilled</u> so can't find alternative employment. Out-dated techniques mean yields are <u>poor</u> and work is usually <u>seasonal</u>, so many rural people are becoming <u>unemployed</u>.

2) <u>Secondary industry</u> (manufacturing) has <u>grown</u> to employ <u>24%</u> of the workforce. Secondary industries are <u>stimulating economic development</u>. They provide people with <u>reliable jobs</u> (compared to <u>seasonal agricultural work</u>), and selling <u>manufactured</u> goods overseas brings more <u>income</u> into India than selling raw materials does. But people may have to do <u>dangerous jobs</u>, e.g. in construction or in factories handling toxic materials, and <u>working conditions</u> are often <u>poor</u> due to lack of regulations.

3) <u>Tertiary</u> (services) and <u>quaternary</u> (knowledge) industries have become a much <u>larger</u> part of the economy, employing <u>34%</u> of the workforce. Lots of this is due to <u>growth</u> in IT firms (especially in the city of <u>Bangalore</u>) and in supplying <u>services</u> for <u>foreign companies</u>, such as customer service centres. But increased <u>automation</u> and a shift towards developing <u>new technologies</u> rather than low-skilled work means that some companies are <u>reducing</u> the number of jobs available — there can be low job <u>security</u>.

Changing economic sectors are so in, dear...

One page down, three to go. Understanding the changes in India's economy will help with the rest of this case study.

Development — India

India is a Key Player in International Trade

International Trade

1) International trade is the import and export of goods and services between countries.

2) Trade is an increasingly important part of India's economy. The government used to control trade by limiting imports and exports. But since 1991, the country has reduced barriers to trade, e.g. by reducing tariffs (mostly taxes on imported goods), so trade with foreign businesses is increasing.

3) India is part of the World Trade Organisation (WTO) and a member of G20, a group of 20 of the world's largest economies. The individual countries that India trades with the most are USA, UAE and China. Neighbouring countries within Asia are also important trading partners.

4) India's main exports are diamonds and chemical products (e.g. medicines) and its main import is crude oil (for transport and industry).

Aid

1) India has been one of the highest receivers of international aid, receiving many loans from IGOs, e.g. the World Bank, as well as individual countries. Until 2015, India received over £200m each year from the UK to tackle poverty.

There's more on aid on page 91.

2) In 1991, India received US $2.2 billion in aid from the IMF in exchange for the government changing its economic policies, e.g. by allowing foreign companies to set up factories in India.

3) However, India also gives aid to neighbouring countries in South Asia, e.g. Bhutan, Afghanistan and Nepal. This gives India more power in the region and access to more resources, e.g. HEP.

The Amount of Public and Private Investment is Changing

1) Before 1991, public investment (investment by the government) was the main type of investment in India. The government prevented private investment in most industries — private businesses needed to get a license before they could start producing goods.

2) After 1991, more industries were opened up to private sector investment. India is trying to attract more foreign investment by relaxing the rules on how much land, property etc. foreign companies can own.

3) Some large TNCs from the USA and Europe outsource manufacturing and IT to India.

4) The government is also encouraging smaller Indian businesses to invest — its 'Startup India' program has made it easier for new businesses to set up, e.g. by reducing paperwork and taxes.

5) Since 2012 the Indian government has been increasing the amount of public investment to make sure economic growth continues, e.g. by upgrading the rail network, constructing new roads and improving broadband connectivity.

Outsourcing is when some of the work is done by another company.

India's Population is Increasing

Between 1985 and 2015 fertility rates (average number of births per woman) fell from 4.5 to 2.4 due to increased use of contraception and more women working instead of having children. Death rates and infant mortality have fallen, partly due to better health care and health education, e.g. encouraging people to wash their hands. This means that:

- India's population has rapidly increased — it grew from about 780 million in 1985, to 1.3 billion in 2015, but the rate of growth has been slowing down.

- Life expectancy has increased from 56 in 1985 to 68 in 2015.

- The majority of the population are young — about 27% are under 14 and the average age is just 30.

- However, since 1985 there are more people of working age and a lower proportion of children — the population pyramid's base is narrowing and the top is widening.

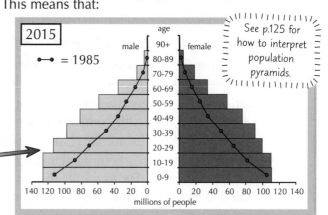

See p.125 for how to interpret population pyramids.

Development — India

CASE STUDY

Inequality is Increasing *but Some Social Factors are Improving*

1) Over the last 30 years, inequality in India has increased — its Gini coefficient rose from 31.9 in 1987 to 35.1 in 2011. Most of the new wealth has gone to making the richest people wealthier, whilst the poorest people stay poor.

2) Lots of people are living in poverty — over 40% of employed people earn less than US $3.10 a day. However, India is also home to many multimillionaires.

3) There have also been some positive social changes:

- There is a growing middle class — as the economy has changed, more people have been able to find work in higher paid jobs, e.g. as call centre assistants, engineers and government officials. These people earn enough to be able to buy consumer goods, e.g. mobile phones, fridges and televisions.

- Education has improved. In 2009 India made primary education free and compulsory — 96% of children now enrol for school. Teaching methods have improved in some areas, e.g. Tamil Nadu. The government is trying to increase the number of pupils who go on to secondary education by building new classrooms, hiring more teachers and providing accommodation for teachers in rural areas.

Geopolitical Relationships *Affect India's Development*

Geopolitics is how geography affects relationships between countries.

Foreign policy — in recent years the Indian government has improved relations with its neighbours (e.g. joining ASEAN, an organisation made up of countries in southeast Asia). It also developed the Act East policy to increase its influence over ASEAN countries and provide security in the region. This increased trade opportunities and promoted India as a global player — foreign companies are more likely to invest, providing jobs and introducing new technology.

Defence — India currently imports a lot of its defence equipment, e.g. aircraft and weapons, but is aiming to build a defence production industry focussed on cyberspace and artificial intelligence (AI). This could create jobs for up to 3 million people. India has third largest military budget in the world — spending more money on the military means that less is available for development.

Military pacts — India historically had strong military ties with Russia, which affected its economic policies, e.g. lack of private investment (see previous page). However, India has recently done a deal with the USA enabling the two countries to use each other's military bases. A better relationship with the USA has increased trade, which is increasing India's development.

Territorial disputes — Pakistan and China both disagree with India over who some of the land on the border belongs to. This has led India to actively build relationships with other nations in the region, e.g. by providing aid, to make sure they side with India if there is conflict.

Technology *and* Connectivity *can Increase Development*

1) The government is promoting technology — it wants everyone to have access to the internet and to use it to bring social development to rural villages, e.g. education and health care.

2) Mobile phone ownership has increased massively — roughly 85% of all Indians now own a mobile phone.

3) Technology and connectivity have increased development for different groups of people. For example:

- Some people have been able to start their own small businesses making them wealthier because they can now make or receive payments online and don't need to travel long distances to find banks.

- Cities such as Hyderabad and Bangalore have developed into international centres for research and development with companies such as Google™ locating there. Many Indians have become very successful software developers and have high-ranking roles in these companies.

- Increasing connectivity through better technology means people can access services even in very remote locations. For example, the government biometric project uses scans of people's fingertips and irises to identify people — this is used e.g. to distribute food rations to the people entitled to them.

Development — India

Rapid Development has had Both Positive Impacts...

Economic
- More companies mean a <u>greater income</u> from <u>tax</u> for the Indian government. This means that there is more money available to spend on improving people's <u>quality of life</u>.
- There are <u>more jobs</u> available and between 2011 and 2014 India's daily <u>wages increased</u> by about 18%. TNCs are a large source of <u>employment</u> — some TNCs employ <u>tens of thousands of people</u>.

Environmental
<u>Increased income</u> from economic development means people can <u>afford</u> to <u>protect</u> the <u>environment</u>. For example, since 1990 India's <u>forest cover</u> has <u>stopped decreasing</u> and <u>started to grow</u>.

Social
- People have <u>more money</u> to <u>improve</u> their <u>life</u>, e.g. access to <u>clean water</u> and <u>medical care</u> when needed.
- Some TNCs run programs to <u>help development</u> in India. For example, companies might help <u>local people</u> in <u>rural villages</u> to become <u>entrepreneurs</u> by providing <u>products</u> for them to <u>sell</u>.

...and Negative Impacts

Social
- <u>Housing</u> and <u>infrastructure</u> can't be built fast enough to keep up with demand — almost a quarter of the <u>urban</u> population live in <u>slums</u>.
- Some <u>jobs</u> in <u>industry</u>, e.g. coal mining, can be <u>dangerous</u> or include <u>poor conditions</u>, which can <u>reduce</u> workers' <u>quality of life</u>.
- Some TNCs have been accused of <u>exploiting</u> workers — people may be forced to work in <u>poor conditions</u>, for <u>long hours</u> and <u>little pay</u>.

Economic
- There is a '<u>brain drain</u>' on rural areas, as <u>educated</u> people move to cities to find <u>work</u>.
- Some <u>profits</u> from TNCs <u>leave India</u>, e.g. many TNCs are based in Europe.
- TNCs may <u>move</u> around India to take <u>advantage</u> of local <u>government incentives</u>. Some companies have been accused of closing factories in <u>certain areas</u> once local <u>tax breaks</u> ended.

Environmental
- India's <u>energy consumption</u> has <u>increased</u> with economic development. Burning <u>fossil fuels</u> releases lots of <u>pollution</u> and <u>greenhouse gases</u>. The <u>10 most polluted cities</u> in the world are in India.
- TNCs can cause <u>environmental problems</u>, e.g. <u>mercury</u>-contaminated glass from a factory in <u>Kodaikanal</u> ended up in a <u>waste dump</u> instead of being <u>safely</u> disposed of.
- <u>Rapid urban growth</u> leads to <u>land</u> and <u>water pollution</u> — lack of <u>infrastructure</u> means that about <u>70%</u> of India's sewage flows <u>untreated</u> into <u>rivers</u>.

The Government is Trying to Improve People's Quality of Life

1) The Indian <u>government</u> wants India to be seen <u>globally</u> as an <u>important</u> country — it's trying to improve India's <u>image</u> by tackling some of the <u>problems</u> caused by <u>rapid development</u>. Some of the <u>management</u> strategies to increase people's <u>quality of life include</u>:
- A <u>large scale solar park</u> scheme (via a World Bank loan) which aims to <u>increase</u> the number of people connected to the <u>national electrical grid</u> and increase <u>economic growth</u> by providing <u>more power</u>. Solar power is also reducing India's reliance on <u>coal-fired power stations</u>, improving <u>air quality</u>.
- <u>Smart cities</u> with <u>affordable</u>, <u>energy-efficient housing</u> and good <u>infrastructure</u> are being built to relieve pressure on existing cities and enable <u>sustainable urban</u> and <u>economic growth</u> in the future.
2) <u>People</u> in India have also been <u>managing</u> the impacts of development to improve <u>quality of life</u>, for example:
- People in Payvihir, Maharashtra, have <u>reforested</u> degraded land near the village, allowing them to grow <u>organic produce</u>. The villagers <u>sell</u> their produce to the <u>increasing</u> number of <u>middle-class</u> people (p.94) in Mumbai. <u>Profits</u> are used to improve <u>health</u>, <u>education</u> and <u>sanitation facilities</u> in the village.

Ohdia — I can't think of a decent gag for these pages...

You might have studied development in a different emerging or developing country — there are a lot to choose from. That's fine, just make sure you have enough information to cover all of the key points on these pages. Don't hold back.

Revision Summary

Hurrah, another section bites the dust. Hopefully you've now developed a good understanding of global development — luckily I've got a big stack of revision summary questions so you can be sure. All the answers are in the section you've just revised, so if you're struggling for an answer, head back to the page and learn it again. Once you've got all of them right, you can head onwards for some lovely resource management.

Measuring Development (p.87) ☑

1) Other than economic, give two ways of defining of development.
2) What is food security?
3) What's the difference between GDP and GDP per capita?
4) What is the HDI?
5) Give one measure of political corruption.

Patterns, Causes and Effects of Uneven Development (p.88-90) ☑

6) In which continents are the most developed countries?
7) Explain one physical factor that can affect how developed a country is.
8) Outline two economic factors that can affect how developed a country is.
9) Give one example of uneven development in the UK.
10) Briefly outline two factors that have led to uneven development in the UK.
11) Explain three ways that uneven development affects people's quality of life.

Increasing Development (p.91) ☑

12) What are inter-governmental agreements?
13) How does international aid reduce uneven development?
14) Explain what is meant by a top-down approach to development.
15) Explain what is meant by a bottom-up approach to development.
16) Give one advantage and one limitation of top-down approaches.
17) Give one advantage of bottom-up development approaches.

Development — Case Study (p.92-95) ☑

Answer these questions for an emerging or developing country you have studied:
18) Give one example of the cultural importance of the country.
19) Give two differences between the core and periphery.
20) How has the balance between primary, secondary, tertiary and quaternary industry changed?
21) Give the key features of the country's involvement in international trade.
22) Outline how the level of private investment has changed.
23) Explain how development has changed the country's population structure.
24) Give three social changes caused by development.
25) Explain two ways that the country's geopolitical relationships are affecting development.
26) Describe how changes in technology are supporting development.
27) Give an example of how development has had an impact on the country's environment.
28) Give an example of a strategy the government is using to improve quality of life.

Natural Resources

Natural resources are pretty darn important, so be resourceful yourself and read all about them...

Natural Resources can be Classified in Four Ways

A natural resource is any part of the environment that people use to meet their needs.
Natural resources can be classified as:

1) Biotic — Living things, e.g. fish or people.
2) Abiotic — Non-living things, e.g. metals or rock.
3) Renewable — Resources which can be replenished in a short timescale, e.g. water or timber (wood).
4) Non-Renewable — Resources that can't be replenished quickly as they take millions of years to form. This means that they can run out, e.g. fossil fuels.

People Exploit the Environment for Food, Water and Energy

1) Fossil Fuels — Coal is removed from the ground by mining at the surface and in deep shafts. Extracting oil and gas involves drilling into underground reserves. It can be done inland (onshore) and at sea (offshore).
2) Fishing — Commercial fishing methods include trawling (towing nets behind boats) and dredging (dragging a metal frame along the seabed to harvest shellfish). Fish farms breed fish in contained spaces.
3) Farming — Farming can be arable (growing crops), pastoral (raising animals) or mixed (both). Industrial farming is increasingly done by machines, e.g. tractors and combine harvesters, rather than people.
4) Deforestation — Trees are chopped down for timber and so that they can be burnt as fuel. They are also removed to make way for power stations, e.g. hydro-electric power (HEP), or to clear land for farming.
5) Water — Water can be extracted directly from rivers, from underground stores (aquifers) or from reservoirs created by dams. Reservoirs provide reliable sources of water which can be transferred from areas of water surplus (an excess of water) to areas with shortages using canals and pipes.

Resource Extraction has Big Impacts on the Environment

Water and Air Quality

1) Fossil Fuels — Fossil fuels release greenhouse gases (p.46) into the atmosphere when they're burned. Waste from mines, e.g. mercury and lead, can pollute groundwater, drinking water and air.
2) Fishing — Oil and petrol can spill from fishing vessels into the sea, causing water pollution.
3) Farming — Artificial fertilisers and pesticides are applied to crops, which can harm or kill organisms if they enter water courses (e.g. rivers).
4) Deforestation — Trees remove CO_2 from the atmosphere, and burning vegetation to clear forest releases CO_2. So deforestation means more CO_2 in the atmosphere, which adds to global warming.
5) Water — Water transfers need lots of energy to pump water over long distances if there isn't a natural downhill route. This may require burning fossil fuels for energy (see above).

Biodiversity

1) Fishing — Some fish species (e.g. cod) are being over-fished, which in turn can reduce the number of other species in the ecosystem.
2) Farming — Removing hedgerows reduces biodiversity in plant and animal species that live in them.
3) Deforestation — Around 70% of all land-based plant and animal species live in forests. Deforestation causes habitats to be lost and species may die out.
4) Water — Dams act as a barrier to species' movements, e.g. salmon that migrate upstream to lay their eggs.

Soil Erosion

1) Farming — The increased use of heavy machinery, e.g. in planting and harvesting, can cause soil erosion.
2) Deforestation — Removing trees exposes the soil and makes it easier for water or wind to erode.

What is a wind turbine's favourite kind of music..?

They're huge metal fans. Learning this lot now will help you breeze through the rest of the topic. Back to the top...

UK Distribution of Resources

The UK may be small but don't let that fool you into thinking there's not much here...

The UK's Natural Resources Include Fertile Soils, Fossil Fuels and Water

A variety of different natural resources are found in the UK:

1) **Soil and Agriculture** — Agriculture in the UK includes arable farming, cattle farming (for milk and beef), hill sheep farming and mixed farming. The kind of agriculture practiced in an area depends on soil type and fertility, climate and terrain, e.g. crops can't grow well in poor soil, with cold and wet conditions.

2) **Forestry** — Timber is one of the main products from forests. The wood is used for building and for products such as furniture and paper. The main type of trees used for timber are conifers because they can cope with wet and cold weather, and they grow very quickly.

3) **Fossil Fuels** — The UK has reserves of coal, oil and gas, which have formed underneath layers of sedimentary rock over millions of years. They're burnt in power stations to generate energy. However, only a very small amount of coal is now mined in the UK.

4) **Water** — Water is used directly by industry (e.g. for cooling in power stations) and in homes (e.g. for washing), but it's also used for generating hydro-electric power (see p.102).

5) **Rocks and Minerals** — Rocks like limestone, slate and granite are important materials for building. Rocks and minerals are dug out of the ground in quarries.

Natural Resources are Unevenly Distributed Across the UK

The map below shows how some natural resources are distributed across the UK.

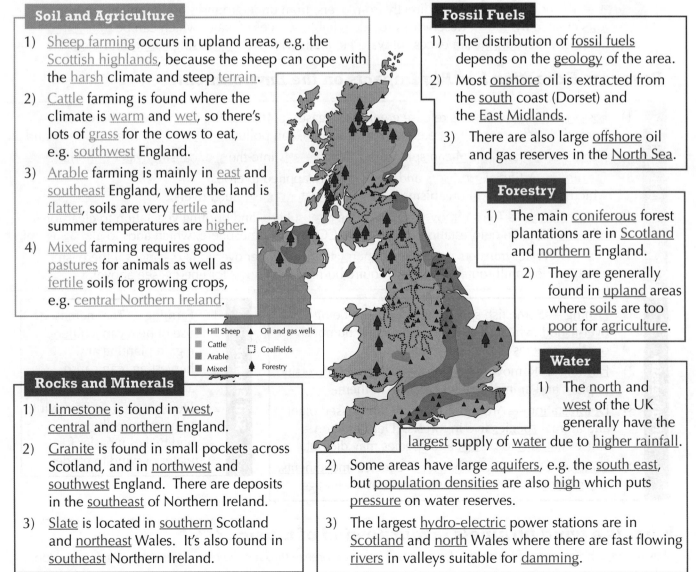

Soil and Agriculture

1) Sheep farming occurs in upland areas, e.g. the Scottish highlands, because the sheep can cope with the harsh climate and steep terrain.

2) Cattle farming is found where the climate is warm and wet, so there's lots of grass for the cows to eat, e.g. southwest England.

3) Arable farming is mainly in east and southeast England, where the land is flatter, soils are very fertile and summer temperatures are higher.

4) Mixed farming requires good pastures for animals as well as fertile soils for growing crops, e.g. central Northern Ireland.

Fossil Fuels

1) The distribution of fossil fuels depends on the geology of the area.

2) Most onshore oil is extracted from the south coast (Dorset) and the East Midlands.

3) There are also large offshore oil and gas reserves in the North Sea.

Forestry

1) The main coniferous forest plantations are in Scotland and northern England.

2) They are generally found in upland areas where soils are too poor for agriculture.

Map key:
- Hill Sheep
- Cattle
- Arable
- Mixed
- ▲ Oil and gas wells
- ▢ Coalfields
- ♠ Forestry

Rocks and Minerals

1) Limestone is found in west, central and northern England.

2) Granite is found in small pockets across Scotland, and in northwest and southwest England. There are deposits in the southeast of Northern Ireland.

3) Slate is located in southern Scotland and northeast Wales. It's also found in southeast Northern Ireland.

Water

1) The north and west of the UK generally have the largest supply of water due to higher rainfall.

2) Some areas have large aquifers, e.g. the south east, but population densities are also high which puts pressure on water reserves.

3) The largest hydro-electric power stations are in Scotland and north Wales where there are fast flowing rivers in valleys suitable for damming.

Global Distribution & Consumption of Resources

There are huge <u>variations</u> in <u>where</u> resources are found in the world, and which countries <u>consume</u> the most.

Global Distributions of Resources Vary

<u>Resources</u> are located <u>unevenly</u> across the world, and there are <u>reasons</u> why:

1) Soil and Agriculture — <u>South</u> and <u>East Asia</u>, <u>North America</u> and <u>South America</u> produce the most <u>food</u> globally. These areas receive significant amounts of <u>rain</u> and <u>sunlight</u> which are <u>ideal conditions</u> for <u>agriculture</u>. The large amounts of <u>vegetation</u> and the <u>warm</u>, <u>wet</u> climate in <u>tropical</u> countries result in lots of <u>decomposition</u> which makes the soils <u>very fertile</u> and the crop yields <u>high</u>.

2) Forestry — <u>Logging</u> for <u>timber</u> takes places in the <u>boreal</u> (coniferous) forests of <u>Canada</u>, northern <u>Europe</u> and <u>Russia</u> as well as the <u>tropical</u> forests of <u>South America</u>, west <u>Africa</u> and southeast <u>Asia</u> (see p.57 for the global distribution of forests).

3) Fossil Fuels — <u>Saudi Arabia</u>, <u>Russia</u> and the <u>USA</u> are the world's biggest producers of <u>oil</u>. <u>Russia</u> and the <u>USA</u> also produce the most <u>gas</u>. <u>China</u> produces the most <u>coal</u>. These countries have large fossil fuel <u>reserves</u> and the necessary <u>equipment</u> and <u>technology</u> to <u>extract</u> it.

4) Water — <u>North America</u>, <u>South America</u> and <u>Northern Europe</u> have the largest global <u>water</u> resources. This is because they receive <u>significant</u> amounts of <u>rain</u>, and also have the <u>infrastructure</u> to <u>capture</u>, <u>store</u> and <u>distribute</u> it.

5) Rocks and Minerals — The highest concentrations of <u>minerals</u> are found in western America, southern Africa and central Asia. The <u>unique geological conditions</u> of these areas has led to the formation of specific minerals, e.g. <u>gold</u> in <u>south Africa</u> and <u>copper</u> down the west coast of <u>South America</u>. Countries must also have the <u>infrastructure</u> to <u>exploit</u> their rock and mineral resources.

Global Energy Consumption is Unevenly Distributed

1) This map shows global <u>energy consumption per person</u> in 2014.

2) <u>Energy consumption</u> is strongly linked to <u>development</u>:

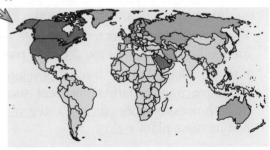

- <u>Developed</u> countries, e.g. Australia and USA, consume <u>lots of energy</u> because people can <u>afford</u> to. Most people have <u>access</u> to <u>electricity</u>, <u>heating</u>, and <u>energy-intensive devices</u> like cars.

- <u>Developing</u> countries, e.g. Chad and Mongolia, consume <u>less energy</u> as they are <u>less able</u> to afford it. Less energy is <u>available</u> and lifestyles are <u>less dependent</u> on high energy consumption.

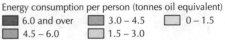

Energy consumption per person (tonnes oil equivalent)

| ■ 6.0 and over | ■ 3.0 – 4.5 | □ 0 – 1.5 |
| ■ 4.5 – 6.0 | ■ 1.5 – 3.0 | |

3) Some regions rely on <u>traditional fuel sources</u>. For example, in <u>sub-Saharan Africa</u>, energy networks are <u>poorly connected</u>, so people rely on <u>biomass</u> like wood for energy. There's <u>little development</u>, so countries <u>can't</u> afford to exploit their <u>energy reserves</u> or improve existing <u>infrastructure</u>.

4) <u>Industrial activities</u> require large amounts of energy, e.g. to <u>power machinery</u> or for <u>transport</u>:

- <u>Manufacturing</u> industries in <u>developed</u> and <u>emerging</u> countries use <u>huge amounts</u> of energy.

- <u>Developing</u> countries have more <u>primary industry</u> (e.g. agriculture), which uses <u>very little</u> energy.

Cake o'clock — the source of my uneven energy consumption...

Well that was a brief dash through the word's natural resources — make sure you learn the general patterns.

1) Explain two factors which affect global energy consumption patterns. [4]

Global Distribution & Consumption of Resources

Pack your emergency rations — we're off to find out how water and food consumption vary around the world.

Global Water Use Varies Significantly

1) This map shows global water consumption per person.

2) North America and central Asia use the most water.

3) Water consumption depends on:

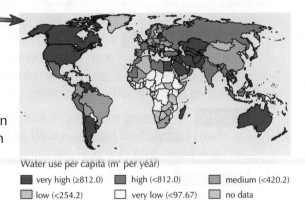

Water use per capita (m³ per year)

- very high (≥812.0)
- high (<812.0)
- medium (<420.2)
- low (<254.2)
- very low (<97.67)
- no data

- Climate — Countries with low rainfall may not have much water available, e.g. Algeria.

- Development — As people's wealth increases, they can afford flushing toilets, showers, dishwashers etc. which increases water use. Wealthy countries are able to invest in schemes to increase water supply if water availability is low, e.g. Australia relies heavily on desalination (removing salt from seawater).

- Industrial activities — Countries with lots of farming, mining and industry, e.g. USA and Argentina, use lots of water because these activities are very water intensive. More traditional societies use less water, e.g. Nomadic herders in Mongolia don't need much water.

Food Consumption also Varies Across the World

The amount of food that countries produce varies. The map on the right shows the production of cereals by country from 2012 to 2014. The production of other food follows a similar pattern.

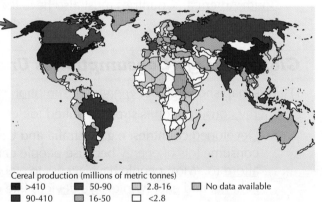

1) East Asia and North America produce a lot of food.

2) Central America and Africa only produce small amounts of food.

Food production is affected by climate — countries that are too hot, too cold or too dry can't produce much food.

It is also affected by the level of development, e.g. the use of mechanised farm equipment (such as tractors) can make processes more efficient and genetic engineering can increase plant yields.

Cereal production (millions of metric tonnes)
- >410
- 90-410
- 50-90
- 16-50
- 2.8-16
- <2.8
- No data available

Daily calorie (kcal) intake per person (2011-2013)
- Over 3539
- 3358 to 3539
- 3266 to 3358
- 3095 to 3266
- 2546 to 3095
- Less than 2546
- No data available

The amount of food people eat also varies across the world. The map on the left shows the daily calorie intake of people in different countries.

1) More developed areas like North America and Europe eat a lot. They can afford to import a large variety of foods and many people have a high income so can buy more food.

2) Less developed areas like Africa, Central America and parts of Asia consume less food per person as people can't afford as much and less food may be available.

3) China and other newly industrialised countries are consuming more as their wealth increases.

All of this reading is building my appetite...

...for even more knowledge. Remember that there are several reasons for variations in resource consumption across the world. Try to think about how levels of development could relate to other factors, e.g. lifestyles, the availability of resources and industrial activities — and what this means for the consumption of energy, water and food.

Meeting Energy Demand

With more than 7.5 billion people in the world, supplying everyone with energy is no walk in the park...

The Global Demand for Energy is Increasing

There are three main reasons why global demand for energy has increased over the last 100 years.

1) Population is increasing — in 2017 the world population was just over 7.5 billion and it's projected to grow to over 9 billion in 2040 — more people means more energy is needed.

2) Economic development — increased wealth in poorer countries means people are buying more things. A lot of these things use energy, e.g. cars, fridges and televisions.

3) Technological advances — more new devices are being created that need energy, e.g. computers and mobile phones. As they become more popular, more energy is needed.

> As energy demands have increased, technological advances in energy generation have increased supply. Now more energy is generated and much less is lost in the process.

There are Pros and Cons to Using Non-Renewable Resources

Energy resources can be renewable or non-renewable (see p.97).
Non-renewable energy resources include fossil fuels and uranium:

1) Fossil fuels include coal, oil and gas. They formed millions of years ago from the remains of dead organisms. They can be extracted from the ground and seabed. Coal is mined, while oil and gas are both extracted via drilling into underground reserves (p.97).

2) Uranium is used to produce nuclear energy — when uranium atoms split lots of heat is produced, which is used to boil water. The steam turns a turbine, generating electricity. Uranium is mined, like coal, from both open pit and underground mines.

Non-renewable energy resources can have positive and negative impacts on people and the environment:

	Positive Impacts	Negative Impacts
People	• Countries with fuel reserves save money by reducing energy imports and can make money from exporting energy. This creates enormous industries which employ millions of people. • Fossil fuels have been used to generate energy for a long time, so they are methods which are proven to work.	• Fossil fuels are a finite resource meaning that they will run out eventually. Relying too heavily on them could lead to energy shortages in the future. • Mining can be very dangerous for workers due to the risks of flooding and cave-ins.
Environment	• Less uranium than fossil fuels is needed to generate the same amount of energy, so less needs to be mined. • Gas is less polluting than other fossil fuels — it releases only 50% of the CO_2 that coal does.	• Mining and drilling remove soil and vegetation. This destroys habitats and reduces biodiversity. • Burning fossil fuels releases CO_2 and other greenhouse gases, causing global warming. • Nuclear waste can be extremely damaging to the environment (see example below).

Example	There are advantages and disadvantages to producing and developing nuclear power: 1) Advantages — nuclear power stations can run almost constantly, so energy supply is consistent. Nuclear energy generation doesn't release CO_2, so doesn't contribute to global warming. 2) Disadvantages — used nuclear fuel is very radioactive and toxic, and can pollute the environment if it is not properly contained. Nuclear power stations are usually very large — many people think they are an eyesore. People also think they are unsafe.

Underground mines — where the alternative moles go to party...

Energy resources is a tricky topic, so take your time and get really comfortable with this page before turning over.

Meeting Energy Demand

Using Renewable Resources also has both Positive and Negative Impacts

There are <u>three</u> main ways of generating <u>renewable</u> energy:

1) <u>Wind turbines</u> use the energy of the <u>wind</u> to <u>generate electricity</u>, either <u>on land</u> or <u>out at sea</u>. The wind turns their blades, which generates power. Turbines are often built in <u>large windfarms</u>.

2) <u>Solar power</u> uses energy from the Sun to <u>heat water</u> and <u>solar cookers</u>. <u>Electricity</u> can also be generated using <u>photovoltaic cells</u> on the roofs of buildings or in large solar farms.

3) <u>Hydro-electric power</u> (HEP) uses the energy of <u>falling water</u>. Water is <u>trapped</u> by a <u>dam</u> and allowed to <u>fall</u> through tunnels, where the <u>pressure</u> of the falling water turns turbines to generate <u>electricity</u>.

They can all have both <u>positive</u> and <u>negative</u> impacts on <u>people</u> and the <u>environment</u>:

	Positive Impacts	Negative Impacts
People	• Unlike <u>fossil fuels</u>, <u>renewable</u> resources like the <u>wind</u> or the <u>Sun</u> will never <u>run out</u>. • <u>Jobs</u> are being created in <u>industries</u> developing renewable energy resources. <u>Countries</u> can make <u>money</u> from <u>exporting</u> renewable energy.	• Renewable energy can be very <u>expensive</u> to <u>generate</u> and <u>consume</u> because the technology is still being <u>developed</u>. • The <u>wind</u> and the <u>Sun</u> are unreliable energy sources. Without the right conditions, energy can't be generated <u>consistently</u>.
Environment	• <u>Renewable</u> energy resources do not release <u>CO$_2$</u> or other greenhouse gases. • <u>Renewable</u> energy resources require much <u>less water</u> to run than non-renewables, so they are <u>less likely</u> to contribute to <u>water shortages</u>.	• Some <u>solar panels</u> are made with <u>toxic chemicals</u> like <u>cadmium</u> which can escape into the environment when they are being mined. • <u>Habitats</u> can be <u>destroyed</u> to make <u>space</u> for <u>solar farms</u>, or <u>flooded</u> when rivers are dammed for <u>HEP</u>.

Example

Producing and developing <u>wind power</u> has <u>advantages</u> and <u>disadvantages</u>:

1) <u>Advantages</u> — wind <u>turbines</u> can be installed by <u>individuals</u> or local <u>communities</u>, which benefits the local <u>economy</u>. <u>Operating</u> costs are very <u>low</u> and wind power is very <u>energy efficient</u> — it <u>outputs</u> significantly <u>more</u> energy than was used to <u>create</u> the turbines.

2) <u>Disadvantages</u> — <u>wind farms</u> produce a <u>constant humming noise</u> which causes <u>noise pollution</u> for people nearby. The <u>spinning blades</u> on <u>wind turbines</u> can <u>kill</u> or <u>injure birds</u> and <u>bats</u>.

Technology can help Resolve Energy Shortages

1) <u>Growing</u> energy <u>demands</u> are putting <u>pressure</u> on <u>existing</u> conventional fossil fuel reserves, e.g. oil and gas.

2) <u>New technologies</u> are being developed to help <u>reach</u> reserves that were previously <u>unexploited</u> because they were <u>too hard</u> to get to.

3) <u>Fracking</u> is a way of <u>extracting</u> natural gas that is <u>trapped</u> in <u>shale rock</u> underground:
   • <u>Liquid</u> is <u>pumped</u> into the shale rock at <u>high pressure</u>.
   • This causes the rock to <u>crack</u> (fracture), releasing the <u>gas</u>, which is collected as it comes out of the well.

4) <u>Fracking</u> could help <u>meet</u> energy <u>demands</u> when conventional fossil fuel reserves are <u>depleted</u>.

5) However, it can have <u>negative</u> impacts on the <u>environment</u>, e.g:
   • Shale gas releases <u>CO$_2$</u> when it is burned, which causes <u>global warming</u> and <u>climate change</u>.
   • <u>Chemicals</u> used in the fracking liquid may <u>pollute</u> groundwater, drinking water and air.
   • It uses <u>lots</u> of <u>water</u>, which is a <u>limited</u> resource.

Extraction Point

Water Table

Fractures

Shale

EXAM QUESTION

Revising energy resources is a fracking good time...

1) *Explain two disadvantages of using renewable energy resources.* [4]

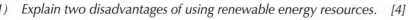

Topic 6 — Resource Management

The Energy Mix

Now you know the ins and outs of energy resources, it's time to find out how countries mix and match them...

The Energy Mix Describes the Sources of Energy a Country Uses

1) Many countries can't supply all of their energy needs from one source. Others may not want to in case something goes wrong with the one source they use, e.g. it becomes more expensive.

2) So, countries use a variety of energy sources instead. The energy mix of a country is the proportion of energy that it gets from different sources. It's usually shown as percentages.

The UK has Several Sources in its Energy Mix

The pie chart below shows the UK's energy mix in 2015. The UK relies on fossil fuels (coal, oil and gas) for most of its energy mix, but uses some nuclear and renewable energy sources too.

1) Nearly 70% of the UK's energy supply is provided by oil and gas.

2) The use of coal is still relatively high, but has fallen due to the closure of mines and the move to less polluting energy sources.

3) The UK doesn't produce enough oil, coal or gas to meet its needs — it imports the rest from other countries. This makes it dependent on international prices.

4) The use of nuclear power has declined since the 1990s but the government are keen to develop new nuclear power stations.

5) Renewable resources form a fairly small proportion of the energy mix, but their use is gradually increasing as the government aims for a more sustainable energy supply (see next page).

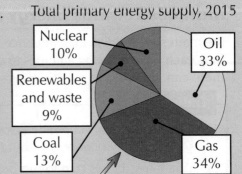

Total primary energy supply, 2015

Nuclear 10%
Renewables and waste 9%
Coal 13%
Oil 33%
Gas 34%

Electricity trade (buying electricity from other countries) made up 1% of the UK's energy mix in 2015, but it's not shown in this pie chart.

The Energy Mix of a Country Depends on lots of Different Things

1) POPULATION — A country with a large and rapidly growing population needs to generate lots of energy as quickly as possible. So fossil fuel sources have often been more attractive than renewable or nuclear because it was cheaper and relatively quick to build the power stations.

> E.g. in 2016, China got 65% of its energy from coal and 9% from renewable sources. However, China is now choosing to invest in large-scale wind and solar farms.

2) WEALTH — Developed nations have high energy consumption and lots of people can afford cars, which rely on oil. Nuclear plants and large-scale wind and solar farms are relatively expensive to build, but changes in public opinion (p.104) are causing governments in developed countries to consider renewable and nuclear energy sources. Developing and emerging countries can't always afford energy infrastructure (e.g. a power grid) and are less dependent on oil — local communities may use biofuels or invest in small-scale solar or wind energy.

The cost of installing wind and solar farms is falling so some countries are investing in these sources instead of fossil fuels.

> E.g. in 2016, France got over 40% of its energy from nuclear power and only 4% from coal, whereas Ethiopia got 91% of its energy from biofuels and waste.

3) AVAILABILITY — Some countries have much greater access to particular sources than others, which relates to their unique geology and their climate.

> E.g. in 2016, the US got 73% of its energy from oil and gas, because it has large oil reserves and has invested heavily in developing fracking (see previous page).

The energy mix is quite exciting but it's not my favourite mix...

...that's pick-n-mix. But you should still make sure you know about the UK's energy mix before you turn the page.

Sustainable Energy Management

Energy resources must meet our current needs and be <u>sustainably managed</u> for the <u>future</u> too.

Sustainable Energy means Future Generations can Meet their Energy Needs

1) <u>Sustainable energy</u> provides energy <u>today</u> without preventing <u>future generations</u> from <u>meeting their energy needs</u>.

2) It's important because the <u>demand</u> for <u>energy</u> is <u>increasing</u> (see p.101) but <u>non-renewable</u> energy resources (such as coal, oil and gas) are <u>running out</u>.

3) Humans need to find <u>new renewable energy sources</u> and use energy <u>more efficiently</u> so that future generations can meet their energy needs.

4) Global concern about the <u>impact</u> that burning <u>fossil fuels</u> has on <u>climate change</u> has led to <u>international agreements</u> to reduce <u>emissions</u> and increase the use of <u>renewable</u> resources.

'Carbon footprints' are a useful way of calculating the amount of greenhouse gases that are produced by a particular activity.

Attitudes Towards Energy Resources Vary between Groups

A stakeholder is anyone with an interest in the issue.

The main stakeholders that influence the energy mix are <u>individuals</u>, <u>organisations</u>, and <u>governments</u>. They each have differing attitudes towards the <u>exploitation</u> and <u>consumption</u> of energy resources. These can also <u>change over time</u>, as societies <u>move</u> from non-renewable to renewable energy resources.

Individuals

1) Many individuals currently favour <u>non-renewable resources</u>, as they provide a <u>cheap</u> and <u>secure</u> supply of energy — but they might not want them being <u>extracted</u> near their <u>homes</u>.

2) When <u>fossil fuels</u> start to <u>run out</u>, the risk of energy <u>shortages</u> will increase unless there has been <u>investment</u> in <u>alternative</u> energy sources. But this can increase the <u>price</u> of energy, so individuals may oppose these developments at first.

3) As <u>environmental awareness</u> increases, some individuals are beginning to favour <u>renewable</u> sources that are more <u>sustainable</u> and aren't as polluting as fossil fuels. However some individuals may <u>oppose</u> new developments, e.g. wind farms in their local area.

Organisations

1) Big <u>TNCs</u> (transnational corporations), e.g. Shell, are involved in <u>extracting</u> and <u>refining</u> fossil fuels and <u>invest</u> a lot of money into the <u>energy sector</u>.

2) Controlling <u>oil reserves</u> gives TNCs lots of <u>power</u> and <u>wealth</u>, which means they may <u>lose</u> money if there is a shift towards using more <u>renewable</u> energy sources.

3) Sustainable energy needs <u>more investment</u> than fossil fuels, increasing the cost of energy — this means other organisations may also <u>favour</u> non-renewable resources.

4) <u>Environmental organisations</u>, e.g. Greenpeace, campaign <u>against</u> fossil fuel <u>extraction</u> and <u>use</u>, because of its negative environmental <u>impacts</u>, and <u>encourage</u> people to use more <u>sustainable</u> energy resources.

Governments

1) Governments want <u>cheap</u>, <u>reliable</u> energy supplies, so they're likely to support the <u>exploitation</u> and <u>use</u> of <u>fossil fuels</u>. However, governments also want to <u>secure</u> energy supplies in the <u>long term</u>, so may be looking into <u>developing</u> nuclear and renewable energy resources for the <u>future</u>.

2) In <u>developed countries</u>, governments are starting to come <u>under pressure</u> from some <u>consumers</u> to <u>protect the environment</u> — this means they want to start using more <u>sustainable energy</u>.

3) Fossil fuels have helped countries to <u>develop</u> and the <u>governments</u> of many <u>emerging</u> countries have <u>concerns</u> about whether sustainable energy sources will <u>continue</u> to help them <u>develop</u>.

Wind energy is a popular sustainable resource — it's got lots of fans...

Make sure you know why the main stakeholders' attitudes towards energy resources vary and why they might change over time — it could be worth some juicy marks in the exam. Then summon a final energy burst for some examples...

Energy Management — Sweden & India

Many countries are trying to switch up their energy resources to become more <u>sustainable</u>. Countries at all levels of development are using more <u>renewable</u> energy sources (or at least thinking about it)...

Sweden is Committed to Sustainable Energy Management

<u>Sweden</u> is a developed country and is one of the most <u>committed</u> countries in the world when it comes to <u>sustainable</u> energy management.

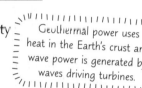

1) <u>Sweden</u> is aiming to get <u>100%</u> of its <u>electricity</u> from <u>renewable</u> energy resources by <u>2040</u>.

2) In 2015, about <u>53%</u> of its energy came from <u>renewable</u> energy resources — mainly <u>hydro-electric power</u> (HEP).

3) The government has set up a policy of '<u>green electricity certification</u>' — a <u>qualification</u> awarded to energy <u>suppliers</u> if their electricity comes from renewable resources such as wind, solar, geothermal or wave power. Companies which <u>sell</u> electricity to customers <u>must</u> buy a <u>proportion</u> of it from green-certified sources.

Geothermal power uses heat in the Earth's crust and wave power is generated by waves driving turbines.

4) Lots of Swedish houses and buildings are '<u>passive</u>' — they don't have any <u>heating</u> at all. Instead they trap the <u>body heat</u> of the people in them by being very well <u>insulated</u> — thick <u>walls</u> and <u>windows</u> make sure that no heat can <u>escape</u> from anywhere in the building. This means that they stay <u>warm</u> without needing to use <u>energy</u> for <u>heating</u>.

5) In 2018 the government increased the <u>road tax</u> paid on <u>petrol</u> or <u>diesel</u> cars, whilst paying a bonus to people who buy <u>electric cars</u>. This has led to more people using <u>electric cars</u>, which can be run on electricity generated using <u>renewable</u> energy resources.

India is an Emerging Country with Ambitious Energy Targets

The <u>2015 Paris Climate Agreement</u> was a <u>pledge</u> made by countries from across the world to <u>limit</u> global warming to <u>2 °C</u>. As part of this agreement, <u>India</u> have set some <u>ambitious targets</u> for using <u>sustainable energy</u>.

1) India is the <u>3rd largest consumer of energy</u> in the world, with increasing energy <u>demands</u> due to:
   - A rapidly growing population.
   - Increasing wealth in the population.
   - Growth of industry.

The increase in energy use means that India's use of fossil fuels will continue to grow.

2) Around <u>55%</u> of India's energy currently comes from <u>coal</u>, but the government has pledged to <u>double</u> the amount of energy that it generates from <u>non-fossil fuel</u> sources by <u>2030</u>. This would represent <u>40%</u> of its power. Most of this energy is to be gained from <u>solar</u> and <u>wind</u> power — India is currently the <u>4th</u> largest producer of <u>wind</u> power in the world.

3) The government has also introduced measures to reduce the use of <u>cars</u> in Indian cities, e.g. developing '<u>Smart Cities</u>' where everything is <u>closer</u> together could <u>reduce</u> fuel consumption for <u>transport</u>.

4) <u>Rural communities</u> that are <u>not connected</u> to the national energy <u>grid</u> (or have an <u>unreliable</u> connection) have set up their <u>own</u> renewable energy-generating projects — e.g. people from <u>Rampura</u> village in Uttar Pradesh built their own <u>solar power plant</u> with support from <u>charities</u>.

5) In the rural state of <u>Bihar</u>, there are power plants which <u>generate</u> electricity by processing <u>rice husks</u> (a <u>waste product</u> from producing rice for food). By 2015 there were <u>84</u> rice husk powered plants operating in Bihar, supplying <u>electricity</u> to around <u>200 000</u> people.

It's very important to set yourself goals and targets...

Challenge yourself to remember some of the statistics from these two examples to put into your exam answers. I once challenged myself to never run a marathon, and I'm proud to say that I'm still going strong. It's all about willpower...

Global Water Distribution

You only need to study <u>one</u> topic out of <u>energy</u> and <u>water</u>, so if you've studied energy resource management, you can skip over this section. If you're studying water, you're in the right place — get ready to dive in...

Fresh Water is Unevenly Distributed Around the World

1) Although the majority of the Earth's surface is covered in water, only about <u>3%</u> of this is <u>fresh water</u> — most of the Earth's water is <u>saline</u> (salty) water in the <u>seas</u> and <u>oceans</u>.

2) Some fresh water is stored as <u>surface water</u> in <u>lakes</u> and <u>rivers</u>. Some of it's stored <u>underground</u> as <u>groundwater</u>, e.g. in <u>aquifers</u> (rocks which hold water). Most of it is <u>frozen</u>, stored in <u>ice caps</u> and <u>glaciers</u>. A small proportion of fresh water is also stored in the <u>atmosphere</u> as <u>clouds</u> and <u>water vapour</u>.

3) The availability of fresh water <u>varies globally</u>, depending on <u>rainfall</u>, <u>evaporation</u>, and where there are water <u>sources</u>. Water availability also depends on whether there are <u>water treatment facilities</u> to make sure that water is <u>clean</u> and <u>safe</u> for <u>people</u> to use.

4) Some countries have a <u>lot</u> of available water, e.g. <u>Canada</u> has <u>high rainfall</u> and <u>low temperatures</u>, which limits rates of <u>evaporation</u>. Other countries have much <u>lower</u> availability of fresh water, e.g. <u>Egypt</u> has a very <u>dry</u> climate and <u>lacks</u> water <u>treatment</u> facilities.

Water resources per capita (m³ per year)

| ■ very high (≥21467) | ■ high (<21467) | ■ medium (<6921) |
| □ low (<2879) | □ very low (<1363) | ■ no data |

5) Water availability is not evenly distributed <u>within</u> countries either. E.g. overall, the <u>UK</u> has fairly <u>low</u> water availability, but this varies <u>locally</u> — some areas have much <u>higher</u> water availability (see p.108).

The Availability of Water Doesn't Always Match Demand

1) The <u>uneven distribution</u> of water availability means that some parts of the world have <u>more water</u> than is needed — this is known as a <u>water surplus</u>. In other areas, there is not <u>enough water</u> to meet everyone's needs — this is called a <u>water deficit</u>.

2) Water <u>deficits</u> generally happen in places with <u>low water availability</u> and <u>high demand</u> for water, e.g. <u>Spain</u> gets a water deficit in the <u>summer</u>, when it has <u>low rainfall</u> but needs a <u>lot</u> of water for <u>agriculture</u>.

3) Places which have <u>plenty of available water</u> and <u>low demand</u> for it tend to have a water <u>surplus</u>, e.g. <u>Canada</u> has a <u>small population</u> for its size and <u>plenty</u> of <u>available fresh water</u> — it has nearly <u>7%</u> of the world's renewable fresh <u>water resources</u> but only <u>0.5%</u> of the world's <u>population</u>.

Water Supply and Demand have Changed over the Past 50 Years

Since the <u>1960s</u>, the pattern of global water <u>availability</u> has <u>changed</u>, while <u>demand</u> for water has <u>increased</u> — water <u>consumption</u> has more than <u>doubled</u> since 1960. These changes have been <u>caused</u> by <u>various factors</u>:

Supply

1) <u>Over-abstraction</u> — <u>aquifers</u> and <u>groundwater</u> have been <u>depleted</u> because people have been using the water <u>faster</u> than it can be <u>replaced</u>.

2) <u>Pollution</u> — <u>chemicals</u> from <u>agriculture</u> and <u>industry</u> have polluted <u>lakes</u> and <u>rivers</u>, making the water <u>unsafe</u> to use.

3) <u>Climate change</u> is causing <u>rainfall</u> to become <u>less reliable</u> in some areas.

Demand

1) Rapid <u>population growth</u> means that the <u>number</u> of people using water has <u>increased</u>.

2) <u>Development</u> — the growth of <u>industry</u> has <u>increased demand</u> for water. Development has also led to more <u>farmers</u> using <u>irrigation</u> instead of relying on <u>rainfall</u>, which increases their water <u>consumption</u>. As people become wealthier, they tend to adopt a <u>lifestyle</u> that uses more water, e.g. using washing machines — this has <u>increased demand</u> for water.

Water lot of stuff to revise...

Well, it looks like a lot, but this page is just about how supply and demand for clean, fresh water aren't always in sync.

Global Water Consumption

Everyone needs water for things like drinking, cooking and washing (at least twice a year, anyway), but the <u>amount</u> of water that gets used and what it's used <u>for</u> depends a lot on <u>where</u> you are in the world.

How Much Water is Used, and What it's Used For, Varies Around the World

1) Water consumption varies a <u>lot</u> around the world — it's generally <u>highest</u> in places with <u>large populations</u>, e.g. <u>India</u> and eastern <u>China</u>.

2) Water is mainly used for <u>agriculture</u> (e.g. irrigating crops), <u>industry</u> (e.g. to cool machinery) and for <u>domestic</u> purposes (e.g. drinking and washing).

3) The <u>proportion</u> of water that countries use for agriculture, industry and domestic purposes also varies, especially between countries at <u>different levels</u> of <u>development</u> (p.88).

Developed Countries Use More Water for Domestic Purposes

Water withdrawals (%)
- Agricultural
- Industrial
- Domestic

UK

1) In general, <u>developed</u> countries use <u>more water</u> per person than <u>developing</u> and <u>emerging</u> countries.

2) Developed countries tend to use more water for <u>domestic</u> uses and <u>industry</u> than for <u>agriculture</u> — e.g. <u>71%</u> of the <u>UK's</u> water consumption is <u>domestic</u>.

3) Developed countries tend to have <u>better water infrastructure</u>, e.g. <u>pipes</u> bring clean water into people's <u>homes</u>. This means that water is <u>easily available</u> for most people.

4) Having <u>cheap</u> and <u>plentiful</u> access to water in the home means that people can use <u>appliances</u> like <u>washing machines</u> and <u>power showers</u> which use a <u>lot</u> of water. People don't have to <u>worry</u> about their water <u>supply</u>, so they are more likely to <u>waste</u> water than people in developing and emerging countries.

5) However, developed countries also have the potential to <u>reduce</u> their water consumption — they have the <u>resources</u> to <u>invest</u> in <u>technologies</u> for managing water <u>efficiently</u>, e.g. <u>smart</u> irrigation systems on <u>farms</u>.

Developing and Emerging Countries Use More Water for Agriculture

1) <u>Developing</u> and <u>emerging</u> countries have <u>lower</u> water consumption per person than <u>developed</u> countries.

2) Many people don't have <u>convenient</u> or <u>affordable</u> access to clean water (see next page), so they might be more <u>careful</u> not to <u>waste</u> water — e.g. people might <u>reuse</u> bathwater to <u>irrigate</u> crops.

<u>Developing</u> countries tend to use most of their water for <u>agriculture</u>, because farming is the basis of their economies — e.g. <u>89%</u> of <u>Tanzania's</u> water use is for agriculture. They have much less <u>industry</u> than <u>developed</u> countries, so there is less <u>demand</u> for water from the industrial sector.

Water withdrawn for agriculture as % of total water withdrawal

- ■ very high (≥87.82)
- ■ high (73.28–87.82)
- ■ medium (51.43–73.28)
- ■ low (10.21–51.43)
- □ very low (<10.21)
- ■ no data

- ■ Agricultural
- ■ Industrial
- ■ Domestic

Tanzania

Brazil

<u>Some emerging</u> countries have <u>growing industry</u>, so this makes up a <u>bigger proportion</u> of their water consumption, e.g. <u>17%</u> of <u>Brazil's</u> water use is for industry.

3) Many <u>developed</u> countries <u>import</u> agricultural and industrial goods that take a lot of water to <u>produce</u>, e.g. beef, cotton and <u>mobile phones</u>, from <u>developing</u> and <u>emerging</u> countries. This is called <u>virtual water importing</u> — it means that <u>developing</u> and <u>emerging</u> countries use a lot of water to <u>produce</u> things that are then <u>consumed</u> in <u>developed</u> countries.

Virtual water — when you almost have a drink...

A country's level of development has a big effect on its patterns of water consumption — make sure you're clear on the main differences and can suggest some reasons for them. That way things will go swimmingly in the exam...

Water Supply Problems

The UK may be famous for being <u>grey</u> and <u>wet</u>, but apparently the <u>rain</u> doesn't fall in the <u>right places</u>...

The Demand for Water Varies Across the UK

1) In the UK, the places with a <u>good supply</u> of water <u>aren't the same</u> as the places with the <u>highest demand</u>:

<u>UK average annual rainfall</u>

■ High
□ Low

<u>UK population density</u>

■ High
■ Medium
□ Low

- The <u>north</u> and <u>west</u> of the UK have <u>high rainfall</u>, which means there's a <u>good supply</u> of water.
- The <u>south east</u> and the <u>Midlands</u> have <u>high population densities</u>, which means there's a <u>high demand</u> for water.
- The <u>south east</u> and <u>Midlands</u> are areas of <u>water deficit</u> (there's a <u>greater demand</u> than <u>supply</u>).
- The <u>north</u> and <u>west</u> are areas of <u>water surplus</u> (there's a <u>greater supply</u> than <u>demand</u>).
- This <u>imbalance</u> between <u>supply</u> and <u>demand</u> can cause <u>water supply problems</u>.

2) There are also <u>seasonal imbalances</u> in water supply and demand — in the <u>winter</u>, rainfall is <u>high</u> and demand is <u>low</u>, while in the <u>summer</u> rainfall is <u>lower</u> and demand is <u>higher</u>.

3) These imbalances mean that <u>transporting</u> and <u>storing</u> water is important, to make sure water is available <u>when</u> and <u>where</u> it's needed:

- <u>Water</u> can be <u>transferred</u> from areas of <u>surplus</u> to areas of <u>deficit</u>, e.g. <u>Birmingham</u> (an area of <u>deficit</u>) is supplied with water from the <u>middle of Wales</u> (an area of <u>surplus</u>).
- Water from <u>winter rainfall</u> can be <u>stored</u> in reservoirs to be used in the summer.

Sharing is important...

4) However, the UK's water <u>infrastructure</u> is <u>ageing</u> — old <u>sewage</u> systems and <u>water pipes</u> are <u>struggling</u> to keep up with the higher <u>volumes</u> of water that need to be treated and transferred to <u>meet demand</u>. The infrastructure is also <u>inefficient</u> — in 2016-17, <u>3.1 billion litres</u> of clean water were estimated to have been <u>lost</u> every day through <u>leaky</u> pipes.

Emerging and Developing Countries also have Water Supply Problems

1) Many emerging and developing countries are unable to provide a <u>supply</u> of <u>high quality</u> (clean) water to the population because they don't have enough <u>water treatment facilities</u>.

- Many people have to <u>carry</u> water to their homes — in 2015, the UN estimated that <u>844 million</u> people did <u>not</u> have access to a safe water source within a <u>30 minute</u> round trip from their homes.
- Over <u>480 000 children</u> die every year from <u>diarrhoea</u>, often caused by drinking <u>contaminated</u> water.

Children carrying water in Haiti

2) In some emerging and developing countries there is also a <u>greater risk</u> of water courses becoming <u>polluted</u> than in developed countries because of the <u>lack of infrastructure</u> for treating <u>sewage</u> and <u>waste water</u>. <u>Laws</u> that protect the <u>environment</u> are often <u>less strict</u> than in developed countries, so industries like <u>mining</u> are more likely to pollute water courses. This <u>reduces</u> the available <u>supply</u> of clean, safe water.

3) Some emerging and developing countries are located in areas with <u>low annual rainfall</u> and a <u>high frequency</u> of <u>droughts</u>, which means there is very low water <u>availability</u> per person, e.g. countries like <u>Mali</u> and <u>Niger</u> in the dry <u>Sahel region</u> of North Africa. Many developing countries also lack the <u>technology</u> and <u>infrastructure</u> to <u>store</u> what rainfall they do receive, and to <u>move</u> water supplies from areas of higher <u>rainfall</u> to areas with higher <u>demand</u>.

EXAM QUESTION

The constant drip of revision is making me need a water transfer...

...but you need to know it — you might have to write about how imbalances cause water supply problems.

1) Suggest two reasons why developing or emerging countries might have water supply problems. [4]

Topic 6 — Resource Management

Exploiting Water Resources

This page has <u>attitude</u>. Well, attitudes about <u>using</u> water and <u>meeting demand</u> for water resources, anyway...

Different Stakeholders have Different Attitudes About Exploiting Water

Different <u>interest groups</u> have <u>different ideas</u> about how water resources should be <u>exploited</u> and <u>consumed</u>. These ideas <u>inform</u> the way that interest groups <u>use</u> water and the role they play in <u>managing</u> water:

Individuals

1) Individual people want to be able to get as much <u>clean</u>, <u>safe water</u> as they <u>need</u> — and to be able to get it <u>easily</u> and <u>cheaply</u>.

2) Different people have different <u>expectations</u> about <u>how much</u> water is <u>enough</u> — e.g. people in <u>developed</u> countries might expect to be able to water their <u>lawns</u> and run <u>washing machines</u> at <u>any time</u> of day, whereas in <u>developing</u> countries, people might think that using <u>treated water</u> for activities like <u>washing clothes</u> is a <u>waste of resources</u>.

> A stakeholder is someone who has an interest in something — usually because they will be affected by decisions that are made about it.

Organisations

1) <u>Charities</u> like <u>WaterAid</u> and <u>UNICEF</u> believe that everyone should be able to use safe, clean water. They carry out work in <u>developing</u> countries to increase people's <u>access</u> to clean water, e.g. installing <u>boreholes</u> and <u>toilets</u>. This <u>increases</u> water <u>consumption</u> but can also <u>reduce</u> the <u>contamination</u> of water sources.

2) Some <u>businesses</u> and <u>industries</u> think that it is acceptable to <u>exploit</u> water resources in an <u>unsustainable</u> way in order to make a <u>profit</u> — e.g. <u>commercial</u> farming of <u>asparagus</u> in <u>Peru</u> makes a lot of <u>money</u> but has led to the <u>depletion</u> of water sources in the area.

Governments

Governments have to <u>balance</u> the needs of <u>citizens</u> and <u>businesses</u>. They need to <u>avoid</u> water <u>shortages</u>, so they have to make sure that <u>industries</u> don't consume <u>too much</u> water — but they also want businesses to <u>stay</u> because they provide <u>jobs</u> and <u>taxes</u>, so they can't <u>restrict</u> water use too much.

Technology Could Help Resolve Shortages of Water Resources

Some <u>stakeholders</u> believe that the <u>best</u> way to <u>meet demand</u> for water is to use <u>technology</u> to overcome <u>supply</u> problems. One example of this is <u>desalination</u>:

1) <u>Desalination</u> is the removal of <u>salt</u> from <u>seawater</u> so that it can be <u>used</u>. There are two main processes that are used — either the seawater can be <u>heated</u> to <u>evaporate</u> it and then <u>condensed</u> to collect the freshwater or the seawater can be passed through a <u>special membrane</u> to remove the salt.

2) It is <u>expensive</u> because <u>energy</u> is needed to <u>heat</u> the water or to <u>force</u> it through the membrane. Most plants are also powered by <u>fossil fuels</u>, though Saudi Arabia is building the world's first <u>large scale</u>, <u>solar powered</u> desalination plant.

3) In the <u>UK</u>, desalination is mainly used during <u>droughts</u>, rather than being the <u>main source of water</u>. E.g. London has a <u>desalination plant</u> on the banks of the River Thames. It can <u>supply</u> enough water for 400 000 homes in times of <u>water shortage</u>.

4) However, <u>wealthy desert countries</u> often use desalination as their main source of clean, drinking water. <u>Dubai</u> supplies <u>98.8%</u> of its water through desalination. It has the <u>largest supply plant</u> in the region, which can produce <u>140 million gallons</u> of desalinated water every day.

5) Desalination plants in countries that are more dependent on them, have developed more <u>efficient technology</u>, e.g. Dubai's new plant is <u>82% efficient</u> compared to about 45% for plants in Europe.

Desalination — when you sea water, you drink it...

Desalination is a popular technology for tackling water shortages — so you need to know it inside out and back to front.

Sustainable Water Management

Deciding on the <u>best way</u> to <u>manage</u> water <u>resources</u> is a tricky business — everyone has their own <u>opinion</u>...

We Need To Manage Water Sustainably to Avoid Running Out

1) Water is <u>crucial</u> for human <u>survival</u>, and it also underpins <u>other</u> important <u>resources</u> — e.g. agriculture needs water to produce <u>food</u>, and most forms of <u>energy</u> production need large volumes of water.

2) The world's water resources are <u>finite</u> — the supply of fresh water is <u>limited</u>. The <u>global demand</u> for water is <u>growing rapidly</u> (see page 106), so we need to <u>manage</u> water <u>sustainably</u> to make sure that there will be <u>enough</u> good quality water resources to meet the <u>needs</u> of <u>future generations</u>.

3) The <u>availability</u> of <u>clean drinking water</u> is very important for the <u>health</u> of the <u>population</u>. The <u>mismanagement</u> of water resources can lead to <u>pollution</u> and <u>lower water quality</u>, which can <u>reduce</u> the <u>supply</u> of clean water and cause <u>water-borne diseases</u> such as <u>dysentery</u> and <u>cholera</u>.

4) Managing water resources is also needed to promote <u>industry</u> and support <u>livelihoods</u>. E.g. <u>flood prevention</u> protects <u>infrastructure</u>, which allows industry to become established. Maintaining the <u>quality</u> of water resources can increase <u>opportunities</u> for <u>leisure</u> and <u>recreation</u>, which can also create <u>jobs</u>.

5) Sustainable water management is needed at <u>every scale</u> — all the way from <u>international</u> treaties between <u>governments</u> to <u>community</u> groups managing <u>local</u> water resources.

Stakeholders Have Different Ideas About Sustainable Management

Individuals

1) Individuals want to have <u>cheap</u>, <u>reliable</u> and <u>convenient</u> access to water in the <u>future</u> — and probably want the same for their <u>children</u> and <u>future generations</u> too.

2) They might also want to have a <u>say</u> in how water is <u>managed</u>, especially if they <u>share</u> the use of a water resource (e.g. a <u>lake</u> or a <u>water pump</u>) with other people. <u>Community-based water management</u> is common in <u>developing countries</u>, e.g. <u>Malawi</u>, where many people do not have their own <u>private</u> water supply and the <u>government</u> doesn't have enough resources to <u>monitor</u> whether water is being used sustainably. For these groups, sustainable management might also mean that <u>everyone</u> has a <u>fair share</u> of the <u>available</u> water resources.

Organisations

1) <u>Environmental</u> organisations, e.g. <u>Waterwise</u>, campaign to encourage people to use water more <u>sustainably</u> and make sure that there is <u>enough water</u> to <u>support wildlife</u>.

2) Some <u>industrial organisations</u> promote the use of <u>technologies</u> which increase <u>efficiency</u> and create <u>alternative</u> water supplies, as this helps them <u>save money</u> on production costs.

3) <u>Private water companies</u> argue that they can manage water more <u>efficiently</u> and <u>cheaply</u> than governments — but if they only have <u>short-term contracts</u> to manage water, they might not want to invest in <u>infrastructure</u> for the <u>long term</u>.

Governments

1) In most countries, the <u>government</u> is seen to have a <u>responsibility</u> to its <u>citizens</u> to make sure they have access to <u>clean</u>, <u>safe</u> and <u>affordable</u> water, and that this can be <u>maintained sustainably</u> in the <u>long term</u>. Governments go about doing this in different ways.

2) In countries where water is managed by <u>private companies</u>, there are <u>government regulation agencies</u>, e.g. <u>Ofwat</u> in the <u>UK</u>, which make sure that water companies aren't <u>charging people too much</u> for water and that they're managing water without harming the <u>environment</u>.

3) Governments also sign up to <u>international agreements</u> on water management, e.g. the <u>1997 UN Convention on International Watercourses</u>. This is particularly important for countries whose water comes from <u>rivers</u> which flow through <u>several</u> countries, e.g. management of the <u>Jordan river basin</u> affects Jordan, Syria, Israel, Lebanon and the disputed territory of the West Bank.

Sustainable water management — a difficult debate to wade into...

There's no single right answer about how we should manage water — so all the more for you to learn. Make sure you can jot down a couple of examples of different stakeholders and what views they might have about managing water.

Water Management — UK and Kenya

You'll need to know some examples of sustainable water management in action in a developed country and in an emerging or developing country. You can use other examples if you've studied them in class.

There are Different Ways of Managing Water Sustainably

Strategies for sustainable management vary a lot at different scales and levels of development:

1) Water management in a developed country:

In the UK, sustainable water management has attempted to tackle two main issues:

- The mismatch between the places with the greatest supply of water and the greatest demand (see page 108).
- Overconsumption — e.g. people consume more water than they need by using things like hosepipes and washing machines.

2) Water management in an emerging country:

Kenya has a different set of challenges:

- Kenya's northern region has a very arid (dry) climate and is vulnerable to water shortages.
- About 70% of people in Kenya don't have access to improved sanitation (toilets and sewage systems) and 38% don't have access to clean drinking water. Many of these people live in rural areas.

International

- In 2000, the UK signed up to the EU Water Framework Directive, which provided new standards for water quality and required the UK to increase its monitoring of water quality and pollution. This has helped identify where management is most needed.

- Kenya receives aid from many international charities and organisations, e.g. Oxfam. These organisations provide funding and technical support to develop water infrastructure, e.g. by working with private companies to install 'water ATMs' in cities.

National

- The UK government funded Plug-it, a scheme that designed training for people working in the water industry, e.g. plumbers, to persuade their customers to choose water-efficient plumbing.
- The Environment Agency changed abstraction licences (permissions for industries and water companies to take water from rivers or groundwater), reducing the amount of water being abstracted by 30 billion litres per year.

- Kenyan law recognises the right to safe water and sanitation as a basic human right, so the government is legally obliged to make sure that everyone has access to clean water. The government set up the Water Services Trust Fund to achieve this — the Fund has run over 800 water projects, e.g. building water kiosks and toilets, reaching over 4 million people.

Regional

- Some regional water boards introduce hosepipe bans during droughts to reduce consumption.
- Regional water companies can also help address supply-demand problems by trading water. In the 1970s, the Ely Ouse to Essex Transfer Scheme was set up to divert water from the River Ely Ouse in Norfolk, where demand is low, to rivers and reservoirs in Essex, where demand is high. This now provides up to 30% of Essex's water supply.

- People from local communities have formed Water Resource Users Associations in the Mara river basin, which includes the popular tourist area of the Maasai Mara. These associations have been monitoring water quality in the river and making sure businesses do not cause pollution — one association took a hotel to court for illegally releasing its sewage into the river.

Individual

- Many people have installed water meters in their homes, so that they are charged for the exact amount of water they use, instead of paying a flat rate. People use less water to save money, e.g. by installing water-efficient washing machines.
- Farmers have adopted water-saving technologies, e.g. rainwater harvesting systems on barn roofs.

- People in Machakos District, a semi-arid rural area, have built sand dams with support from international charities. The dams are easy and cheap to build. Water gathers in the sand behind the dam during the short rainy season. The sand stops the water from evaporating.

I hope sustainable water management isn't a wild Ouse chase...

1) Using a named example of a developing or emerging country, explain how water resources have been managed in a sustainable way. [8]

Revision Summary

Hope you're still well hydrated and full of energy, because here's a lovely page of revision summary questions. Remember, you've got to study Resource Management, but then you only need to do <u>one</u> option from Energy and Water. As always, all the answers you need are on the pages you (should) have just learnt — if you get stuck on a question, go back and revise the page again.

<u>Natural Resources (p.97-98)</u> ☑

1) Explain the difference between biotic and abiotic resources.
2) Describe two ways that resource extraction can lead to reduced biodiversity.
3) Give three types of natural resources which are found in the UK.
4) Describe the distribution of forestry in the UK.

<u>Global Distribution and Consumption of Resources (p.99-100)</u> ☑

5) a) Which countries produce the most fossil fuels?
   b) Give two reasons why they are the biggest producers.
6) How do increasing levels of development affect a country's energy consumption?
7) Give two reasons why water consumption is usually higher in developed countries.
8) How is food consumption changing in emerging countries?

<u>Energy Resource Management (p.101-105)</u> ☑

9) Give three reasons why demand for energy has increased over the last 100 years.
10) Give two advantages and two disadvantages of using non-renewable energy resources.
11) a) Give three examples of renewable energy sources.
    b) Give two positive impacts of renewable energy sources on the environment.
12) What is fracking?
13) Explain what the energy mix of a country is.
14) True or false: 20% of the UK's energy mix comes from nuclear power.
15) Define sustainable energy management.
16) a) Give two examples of stakeholders in energy resource management.
    b) For each stakeholder, explain how they might think energy resources should be used.
17) Describe an example of sustainable energy management in a developing or emerging country.

<u>Water Resource Management (p.106-111)</u> ☑

18) Describe the global distribution of fresh water availability.
19) What is a water deficit?
20) Give three reasons why global water supply has decreased over the last 50 years.
21) Explain why developed countries use more water for domestic uses than developing countries.
22) Explain what is meant by a seasonal imbalance in water supply and demand.
23) What attitudes might a government have towards water exploitation and consumption?
24) Why is desalination expensive?
25) How does sustainable water management help maintain the health of the population?
26) Suggest two opinions which different organisations might have about sustainable water management.
27) Give one way that the government in a developed country has attempted to manage its water sustainably.
28) Describe an example of a scheme to manage water sustainably in a developing or emerging country.

Fieldwork

Ah, <u>fieldwork</u>. Time to venture into the <u>outside world</u> armed only with a <u>clipboard</u> and a <u>geographical hat</u>*...

*Geographical hat not always supplied.

You have to Write About Two Fieldwork Investigations in the Exam

1) Fieldwork is <u>assessed</u> in the first two sections (<u>Sections A</u> and <u>B</u>) of <u>Paper 3</u>. There's no <u>coursework</u>, but in the exam you need to be able to <u>write about</u> fieldwork that you have done.

2) You need to have done at least one <u>physical</u> and one <u>human</u> fieldwork investigation. The <u>physical</u> one will be on <u>either</u> river landscapes <u>or</u> coastal landscapes. The <u>human</u> one will be on <u>either</u> central/inner urban areas <u>or</u> rural settlements. You'll be asked about <u>both</u> your physical and human fieldwork investigation in the exam.

Your teacher will tell you which topics you're doing.

3) The fieldwork part of the exam has <u>two</u> types of questions:

- You'll have to answer questions about <u>your investigation</u> — you might be asked about your <u>question</u> or <u>hypothesis</u>, your <u>methods</u>, what <u>data</u> you <u>collected</u> and <u>why</u>, how you <u>presented</u> and <u>analysed</u> it, how you could <u>extend your research</u> and so on.

- You'll also be asked about fieldwork in <u>unfamiliar</u> situations. You might have to answer questions about <u>techniques</u> for <u>collecting data</u>, how to <u>present data</u> you've been given or how <u>useful</u> the <u>different techniques</u> are.

For Each of your Investigations, You'll Need to Know...

1 Why You Chose Your Question

You may need to explain <u>why</u> the question or hypothesis you chose is <u>suitable</u> for a <u>geographical investigation</u>.

If you studied <u>different sites</u> in the <u>study area</u>, make sure you know <u>why</u> they were <u>suitable</u> for the study. This could include that they gave a <u>good overall representation</u> of the study area or that they could be <u>compared</u> (if your investigation was a <u>comparison</u>).

2 How and Why You Collected Data

You may need to <u>describe</u> and <u>justify</u> what data <u>you collected</u>. This includes whether it was <u>primary data</u> (data that you collected <u>yourself</u>) or <u>secondary</u> data (data that <u>someone else</u> collected and you <u>used</u>), <u>why</u> you collected or used it, <u>how</u> you <u>measured</u> it and <u>how</u> you <u>recorded</u> it.

3 How You Processed and Presented Your Data

The way you <u>presented</u> your data, and <u>why</u> you <u>chose</u> that option, could come up.

You may need to <u>describe what you did</u>, <u>explain</u> why it was <u>appropriate</u>, and discuss <u>how</u> you <u>adapted</u> your presentation method for <u>your data</u>.

You might also be asked for a <u>different way</u> you <u>could</u> have presented your data.

There's more on analysing, concluding and evaluating on page 115.

4 What Your Data Showed

You'll need to know:

- A <u>description</u> of your data.
- How you <u>analysed</u> your data.
- An <u>explanation</u> of your data.

This might include <u>links</u> between your <u>data sets</u>, the <u>statistical techniques</u> you used, and any <u>anomalies</u> (odd results) in the data that you spotted.

There's more on statistical techniques on pages 128-129.

5 The Conclusions You Reached

This means you may need to <u>explain how</u> your data provides <u>evidence</u> to <u>answer</u> the <u>question</u> or <u>support</u> the <u>hypothesis</u> you set at the <u>beginning</u>.

6 What Went Well, What Could Have Gone Better

You might be asked to <u>evaluate</u> your fieldwork:

- Were there <u>problems</u> in your <u>data collection methods</u>?
- Were there <u>limitations</u> in your <u>data</u>?
- What <u>other data</u> would it have been <u>useful</u> to have?
- How <u>reliable</u> are your <u>conclusions</u>?

No, you can't get a tractor to do your field work for you...

Don't worry if your fieldwork doesn't quite go to plan. It's more important that you can write about it and say why things went wrong. It does help if you at least attempt to make it work though — another read through won't go amiss.

Completing Fieldwork

The <u>fun</u> part of fieldwork is <u>going out</u> and <u>doing it</u> — but before you grab your <u>anorak</u> and rush out the door, there are a couple of <u>important things</u> you need to <u>keep in mind</u>...

You Need to Know How You're Going to Collect Your Data

1) There are <u>rules</u> set by the <u>exam board</u> about the <u>type</u> of <u>data</u> that you have to <u>collect</u> in your <u>fieldwork</u>.

2) You might need to use <u>specialist techniques</u> to collect your data. For example, you may need to measure the <u>gradient</u> of a <u>beach</u> using a <u>clinometer</u> or <u>pantometer</u>, or the <u>velocity</u> of a river by using a <u>flow meter</u> or timing <u>how long</u> it takes for a <u>float</u> to <u>travel</u> between two points.

3) To get the <u>best results</u>, you'll need to know <u>how</u> to <u>carry out</u> these techniques <u>accurately</u> and <u>consistently</u>. In the exam, you could get asked to <u>explain why</u> you <u>chose</u> the method you used.

There are Different Types of Data that You Can Collect

1) There are <u>two</u> types of data that you can use in your investigations — <u>primary</u> and <u>secondary</u> (see p.113).

2) Sometimes, you'll need to use <u>sampling techniques</u> when you're collecting <u>primary</u> data:

- <u>Random sampling</u> is where samples are chosen at <u>random</u>, e.g. picking pebbles on a beach.
- <u>Systematic sampling</u> is where samples are chosen at <u>regular intervals</u> — this is useful in places where what you want to investigate <u>changes frequently</u>, e.g. the number of pedestrians in an area.
- <u>Stratified sampling</u> is where you choose samples from <u>different groups</u> to get a <u>good overall representation</u>. This type of sampling is useful if you need to collect people's <u>perceptions</u>, e.g. of pollution in their area, and need to ask people of <u>different ages</u>.

3) The data you collect can be <u>quantitative</u> or <u>qualitative</u>:

- <u>Quantitative data</u> is <u>numerical data</u>, e.g. the <u>number</u> of <u>pedestrians</u> in an urban area. It's based on things you can <u>measure</u>.
- <u>Qualitative data</u> is based on information that <u>can't</u> be measured, e.g. <u>opinions</u>. For your fieldwork investigations, it's <u>likely</u> that you'll need to collect data on people's <u>views</u>, e.g. what <u>residents</u> think about <u>quality of life</u> in their area.

4) You need to use at least <u>two</u> secondary data sources for <u>each</u> of your <u>investigations</u>. <u>One</u> of these <u>must</u> be a source from a list <u>decided</u> by the <u>exam board</u>. The source that you <u>have</u> to use <u>depends</u> on which <u>investigation</u> you're carrying out:

If you're unsure about what sources you should use, check with your teacher.

- GEOLOGY MAPS — for <u>Investigating Physical Environments</u> (<u>coastal landscapes</u>)
- FLOOD RISK MAPS — for <u>Investigating Physical Environments</u> (<u>river landscapes</u>)
- CENSUS DATA — for <u>Investigating Human Environments</u> (<u>urban areas</u> and <u>rural settlements</u>)

You Need to Think About Health and Safety

1) You'll need to think about <u>safety</u> when choosing the sites you're going to study.

2) You need to know how to carry out a <u>risk assessment</u> for the <u>sites</u> you choose to study:

- Identify the <u>specific risks</u> at the site,
- Give them a <u>risk rating</u> up to <u>10</u> (where 10 is the <u>most severe</u> risk),
- Write down how they can be <u>managed</u>.

E.g.

Risk Identified	Risk Rating	How can it be managed?
Risk of accidents whilst surveying traffic passing through junction.	7	Wear a fluorescent vest and choose a safe place to stand away from the traffic flow.

Pantometers — useful for measuring a dog's stick-chasing field work...

'But what do I do with all the data I've collected?', I hear you cry — just wander over to the next page and I'll explain...

Geographical Investigations — Fieldwork

Analysing, Concluding and Evaluating

Analysis, conclusions and evaluations can be pretty tricky, so here's a load of stuff to help you with them.

You need to Describe and Explain what the Data Shows

Analysing and interpreting data is about:

1) Describing what the data shows — you need to describe any patterns and correlations (see page 124) and look for any anomalies. Make sure you use specific points from the data and reference what graph, table etc. you're talking about. You might also need to make comparisons between different sets of data. Statistical techniques (see pages 128-129) help make the data more manageable, so it's easier to spot patterns and make comparisons.

2) Explaining what the data shows — you need to explain why there are patterns and why different data sets are linked together. Use your geographical knowledge to help you explain the results and remember to use geographical terms.

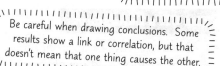
For both of your investigations you need to be able to say how the physical environment affects people — or how people affect the environment.

Conclusions are a Summary of the Results

A conclusion is a summary of what you found out in relation to the original question. It should include:

Be careful when drawing conclusions. Some results show a link or correlation, but that doesn't mean that one thing causes the other.

1) A summary of what your results show.

2) An answer for the question you are investigating, and an explanation for why that is the answer.

3) An explanation of how your conclusion fits into the wider geographical world — think about how your conclusion and results could be used by other people or in further investigations.

Evaluations Identify Problems in the Investigation

Evaluation is all about self assessment — looking back at how good or bad your study (or the data you are given in the exam) was. You need to be able to:

1) Identify any problems with the methods used and suggest how they could be improved. Think about things like the size of the data sets, if any bias (unfairness) slipped in and if other methods would have been more appropriate or more effective.

2) Describe how accurate the results are and link this to the methods used — say whether any errors in the methods affected the results.

3) Comment on the validity of your conclusion. You need to talk about how problems with the methods and the accuracy of the results affect the validity of the conclusion. Problems with methods lead to less reliable and accurate results, which affects the validity of the conclusion.

> Accurate results are as near as possible to the true answer — they have few errors.
> Reliable means that data can be reproduced.
> Valid means that the data answers the original question and is reliable.

For example:

> I concluded that the river flowed faster further downstream. However, one problem with my data collection method was that it was difficult to put the float in at exactly the same point each time. This reduced the accuracy of my measurements. To make my investigation more accurate, I could have placed a tape measure across the river to mark the exact point of entry. Another problem was that I only took two readings at each site and I only used one upstream site and one downstream site. To make my data more reliable I could have taken more readings at each site, and used a larger number of sites both upstream and downstream. These improvements would have produced a more valid conclusion.

Evaluation — could do with a hair cut, otherwise fine...

Bit of a weird one this — you need to remember how you analysed your data, the conclusion of your investigations and the evaluation for your studies. So make sure you have some points ready to go before you hit the exam. But you also need to be able to analyse, conclude and evaluate based on someone else's data that you might be given in the exam.

Geographical Investigations — UK Challenges

Knowing all the facts isn't quite enough to get you through your exams — you'll also have to use what you've learnt to interpret resources and write a balanced argument about a geographical challenge. Crumbs.

Geographical Investigations involve Analysing and Interpreting Information

Section C of Paper 3 (Geographical Investigations) tests you on a range of topics from the course.
In the exam, you'll be given a resource booklet with loads of information about a geographical challenge that the UK is facing. The challenge will be linked to one or more of four different themes:

1 **Resource Consumption and Environmental Sustainability**

- Population pressures on resource use and ecosystems.
- Sustainable transport options.

2 **Settlement, Population and Economic Challenges**

- Uneven development between different regions of the UK.
- Development of greenfield vs. brownfield sites.
- Migration statistics and different attitudes towards migration.

3 **The UK's Landscape**

- Different ways of approaching conservation and development in National Parks.
- Flood management strategies for rivers and coasts.

4 **Climate Change**

- Uncertainty about how the UK's climate will be affected by global climate change.
- How climate change will affect people and landscapes.
- Local and national responses to climate change in the UK.

You'll have to answer questions using the information you're given and your knowledge of the UK's human and physical geography from the rest of the course. There'll also be a longer answer question where you'll need to consider a geographical issue related to the information you've been given and make judgements about it (see below).

There'll be Lots of Different Information Sources in the Resource Booklet

1) The booklet could include several different types of information, such as maps, graphs, photographs, diagrams, statistics, newspaper articles and quotes from people involved.

2) The information you're given is there to help you answer the questions in the exam paper. Each question will be linked to certain parts of the resource booklet.

3) Some questions will probably ask you to demonstrate geographical skills, including reading graphs and charts (see pages 123-127) and calculating statistics (see pages 128-129).

Use All the Information to Write Your Longer Answer

1) You'll be asked to use your knowledge and the information in the resource booklet to discuss a geographical challenge that the UK is facing, e.g. discussing the idea that the UK should address its housing shortage by developing greenfield sites.

2) There's no single right or wrong answer — but you need to be able to justify your argument, so make sure you can use the data from the resource booklet to support it.

3) Whatever your view is, you need to give a balanced argument. Try to think of the positive and negative impacts that the issue may have on people and the environment.

4) It's likely to be a complex issue with lots of different parties involved. So think about the different viewpoints that different groups of people might have.

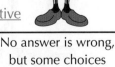

No answer is wrong, but some choices are hard to justify...

Colouring in a map while underwater — a real geographical challenge...

It may sound a bit daunting, but the resource booklet will give you most of what you need to write great answers. Just remember to back up your answer using facts and figures from the resource booklet, and the job's a good 'un.

Answering Questions

Here are some lovely <u>techniques</u> and <u>skills</u> you'll need for your exams. First, answering questions properly...

Make Sure you Read the Question Properly

It's easy to <u>misread</u> the question and write about the <u>wrong thing</u>. Here are some tips to help you <u>avoid</u> this:

1) Figure out if it's a <u>case study question</u> — if the question wording includes 'using <u>named examples</u>' or 'for a <u>named</u> country' you need to include a case study or examples you've learnt about.

2) <u>Underline</u> the <u>command words</u> in the question (the ones that tell you <u>what to do</u>):

When writing about differences, '<u>whereas</u>' is a good word to use in your answers, e.g. 'Australia is a developed country, whereas Ethiopia is a developing country.'

These questions don't normally have a <u>right</u> or <u>wrong</u> answer — the important thing is that you give <u>reasons</u>.

Command word	Means write about...
Describe	what it's <u>like</u>
Explain	<u>why</u> it's like that (i.e. give <u>reasons</u>)
Compare	the <u>similarities</u> AND <u>differences</u>
Suggest why	give <u>reasons</u> for
Evaluate	<u>judge</u> the <u>success</u> of something
Examine	different <u>components</u> or <u>processes</u> and how they <u>interact</u>
Assess	<u>weigh up</u> all factors
Discuss	give <u>both sides</u> of an <u>argument</u>

If a question asks you to describe a <u>pattern</u> (e.g. from a map or graph), make sure you identify the general pattern, then refer to any <u>anomalies</u> (things that <u>don't</u> fit the general pattern). E.g. to answer 'describe the global distribution of deserts', <u>first</u> say that they're mostly between 15° and 35° north and south of the equator, <u>then</u> mention that a few aren't (e.g. the Gobi desert).

3) <u>Underline</u> the <u>key words</u> (the ones that tell you what it's <u>about</u>), e.g. glaciers, immigration, energy supply.

4) If the question says '<u>using Figure 2</u>', bloomin' well <u>make sure</u> you've talked about <u>what Figure 2 shows</u>. <u>Don't</u> just wheel out all of your <u>geographical knowledge</u> and forget all about the photo you're <u>supposed</u> to be <u>talking about</u>. <u>Re-read</u> the <u>question</u> and your <u>answer</u> when you've <u>finished</u>, just to check.

Some Questions are Level Marked

Questions worth <u>8 marks or more</u> with longer written answers are <u>level marked</u>, which means you need to do these <u>things</u> to get the <u>top level</u> and a <u>high mark</u>:

1) <u>Read</u> the question properly and figure out a <u>structure</u> for your answer before you start. Your answer needs to be well <u>organised</u> and <u>structured</u>, and written in a <u>logical</u> way.

2) If it's a <u>case study</u> question, include plenty of <u>relevant details</u>:

- This includes things like <u>place names</u>, <u>dates</u>, <u>statistics</u>, names of <u>organisations</u> or <u>companies</u>.
- Don't forget that they need to be <u>relevant</u> though — it's no good including the exact number of people killed in a tropical cyclone when the question is about <u>responses</u> to a cyclone.

3) Some questions have <u>4 extra marks</u> available for <u>spelling</u>, <u>punctuation</u> and <u>grammar</u>. To get <u>top marks</u> you need to:

- Make sure your <u>spelling</u>, <u>punctuation</u> and <u>grammar</u> are <u>consistently correct</u>.
- Write in a way that makes it <u>clear</u> what you mean.
- Correctly use a <u>wide range</u> of <u>geographical terms</u> (e.g. sustainable development).

Explain the similarities and differences between compare and assess...

Level marked questions are a great opportunity to really impress the examiner with your knowledge of geography and score some juicy marks in the exam. These types of questions often ask you to assess, evaluate, examine or discuss something. The differences between the meanings of some of these command words can be quite subtle, so get learnin'.

Maps

Maps, glorious maps... there's nothing better. OS® maps are my personal favourite, but these aren't bad.

Latitude and Longitude are Used for Global Coordinates

1) The position of anywhere on Earth can be given using coordinates if you use latitude and longitude.

2) Lines of latitude run horizontally around the Earth. They measure how far north or south from the equator something is.

3) Lines of longitude run vertically around the Earth. They measure how far east or west from the Prime Meridian (a line of longitude running through Greenwich in London) something is.

4) Latitude and longitude are measured in degrees.

5) For example, the coordinates of London are 51° N, 0° W. New York is at 40° N, 74° W.

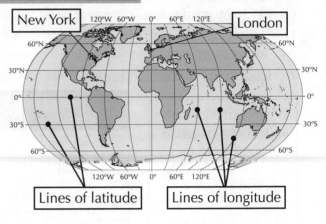

Describing Distributions on Maps — Describe the Pattern

1) In your exam you could get questions like, 'use the map to describe the distribution of tropical cyclones' and 'explain the distribution of deforestation'.

2) Describe the general pattern and any anomalies (things that don't fit the general pattern).

3) Make at least as many points as there are marks and use names of places and figures if they're given.

4) If you're asked to give a reason or explain, you need to describe the distribution first.

Figure 1 — Population density of Britain

Key
■ 600 to 5000 persons per km^2
■ 400 to 599 persons per km^2
□ 200 to 399 persons per km^2
□ 0 to 199 persons per km^2

Q: Use Figure 1 to explain the pattern of population density in Britain.

A: The London area has a very high population density (600 to 5000 per km^2). There are also areas of high population density (400 to 599 per km^2) in the south east, the Midlands and north west of England. These areas include major cities (e.g. Birmingham and Manchester). More people live in and around cities because there are better services and more job opportunities than in rural areas. Scotland and Wales have the lowest population densities in Britain (less than 199 per km^2)...

You could be given two maps to use for one question — link information from the two maps together.

Describing Locations on Maps — Include Details

1) In your exam you could get a question like, 'describe the location of cities in ...'.

2) When you're asked about the location of something say where it is, what it's near and use compass points.

3) If you're asked to give a reason or explain, you need to describe the location first.

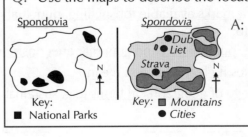
Spondovia

Spondovia
● Dub
● Liet
Strava

Key:
■ National Parks

Key: ■ Mountains
● Cities

Q: Use the maps to describe the location of the National Parks.

A: The National Parks are found in the south west and north east of Spondovia. They are all located in mountainous areas. Three of the parks are located near to the city of Strava.

Describing maps — large, cumbersome, impossible to fold...

...but I love them really. Give me a paper map over some digital device — or worse, a GPS satnav type thing. Yuck. Make sure you're happy with latitude and longitude, then practise describing a map using lots of lovely details.

Geographical Skills

Maps

This page has more <u>dots</u> and <u>lines</u> than the Morse code highlights of the last footy match of the season...

Dot Maps Show Distribution and Quantity Using Identical Symbols...

1) Dot maps use <u>identical dots</u> to show how something is <u>distributed</u> across an <u>area</u>.

2) Use the <u>key</u> to find out what <u>quantity</u> each dot represents.

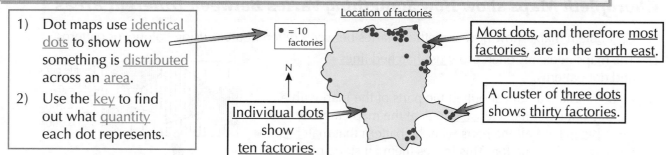

Location of factories

● = 10 factories

N

Most dots, and therefore <u>most factories</u>, are in the <u>north east</u>.

A cluster of <u>three dots</u> shows <u>thirty factories</u>.

Individual dots show <u>ten factories</u>.

...Proportional Symbol Maps use Symbols of Different Sizes

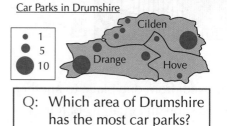

Car Parks in Drumshire

● 1
● 5
● 10

Cilden

Drange   Hove

1) <u>Proportional symbol maps</u> use symbols of different <u>sizes</u> to represent different <u>quantities</u>.

2) A <u>key</u> shows the <u>quantity</u> each <u>different sized</u> symbol represents. The <u>bigger</u> the symbol, the <u>larger</u> the amount.

3) The symbols might be <u>circles</u>, <u>squares</u>, <u>semi-circles</u> or <u>bars</u>, but a <u>larger symbol</u> always means a <u>larger amount</u>.

Q: Which area of Drumshire has the most car parks?

A: Drange, with 20.

Isolines on Maps Link up Places with Something in Common

1) <u>Isolines</u> are lines on a map <u>linking</u> up all the places where something's the <u>same</u>, for example:
   - <u>Contour lines</u> are isolines linking up places at the same <u>altitude</u>.
   - In <u>bathymetric charts</u> of the <u>ocean</u>, isolines link up places at the same <u>depth</u>.
   - Isolines on a <u>weather map</u> (called <u>isobars</u>) link together all the places where the <u>pressure's</u> the same.

2) Isolines can be used to link up lots of things, e.g. <u>average temperature</u>, <u>wind speed</u> or <u>rainfall</u>.

3) Isolines are normally <u>labelled</u> with their <u>value</u>. The <u>closer together</u> the <u>lines</u> are, the <u>steeper</u> the <u>gradient</u> (how quickly the thing is changing) <u>at that point</u>.

1 Reading Isoline Maps

1) <u>Find</u> the place you're interested in on the map and if it's on a <u>line</u> just <u>read</u> off the value.

2) If it's <u>between</u> two lines, you have to <u>estimate</u> the value.

Q: Find the average annual rainfall in Port Portia and on Mt. Mavis.

A: Port Portia is between the lines for 200 mm and 400 mm so the rainfall is likely to be around 300 mm per year.
Mt. Mavis is on an isoline so the rainfall is 1000 mm per year.

Average annual rainfall on Itchy Island (mm per year)

N

600
500   600
1000
500
800
Mt. Mavis
600
Port Portia
400
200

2 Completing Isoline Maps

1) Drawing an isoline's like doing a <u>dot-to-dot</u> — you just join up all the dots with the <u>same numbers</u>.

2) Make sure you don't <u>cross</u> any <u>other isolines</u> though.

Q: Complete on the map the isoline showing an average rainfall of 600 mm per year.

A: See the red line on the map.

When it comes to maps, the key is, er, key...

No matter whether you've got identical dots, proportional symbols or wavy lines, the key to correctly interpreting the map is to understand what each symbol means. The title helps here, but you really need to check the key carefully.

Maps

Three more maps, with three more ludicrous names. Well the last two aren't that bad, but this first one — choropleth, sounds like a treatment at the dentist.

Choropleth Maps show How Something Varies Between Different Areas

1) Choropleth maps show how something varies between different areas using colours or patterns.

2) The maps in exams often use cross-hatched lines and dot patterns.

3) If you're asked to talk about all the parts of the map with a certain value or characteristic, look at the map carefully and put a big tick on all the parts with the pattern that matches what you're looking for. This makes them all stand out.

4) When you're asked to complete part of a map, first use the key to work out what type of pattern you need. Then carefully draw on the pattern, e.g. using a ruler.

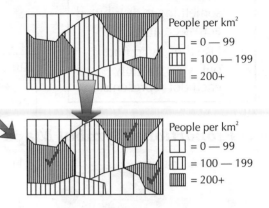

Flow Lines show Movement

1) Flow line maps have arrows on, showing how things move (or are moved) from one place to another.

2) They can also be proportional symbol maps — the width of the arrows show the quantity of things that are moving.

Q: From which area do the greatest number of people entering the UK come from?

A: USA, as this arrow is the largest.

Q: The number of people entering the UK from the Middle East is roughly half the number of people entering from the USA. Draw an arrow on the map to show this.

A: Make sure your arrow is going in the right direction and its size is appropriate (i.e. half the width of the USA arrow).

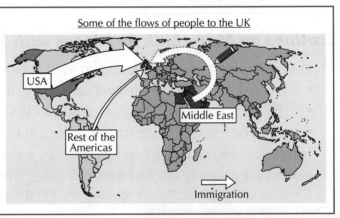

Some of the flows of people to the UK

Desire Lines show Journeys

1) Desire line maps are a type of flow line as they show movement too.

2) They're straight lines that show journeys between two locations, but they don't follow roads or railway lines.

3) One line represents one journey.

4) They're used to show how far all the people have travelled to get to a place, e.g. a shop or a town centre, and where they've come from.

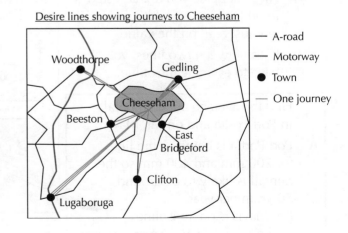

Desire lines showing journeys to Cheeseham

Desire lines — I'm sure my palm reader mentioned those...

...unfortunately I'm not as good at seeing the future as she is* so I can't predict if any of these maps are going to come up in your exam. They could do though, so make sure you know what they are and how to read them.

*If you're wondering, I'm going to meet a short, fair stranger very soon...

Ordnance Survey Maps

Next up, the dreaded <u>Ordnance Survey®</u> <u>maps</u>. Don't worry, they're easy once you know how to use 'em.

Learn These Common Symbols

Ordnance Survey (OS®) maps use lots of <u>symbols</u>. It's a good idea to learn some of the most <u>common ones</u> — like these:

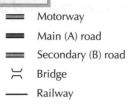

▬▬	Motorway
▬▬	Main (A) road
▬▬	Secondary (B) road
⌤	Bridge
——	Railway

— · — ·	County boundary
	National Park boundaries
▭	Building
⬤	Bus station

┈┈┈	Footpaths
⚹	Viewpoint
i	Tourist information centre
P	Parking
+ ♦ ●	Places of worship

You have to be able to Understand Grid References

You need to be able to use <u>four figure</u> and <u>six figure</u> grid references for your exam.

Q: Give the four figure and six figure grid reference for the place of worship.

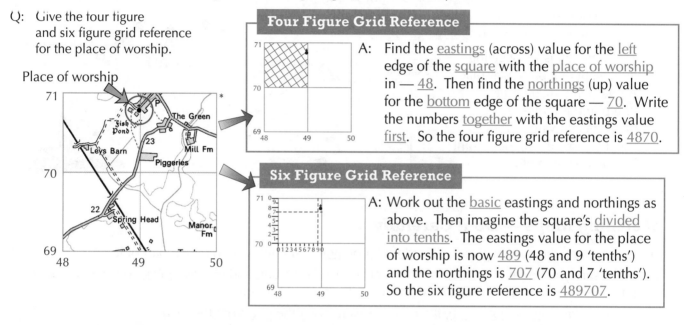

Place of worship

Four Figure Grid Reference

A: Find the <u>eastings</u> (across) value for the <u>left</u> edge of the <u>square</u> with the <u>place of worship</u> in — <u>48</u>. Then find the <u>northings</u> (up) value for the <u>bottom</u> edge of the square — <u>70</u>. Write the numbers <u>together</u> with the eastings value <u>first</u>. So the four figure grid reference is <u>4870</u>.

Six Figure Grid Reference

A: Work out the <u>basic</u> eastings and northings as above. Then imagine the square's <u>divided into tenths</u>. The eastings value for the place of worship is now <u>489</u> (48 and 9 'tenths') and the northings is <u>707</u> (70 and 7 'tenths'). So the six figure reference is <u>489707</u>.

You need to Know your Compass Points

You've got to know the compass — for giving <u>directions</u>, saying <u>which way</u> a <u>river's flowing</u>, or knowing what they mean if they say 'look at the river in the <u>NW</u> of the map' in the exam. Read it <u>out loud</u> to yourself, going <u>clockwise</u>.

North
West — East **OR** Never
South   Wheat — Eat
         Soggy

You Might have to Work Out the Distance Between Two Places

To work out the <u>distance</u> between <u>two places</u> on a <u>map</u>, use a <u>ruler</u> to measure the <u>distance</u> in <u>cm</u> then <u>compare</u> it to the scale to find the distance in <u>km</u>.

Q: What's the distance from the bridge (482703) to the place of worship (489707)?

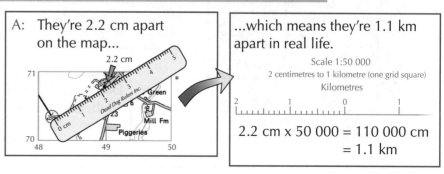

A: They're 2.2 cm apart on the map...

...which means they're 1.1 km apart in real life.

Scale 1:50 000
2 centimetres to 1 kilometre (one grid square)
Kilometres

2.2 cm x 50 000 = 110 000 cm
= 1.1 km

Learn the common cymbals — and really annoy your neighbours...

I told you OS maps aren't as bad as you thought. If a bedraggled walker who's been out in the rain for five hours with only a cup of tea to keep them going can read them, then so can you. Get ready for some more map fun...

Ordnance Survey Maps

Almost done with <u>map skills</u> now. Just this final page looking at <u>contour lines</u> and <u>sketching</u> from Ordnance Survey® maps or photographs to deal with then you're free, free I tell you... (well, free from maps anyway).

The Relief of an Area is Shown by Contours and Spot Heights

1) <u>Contour lines</u> are the <u>browny-orange lines</u> drawn on maps — they join points of <u>equal height</u> above sea level (<u>altitude</u>).

2) They tell you about the <u>relief</u> of the land, e.g. whether it's hilly or flat.

3) They show the <u>height</u> of the land by the <u>numbers</u> marked on them. They also show the <u>steepness</u> of the land by how <u>close together</u> they are (the <u>closer</u> they are, the <u>steeper</u> the slope).

4) For example, if a map has <u>lots</u> of contour lines on it, it's probably <u>hilly</u> or <u>mountainous</u>. If there are only a <u>few</u> it'll be <u>flat</u> and often <u>low-lying</u>.

5) A <u>spot height</u> is a <u>dot</u> giving the height of a particular place. A <u>trigonometrical point</u> (trig point) is a <u>blue triangle</u> plus a height value. They usually show the <u>highest point</u> in that area (in metres).

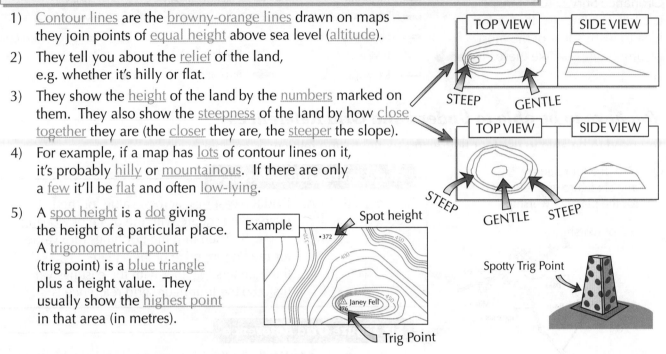

Sketching Maps — Do it Carefully

1) In the <u>exam</u>, they could give you a <u>map</u> or <u>photograph</u> and tell you to <u>sketch</u> part of it.

2) Make sure you figure out <u>what bit</u> they want you to sketch out, and <u>double check</u> you've <u>got it right</u>. It might be only <u>part</u> of a lake or a wood, or only <u>one</u> of the roads.

3) If you're <u>sketching</u> an <u>OS® map</u>, it's a good idea to <u>copy</u> the <u>grid</u> from the map onto your sketch paper — this helps you to copy the map <u>accurately</u>.

4) Draw your sketch <u>in pencil</u> so you can <u>rub it out</u> if it's <u>wrong</u>.

5) Look at how much <u>time</u> you have and <u>how many marks</u> it's worth to decide how much <u>detail</u> to add.

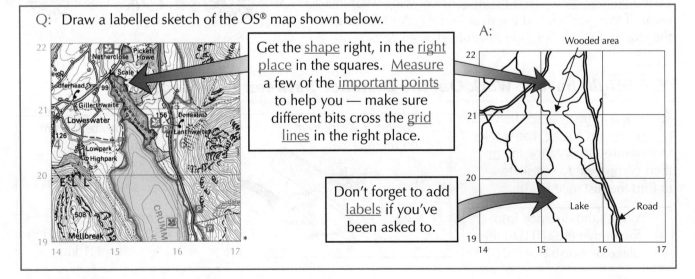

Q: Draw a labelled sketch of the OS® map shown below.

Get the <u>shape</u> right, in the <u>right place</u> in the squares. <u>Measure</u> a few of the <u>important points</u> to help you — make sure different bits cross the <u>grid lines</u> in the right place.

Don't forget to add <u>labels</u> if you've been asked to.

What a relief that's over...

When you're sketching a copy of a map or photo see if you can lay the paper over it — then you can trace it (sneaky). Anyway, that may be it for maps, but you're not quite free yet... It's time to rock the charts and graphs. Oh yeah.

Charts and Graphs

Stand by for <u>charts</u> and <u>graphs</u>. Make sure you can <u>interpret</u> (read) and <u>construct</u> (draw) each of them...

Describing what Graphs Show — Include Figures from the Graph

1) When <u>describing</u> graphs make sure you mention:

2) The general pattern — when it's <u>going up</u> and <u>down</u>, and any <u>peaks</u> (highest bits) and <u>troughs</u> (lowest bits).

3) Any <u>anomalies</u> (odd results).

4) Specific <u>data points</u>.

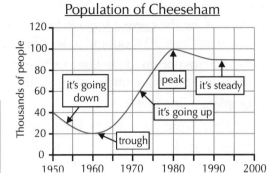

Population of Cheeseham

Q: Use the graph to describe population change in Cheeseham.

A: The population halved between 1950 and 1960 from 40 thousand people to 20 thousand people. It then increased to 100 thousand by 1980, before falling slightly and staying steady at 90 thousand from 1990 to 2000.

Bar Charts — Draw the Bars Straight and Neat

To <u>read</u> a bar chart:

1) Read along the <u>bottom</u> to find the <u>bar</u> you want.

2) To find out the <u>value</u> of a bar in a <u>normal</u> bar chart — go from the <u>top</u> of the bar <u>across</u> to the <u>scale</u>, and <u>read off</u> the number.

3) To find out the <u>value</u> of <u>part</u> of the bar in a <u>divided</u> bar chart — find the <u>number at the top</u> of the part of the bar you're interested in, and <u>take away</u> the <u>number at the bottom</u> of it (see example below).

To <u>complete</u> a bar chart:

1) First find the number you want on the <u>vertical scale</u>.

2) Then <u>trace</u> a line across to where the <u>top</u> of the bar will be with a <u>ruler</u>.

3) Draw in a bar of the <u>right size</u> using a <u>ruler</u>.

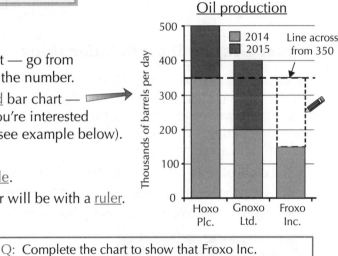

Oil production

Q: How many barrels of oil did Hoxo Plc. produce per day in 2015?

A: 500 000 – 350 000 = <u>150 000 barrels</u> per day

Q: Complete the chart to show that Froxo Inc. produced 200 000 barrels of oil per day in 2015.

A: 150 thousand (2014) + 200 thousand = <u>350 000 barrels</u>. So draw the bar up to this point.

Histograms are a Lot Like Bar Charts

1) <u>Histograms</u> are very <u>similar</u> to <u>bar charts</u>, but they have a <u>continuous scale</u> of <u>numbers</u> on the <u>bottom</u> and there <u>can't</u> be any <u>gaps between the bars</u>.

2) You can use <u>histograms</u> when your <u>data</u> can be divided into <u>intervals</u>, like <u>this</u>:

3) You <u>draw</u> and <u>plot</u> them just like a <u>bar chart</u>, but you have to make sure that the bars are all the <u>correct width</u>, as well as the <u>correct height</u>.

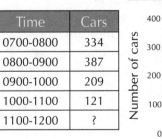

Time	Cars
0700-0800	334
0800-0900	387
0900-1000	209
1000-1100	121
1100-1200	?

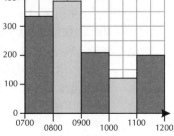

Number of cars passing a point

Q: How many cars were recorded between 1100 and 1200?

A: Trace a line from the top of the 1100-1200 bar and read the answer off — <u>200 cars</u>.

The top forty for sheep — the baaaaaaaaaaaaa chart...

Something to watch out for with bar charts (and line graphs on the next page) is reading the scale — check how much each division is worth before reading them or completing them. Don't assume each division is worth one...

Geographical Skills

Charts and Graphs

'More charts and graphs' I hear you cry — well OK, your weird wishes are my command.

Line Graphs — the Points are Joined by Lines

To read a line graph:

1) Read along the correct scale to find the value you want, e.g. 20 thousand tonnes or 1920.

2) Read across or up to the line you want, then read the value off the other scale.

To complete a line graph:

1) Find the value you want on both scales.

2) Make a mark (e.g. ×) at the point where the two values meet on the graph.

3) Using a ruler, join the mark you've made to the line that it should be connected to.

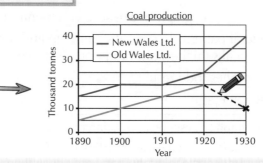

Coal production

Q: Complete the graph to show that Old Wales Ltd. produced 10 thousand tonnes of coal in 1930.

A: Find 1930 on the bottom scale, and 10 thousand tonnes on the vertical scale. Make a mark where they meet, then join it to the blue line with a ruler.

Scatter Graphs Show Relationships

Scatter graphs tell you how closely related two things are, e.g. altitude and air temperature. The fancy word for this is correlation. Strong correlation means the two things are closely related to each other. Weak correlation means they're not very closely related. The line of best fit is a line that goes roughly through the middle of the scatter of points and tells you about what type of correlation there is. Data can show three types of correlation:

1) Positive — as one thing increases the other increases.

2) Negative — as one thing increases the other decreases.

3) None — there's no relationship between the two things.

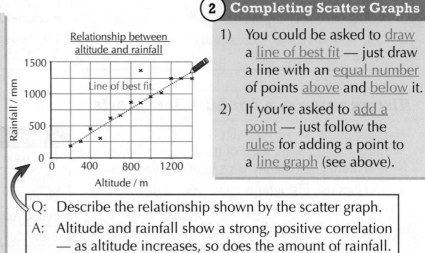

1 Reading Scatter Graphs

1) If you're asked to describe the relationship, look at the slope of the graph, e.g. if the line's moving upwards to the right it's a positive correlation. You also need to look at how close the points are to the line of best fit — the closer they are the stronger the correlation.

2) If you're asked to read off a specific point, just follow the rules for a line graph (see above).

Relationship between altitude and rainfall

Q: Describe the relationship shown by the scatter graph.

A: Altitude and rainfall show a strong, positive correlation — as altitude increases, so does the amount of rainfall.

2 Completing Scatter Graphs

1) You could be asked to draw a line of best fit — just draw a line with an equal number of points above and below it.

2) If you're asked to add a point — just follow the rules for adding a point to a line graph (see above).

- You can use your line of best fit to make predictions by reading off values from the graph (interpolation).

- If you're confident that your best fit line will continue, you can extend it beyond the data you have collected. This means you can make predictions outside the range of data you collected (extrapolation).

Sorry darling, we've got no relationship — look at our scatter graph...

Line graphs and scatter graphs with a line of best fit are pretty similar, but don't get them confused — however much you might want to, it's not always ok to go around joining dots up. Study this page 'til you're seeing lines in your sleep.

Geographical Skills

Charts and Graphs

Chart or graph, tomayto or tomarto, Daddy or chips. I think I've lost it. Please continue as normal.

Pie Charts *Show Amounts or Percentages*

The important thing to remember with pie charts is that the whole pie = 360°.

1 Reading Pie Charts

1) To work out the % for a wedge of the pie, use a protractor to find out how large it is in degrees.

2) Then divide that number by 360 and times by 100.

3) To find the amount a wedge of the pie is worth, work out your percentage then turn it into a decimal. Then times the decimal by the total amount of the pie.

Q: Out of 200 people, how many used a pogostick?
A: 126 – 90 = 36°, so (36 ÷ 360) × 100 = 10%, so 0.1 × 200 = 20 people.

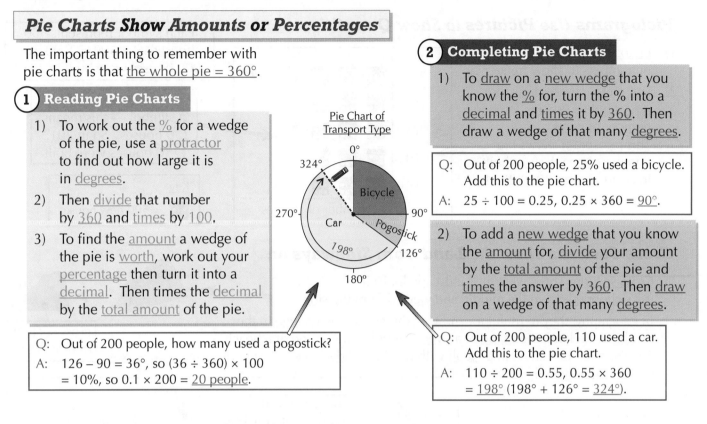

Pie Chart of Transport Type

2 Completing Pie Charts

1) To draw on a new wedge that you know the % for, turn the % into a decimal and times it by 360. Then draw a wedge of that many degrees.

Q: Out of 200 people, 25% used a bicycle. Add this to the pie chart.
A: 25 ÷ 100 = 0.25, 0.25 × 360 = 90°.

2) To add a new wedge that you know the amount for, divide your amount by the total amount of the pie and times the answer by 360. Then draw on a wedge of that many degrees.

Q: Out of 200 people, 110 used a car. Add this to the pie chart.
A: 110 ÷ 200 = 0.55, 0.55 × 360 = 198° (198° + 126° = 324°).

Dispersion Diagrams *Show the Frequency of Data*

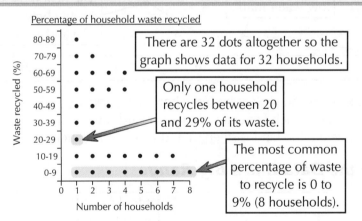

Percentage of household waste recycled

There are 32 dots altogether so the graph shows data for 32 households.

Only one household recycles between 20 and 29% of its waste.

The most common percentage of waste to recycle is 0 to 9% (8 households).

1) Dispersion diagrams are a bit like a cross between a tally chart and a bar chart.

2) The range of data that's measured goes on one axis. Frequency goes on the other axis.

3) Each dot represents one piece of information — the more dots there are in a particular category, the more frequently that event has happened.

4) The dispersion diagram on the left shows the percentage of household waste that's recycled for households in a particular village.

Population Pyramids *Show the Structure of a Population*

1) Population pyramids are a bit like two bar charts on their sides.

2) It's a way of showing the population of a country by age and gender.

3) The number of people goes on the horizontal axis, and the age groups go on the vertical axis. The left side is the male population and the right side is the female population.

There are a few people over 80.

There are lots of people aged 0-9.

Pie charts aren't bad, but I prefer cake...

Hmm, who'd have thought pie could be so complicated. Don't panic though, a bit of practice and you'll be fine. And don't worry, there are only four more pages to go in the whole book. Congratulations — I'm so proud of you, sniff.

Geographical Skills

Charts and Graphs

What a lovely surprise — some <u>more</u> charts and graphs for you to <u>get to grips</u> with...

Pictograms Use Pictures to Show Quantities

1) <u>Pictograms</u> use <u>symbols</u> instead of <u>numbers</u> to show frequency.

2) In a pictogram each <u>picture</u> or <u>symbol</u> represents a <u>certain number of items</u>. This <u>pictogram</u> shows the <u>number of new houses</u> built in Bogdon from 2010-2014:

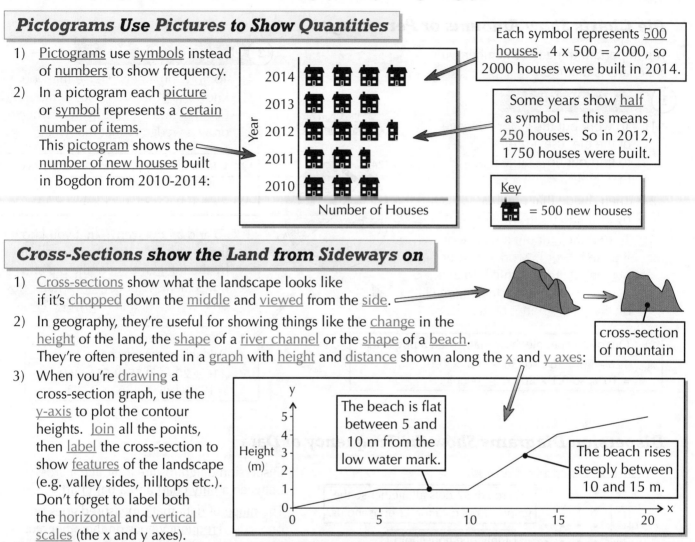

Each symbol represents <u>500 houses</u>. 4 x 500 = 2000, so 2000 houses were built in 2014.

Some years show <u>half</u> a symbol — this means <u>250</u> houses. So in 2012, 1750 houses were built.

Key

= 500 new houses

Number of Houses

Cross-Sections show the Land from Sideways on

1) <u>Cross-sections</u> show what the landscape looks like if it's <u>chopped</u> down the <u>middle</u> and <u>viewed</u> from the <u>side</u>.

cross-section of mountain

2) In geography, they're useful for showing things like the <u>change</u> in the <u>height</u> of the land, the <u>shape</u> of a <u>river channel</u> or the <u>shape</u> of a <u>beach</u>. They're often presented in a <u>graph</u> with <u>height</u> and <u>distance</u> shown along the <u>x</u> and <u>y axes</u>:

3) When you're <u>drawing</u> a cross-section graph, use the <u>y-axis</u> to plot the contour heights. <u>Join</u> all the points, then <u>label</u> the cross-section to show <u>features</u> of the landscape (e.g. valley sides, hilltops etc.). Don't forget to label both the <u>horizontal</u> and <u>vertical</u> <u>scales</u> (the x and y axes).

The beach is flat between 5 and 10 m from the low water mark.

The beach rises steeply between 10 and 15 m.

4) If you're <u>interpreting</u> a cross-section graph, make sure you look at both the <u>horizontal</u> and <u>vertical</u> <u>scales</u> carefully. Describe the <u>general trends</u>, e.g. the beach generally slopes upwards away from the sea, and then pick out the <u>key features</u>, e.g. where the land is <u>steepest</u> and where it is <u>flatter</u>.

Logarithmic Scales Are Used When the Data Has a Big Range

1) Logarithmic scales are a way of presenting data with a very <u>big range</u> (the difference between the highest value and the lowest — see p.128) <u>without</u> having to draw an <u>enormous</u> graph.

2) The <u>intervals</u> between the <u>points</u> on a logarithmic scale get <u>bigger</u> each time, like on the <u>y-axis</u> of this graph.

This interval represents 256 000 people.

This interval represents 2000 people.

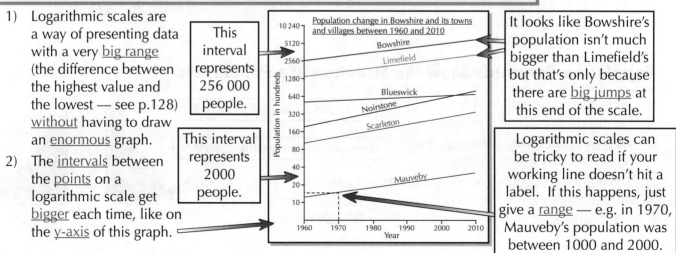

Population change in Bowshire and its towns and villages between 1960 and 2010

It looks like Bowshire's population isn't much bigger than Limefield's but that's only because there are <u>big jumps</u> at this end of the scale.

Logarithmic scales can be tricky to read if your working line doesn't hit a label. If this happens, just give a <u>range</u> — e.g. in 1970, Mauveby's population was between 1000 and 2000.

A bit of revision helps to avoid cross sections in exams...

...so learn this page 'til you can't see for pictograms and you're dreaming in cross-sections and logarithmic scales.

Charts and Graphs

Yep, you guessed it — there are <u>even more</u> charts and graphs to learn. These are the <u>last ones</u>, I <u>promise</u>.

Radial Graphs Often Show Directional Data

1) <u>Radial graphs</u> have <u>axes</u> that go round in a <u>circle</u>.
2) They often show <u>directional data</u>.
3) The most <u>common</u> radial diagram is a <u>wind rose</u>. The bars point in different <u>directions</u> to show which way the wind is <u>blowing from</u>. <u>How far</u> the bar reaches from the centre shows <u>how often</u> winds blow from that direction.

Winds from the south and west are more common than from the north and east.

The wind blows from the west about 14% of the time.

Radial graphs are sometimes called rose charts.

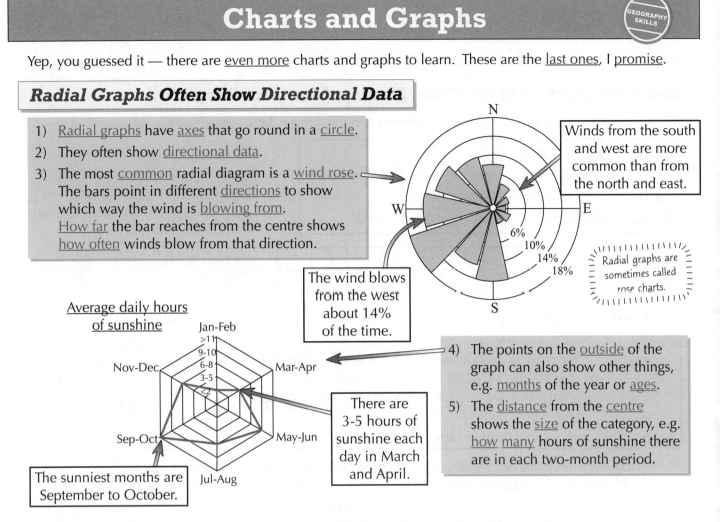

Average daily hours of sunshine

The sunniest months are September to October.

There are 3-5 hours of sunshine each day in March and April.

4) The points on the <u>outside</u> of the graph can also show other things, e.g. <u>months</u> of the year or <u>ages</u>.
5) The <u>distance</u> from the <u>centre</u> shows the <u>size</u> of the category, e.g. <u>how many</u> hours of sunshine there are in each two-month period.

Triangular Graphs Show Percentages Split into Three Categories

1) To read a triangular graph, start by <u>finding the point</u> you want on the graph.
2) <u>Follow</u> the <u>line</u> that goes <u>down</u> from the <u>point</u> to the <u>lowest end</u> of the <u>scale</u> and record the percentage.
3) Then <u>turn the graph around</u> so that the next axis is at <u>the bottom</u>, <u>follow</u> the <u>line</u> down to the lower end of the scale and record that percentage.
4) Do the same for the <u>third axis</u>.
5) The three readings should <u>add up</u> to <u>100%</u>.
6) The graph on the right shows the age distribution of three populations. There are <u>three age groups</u> so a triangular graph can be used. <u>Each point</u> represents <u>one population</u>.

On this scale the lowest end is on the <u>left</u>, so to find the percentage you follow the line down and towards the left of the scale.

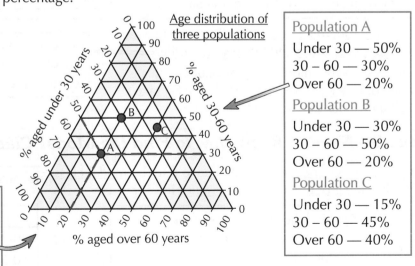

Age distribution of three populations

Population A
Under 30 — 50%
30 – 60 — 30%
Over 60 — 20%

Population B
Under 30 — 30%
30 – 60 — 50%
Over 60 — 20%

Population C
Under 30 — 15%
30 – 60 — 45%
Over 60 — 40%

Make sure you don't miss the point...

It might take a moment for you to get your head around a triangular graph, but don't worry — just follow the instructions above, take your time, and you'll be able to read it standing on your head before you know it.

Statistics

EEEK, it's a page about <u>maths</u>. In a <u>geography</u> book. Still, it should all be <u>very familiar</u> from <u>maths lessons</u>...

Learn the Definitions for Mode, Median, Mean and Range...

<u>Mode</u>, <u>median</u> and <u>mean</u> are measures of <u>average</u> and the <u>range</u> is how <u>spread out</u> the values are:

<u>MODE</u> = <u>MOST</u> common
<u>MEDIAN</u> = <u>MIDDLE</u> value (when values are in order of size)
<u>MEAN</u> = <u>TOTAL</u> of items ÷ <u>NUMBER</u> of items
<u>RANGE</u> = <u>DIFFERENCE</u> between highest and lowest

<u>REMEMBER</u>:

<u>Mode</u> = <u>most</u> (emphasise the 'mo' in each when you say them)
<u>Median</u> = <u>mid</u> (emphasise the m*d in each when you say them)
<u>Mean</u> is just the <u>average</u>, but it's <u>mean</u> 'cos you have to work it out.

Sample	1	2	3	4	5	6	7
River discharge (cumecs)	184	90	159	142	64	64	95

Q: Calculate the mean, median, mode and range for the river discharge data shown in the table above.
A: • The mode is the most common value = <u>64</u>.
   • To find the median, put all the numbers in order and find the middle value:
      64, 64, 90, <u>95</u>, 142, 159, 184. So the median is <u>95</u>.
   • Mean = $\dfrac{\text{total of items}}{\text{number of items}}$ = $\dfrac{184 + 90 + 159 + 142 + 64 + 64 + 95}{7}$ = $\dfrac{798}{7}$ = <u>114</u>
   • The range is the difference between highest and lowest value, i.e. 184 − 64 = <u>120</u>

When there are two middle numbers, the median is halfway between the two.

1) Each of these methods has <u>weaknesses</u>. The <u>mean</u> and the <u>range</u> are affected by any <u>outliers</u> (values that are a lot <u>bigger</u> or <u>smaller</u> than most of the other values) — this reduces their <u>accuracy</u>.

2) In some data sets, there might be <u>more than one mode</u> — or each value might be <u>different</u>, meaning there <u>isn't</u> a mode.

3) If you have a <u>large</u> set of data, it takes <u>longer</u> to calculate the <u>median</u>.

As well as finding the <u>median</u> (the middle value in a list), you can also find the <u>upper</u> and <u>lower quartiles</u> — the values a <u>quarter</u> (25%) and <u>three-quarters</u> (75%) of the way through the <u>ordered data</u>.

Q: The number of shoppers in each shop in a village were counted. Find the median and the quartiles of the data set.

A: 2, 3, 6, 6, 7, 9, 13, 14, 17, 22, 22
   | Lower quartile | Median | Upper quartile |

1) The <u>interquartile range</u> is the <u>difference between</u> the <u>upper quartile</u> and the <u>lower quartile</u>.

2) It contains the middle <u>50%</u> of values — this is one of its <u>weaknesses</u> because it <u>doesn't</u> take <u>all</u> the values into account.

Q: Find the interquartile range of the number of shoppers.
A: 17 − 6 = <u>11</u>

You also Need to Know How to Find the Modal Class

If your data is <u>grouped</u> you might need to find the <u>modal class</u>. This is just the <u>group</u> with the <u>most values</u> in.

Q: Find the modal class of the population data shown in the table.
A: Modal class = <u>20-39 years</u>

Age	Number of people
0-19	21
20-39	37
40-59	27
60+	15

Remember, the modal class will be the group — not how many items are in that group.

This page is mean — wish I was still on those maps pages...

Sheesh, I wasn't expecting so much stats in a geography book. But here it is, so you might as well learn it before it comes up in your exam. Anyway, this is the penultimate page in the book so once you've cracked it, you're on the home straight.

Statistics

Phew, you've made it to the last page — just a few more statistics to look at, then it's time for a nap.

You Need to be Able to Calculate Percentages and Percentage Change...

To give the amount X as a percentage of a sample Y, you need to divide X by Y and multiply by 100.

> Q: This year, 35 out of the 270 houses in Foxedapolice were burgled.   A: $35 \div 270 \times 100$
>   Calculate the percentage of houses burgled in Foxedapolice.   = 13%

Calculating percentage change lets you work out how much something has increased or decreased.
You use this formula:

$$\text{Percentage change} = \frac{\text{final value} - \text{original value}}{\text{original value}} \times 100$$

A positive value shows an increase and a negative value shows a decrease.

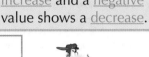

> Q: Last year in Foxedapolice, only 24 houses were burgled.
>   Calculate the percentage change in burglaries in Foxedapolice.
>
> A: $\frac{35 - 24}{24} \times 100 = \underline{46\% \text{ increase}}$ in the number of burglaries in Foxedapolice.

Percentiles Tell You Where in Your Data Set a Data Point Lies

1) Percentiles are useful if you want to compare the value of one data point to the rest of your data.

2) To find a percentile, you rank your data from smallest to largest,
   then divide it into one hundred equal chunks. Each chunk is one percentile.

3) This means that each percentile represents one percent of the data, and so the value of a percentile
   tells you what percentage of the data has a value lower than the data points in that percentile.

> E.g. Sid the Stone is in the 90th percentile for weight in his section of the
> river bed. This means that 90% of the stones are lighter than Sid.

4) Percentiles can be used to give a more realistic idea of the spread of data than the range —
   by finding the range between the 10th and 90th percentiles in a data set (the middle 80% of the data),
   you can look at the spread of the data while ignoring any outlying results.

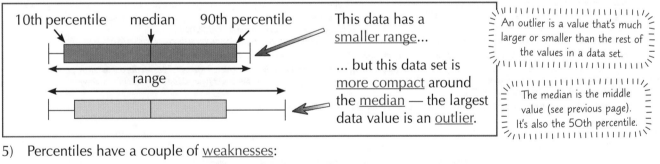

10th percentile   median   90th percentile

range

This data has a smaller range...

... but this data set is more compact around the median — the largest data value is an outlier.

An outlier is a value that's much larger or smaller than the rest of the values in a data set.

The median is the middle value (see previous page). It's also the 50th percentile.

5) Percentiles have a couple of weaknesses:
   - Any outliers in the data set are given the highest or lowest percentile.
   - If a lot of the data is very close to the mean, any differences are exaggerated by percentiles.

A Ratio Can be Used to Show a Proportion

1) A ratio shows how two amounts compare to each other — they're one way of showing a proportion.

2) They're written like this ⟹ 1 : 10. E.g. 'Droughts and storms occurred in
   the ratio 1 : 10.' This means that for every 1 drought, there were 10 storms.

Percentiles — found in every mathematician's bathroom...

Well, that's your lot for skills. I know this has been a big ol' section, but it's all important stuff, so there's no excuse for not learning it. Now it's officially time for that nap — you should have nothing but sweet geographical dreams.

Acknowledgements

Topographic map of the United Kingdom on page 2 and page 4 by Captain Blood, Licensed under the Creative Commons Attribution-Share Alike 3.0 Unported license. http://creativecommons.org/licenses/by-sa/3.0/deed.en

Photograph on p.2 (River Avon, Cairngorms) © Clive Giddis/p.2 (Glaslyn) © Bill Boaden/p.2 (the Weald) © Peter Jeffery/p.4 (Giant's Causeway) © Kenneth Allen/p.5 (Llyn Idwal) © Dudley Smith/p.5 (dry valley) © Colin Smith/p.9 (Porthcothan rocks) © Val Pollard/p.10 and p.16 (Old Harry Rock) © Raymond Knapman/p.11 (Spurn Head Spit) © Mat Fascione/p.13 (coastal quarry) © Mike Faherty/p.15 (landslides near Chapman's Pool) © Robin Webster/p.16 (Lulworth Cove) © nick macneill/p.16 (Chesil Beach) © Eugene Birchall/p.19 (River Eden at Salkeld) © Greg Fitchett/p.19 (Hell Gill Force) © Roger Templeman/ p.19 (River Eden at Appleby-in-Westmorland)© Steve Daniels/ p.19 (River Eden floodplain) © Rose and Trev Clough/p.20 (carbonation weathering) © Peter Standing/p.20 (landslip at Tofthead) © Anne Burgess/p.22 (interlocking spurs) © Bob Bowyer/p.24 (River Brue) © Richard Webb/p.26 (River Kent) © Karl and Ali/p.27 (River Liffey Dredger) © David Dixon/p.28 (deforestation) © David Maclennan/p.29 (Hardwicke Circus under water) © Rose and Trev Clough/p.29 (flooding aftermath in Cumbria) © Rose and Trev Clough/p.30 (Clywedog Dam) © Jeremy Bolwell/p.30 (Girton grasslands) © Richard Croft/p.40 (Nant Ffrancon valley) © Meirion/p.40 (moraine around Llyn Idwal) © N Chadwick/p.40 (truncated spur) © John Smith/p.40 (Llyn Idwal) © Dudley Smith/p.41 (old quarry in Gwynedd) © Eric Jones/p.52 (drought conditions) © John Sutton/p.61 (heather on the cliffs) © Steve Daniels/p.62 (bluebells in Dole Wood) © Rex Needle/p.72 (Taylor's Green, Forest of Dean) © Stuart Wilding/p.72 (coppice stool) © Roger Jones/p.75 (overcrowding in city) © Alan Murray-Rust/p.78 (skyscraper at Canary Wharf) © Christine Matthews/p.78 (terraced houses) © Dr Neil Clifton/p.81 (upper shopping area at Bluewater) © Elliott Simpson/p.109 (desalination plant) © Octal. Licensed under the Creative Commons Attribution-Share Alike 2.0 Generic license. http://creativecommons.org/licenses/by-sa/2.0/

Geological map of the UK on page 3 from the British Geological Survey ©UKRI/UK climate data on page 47 © Crown Copyright, the Met Office/Scotland life expectancy on page 89 source: National Records of Scotland/Oil and gas areas for map on page 98 from the Oil & Gas Authority. Contain public sector information licensed under the Open Government Licence v3.0. http://www.nationalarchives.gov.uk/doc/open-government-licence/version/3/

Map extracts on pages 5, 6, 12, 25, 37, 121 & 122 and symbols on page 121 reproduced with permission from Ordnance Survey® © Crown copyright 2019 03 100094041

Map on page 40 contains OS data © Crown copyright and database right 2016

Historical climate graph on page 47 based on Palaeogeography, Palaeoclimatol., Palaeoecol., 1 (1965) 13-37, H. H. Lamb, The early medieval warm epoch and its sequel, p25, Copyright © 1965, with permission from Elsevier.

Map of UK annual temperature 1971-2000 on page 47 © Crown Copyright, the Met Office. Contains public sector information licensed under the Open Government Licence v1.0. http://www.nationalarchives.gov.uk/doc/open-government-licence/version/1/

Data used to compile the UK average rainfall map on pages 47 and 108 from the Manchester Metropolitan University.

Image of Hurricane Katrina on page 49 source: Jeff Schmaltz, MODIS Rapid Response Team, NASA/GSFC

Image of New Orleans flood defences on page 50 source: U.S. Army Corps of Engineers

Image of Cyclone Nargis on page 51 source: NASA

Map of global drought distribution on page 53 from Aqueduct Global Maps 2.1 Indicators. Constructing Decision-Relevant Global Water Risk Indicators by Francis Gassert, Paul Reig, Tien Shiao, Matt Luck, Research Scientist, ISciences LLC and Matt Landis Research Scientist, ISciences LLC - April 2015/ Data used to produce the Gini coefficient map on page 88 and Gini coefficient for UK data on page 89 from The World Bank Indicators: GINI index (World Bank estimate)/Income distribution statistics in UK on page 89 from the World Bank: Income share held by highest 10%/India employment data on page 92 and population and birth rate data on page 93, Gini coefficient data for India on page 94, mobile phone ownership data on page 94 and HEP use in Sweden on page 105 from The World Bank: World Development Indicators. Licensed under the Creative Commons Attribution International 4.0 License (CC BY 4.0). https://creativecommons.org/licenses/by/4.0/legalcode

Source used to produce the map of UK Ecosystems on page 61: The Corine Land Cover data for 2012 "Copyright rests with the European Commission; Acknowledgement: Produced by the University of Leicester, The Centre for Landscape and Climate Research and Specto Natura and supported by Defra and the European Environment Agency under Grant Agreement 3541/B2012/R0-GIO/EEA.55055 with funding by the European Union. This resource is made available under the terms of the Open Government Licence v3.0. http://www.nationalarchives.gov.uk/doc/open-government-licence/version/3/."

Population distribution data used to construct map on page 76, city growth data on page 76, business start-up data on page 76, Canary Wharf population data on page 78, ethnicity data on page 79, immigration data on page 79, place of birth data on page 79, unemployment data on page 89, average household income data used in text and to construct map on page 89, England life expectancy on page 89, data used to construct map of UK population density on page 108 and page 118, immigration data used to construct flow map on page 120 from the Office for National Statistics/Average wages data on page 76, Huddersfield and London wages on page 89 from ONS, Annual Survey of Hours and Earnings (ASHE)/Coal areas for map on page 98 Source: The Coal Authority. Contains OS data © Crown Copyright and database right 2018. Licensed for reuse under the Open Government Licence v3.0. https://www.nationalarchives.gov.uk/doc/open-government-licence/version/3/

Satellite image on page 77 courtesy of NASA/GSFC/MITI/ERSDAC/JAROS, and U.S./Japan ASTER Science Team

London national immigration data on page 79/data used to construct map of deprivation in London on page 80/data for recycling in London on page 81. Contain public sector information licensed under the Open Government Licence v3.0. http://www.nationalarchives.gov.uk/doc/open-government-licence/version/3/

Map of London boroughs on page 80 produced using data from http://data.london.gov.uk/documents/Geography-licensing.pdf. Contains National Statistics data © Crown copyright and database right [2012] & Contains Ordnance Survey data © Crown copyright and database right [2012]. Licensed under the terms of the Open Government Licence v3.0. https://www.nationalarchives.gov.uk/doc/open-government-licence/version/3/

Satellite map of Lagos on page 82 made with Landsat imagery courtesy of NASA Goddard Space Flight Center and U.S. Geological Survey

Map overlays showing changing extent of Lagos on page 82 adapted from Planning, Anti-planning and the Infrastructure Crisis Facing Metropolitan Lagos, page 373, by Matthew Gandy and from Sawyer, Lindsay. 'Piecemeal Urbanisation at the Peripheries of Lagos'. African Studies, 9 June 2014, 1–19, by Lindsay Sawyer https://doi.org/10.1080/00020184.2014.925207.

Data used to produce the HDI map on page 88 © Copyright 2016 United Nations Development Programme.

Chad infant mortality data on page 90 source: Central Intelligence Agency

DRC development data on page 90 from Millennium Development Goals Indicators, by Department of Economic and Social Affairs. © United Nations 2019. Accessed 25.03.2019. Reprinted with the permission of the United Nations.

Urban Population data for Bihar and Maharashta on page 92 © Office of the Registrar General & Census Commissioner, India.

Population and HDI data for Maharashtra and Bihar on page 92 source: India Human Development Report 2011, IAMR and Planning Commission

GDP per capita data for Maharashtra and Bihar on page 92 from statisticstimes.com

India average age data and population pyramid data (2015) on page 93 from The World Factbook. Washington, DC: Central Intelligence Agency, 2019

India population pyramid data (1985) on page 93 from Annual Urban Population at Mid-Year, by UN Population Division, © 2019 United Nations. Reprinted with the permission of the United Nations. https://esa.un.org/unpd/wup/DataQuery/

India earnings data on page 94 from 2015 Human Development Report, United Nations Development Programme from hdr.undp.org. Licensed for re-use under the Creative Commons Attribution 3.0 IGO license. https://creativecommons.org/licenses/by/3.0/igo/

Primary education enrolment data on page 94 source: UNESCO Institute for Statistics (UIS), http://uis.unesco.org

Global energy consumption map on page 99 © BP Statistical Review of World Energy 2016.

UK energy supply pie chart on page 103 based on IEA Statistics, World Energy Balances © OECD/IEA 2016, www.iea.org/statistics. Licence: www.iea.org/t&c; as modified by Coordination Group Publications Ltd.

Global maps of water use per capita, food production and food consumption on page 100 and water use data used to construct pie charts on page 107 source: FAO. 2016. AQUASTAT Main Database, Food and Agriculture Organization of the United Nations (FAO). Website accessed on 28/02/2019.

World water resources map on page 106 and agriculture water use map on page 107 source: FAO. 2016. AQUASTAT website. Food and Agriculture Organization of the United Nations (FAO). Website accessed on 28/02/2019.

Every effort has been made to locate copyright holders and obtain permission to reproduce sources. For those sources where it has been difficult to trace the copyright holder of the work, we would be grateful for information. If any copyright holder would like us to make an amendment to the acknowledgements, please notify us and we will gladly update the book at the next reprint. Thank you.

Index